ONE HEARTBEAT II

ONE HEARTBEAT II
The Road to the National Championship

Mack Brown
and Bill Little

bright sky press

ALBANY, TEXAS

bright sky press

Box 416, Albany, Texas 76430

10   9   8   7   6   5   4   3   2   1

Library of Congress Cataloging-in-Publication Data
Brown, Mack, 1951 –
    One heartbeat II: the road to the national championship /
Mack Brown and Bill Little.
    p. cm.
ISBN-13: 978-1-931721-76-9 (hardcover with dust jacket :
    alk. paper) 1. Football –Coaching—Philosophy.
    2. Teamwork (Sports) 3. Leadership. 4. Texas
    Longhorns (Football Team) 5. University of Texas
    at Austin—Football. I. Little, Bill, 1942- II. Title.

    GV954.4.B76 2006
    796.33207'7—dc22
        2006016558

ONE HEARTBEAT II
Edited by: Jenna Hays McEachern
Design by: Tina Taylor, T2 Design
Photos courtesy of: Jan Allgood, Chris Carson, Robert
Pandya / *Alcalde Magazine*, Jim Sigmon, Susan Sigmon,
and the Brown family collection.

Printed in the USA

To Dad and Granddad, whose examples led me to become a coach
To Mom and Grandmother, for their strong will and confidence
To Watson and Mel, for being great brothers
And to Sally and the kids, for their love and support

—Mack Brown

To Kim and the kids and their families
To all of those who have encouraged me
To those who are touched by the written word
And to those who work and play in the spirit of *one heartbeat*

—Bill Little

One Heartbeat II is dedicated to the players, coaches, and staff of the Texas Longhorn football team. Special thanks to the Tournament of Roses officers and committee, whose faith created the match-up with Michigan in 2005, and whose cooperation and support helped make the 2006 game for the 2005 national championship a wonderful experience.

It is with sincere appreciation that we acknowledge the work of the Texas high school coaches, and the love and caring of the parents who helped mold the early years of the 2005 national champions.

Finally, this is for the fans of college football, who witnessed a remarkable season and a classic game in Texas's 41-38 victory over Southern Cal in the BCS national championship, and for the legion of Texas Longhorn supporters, who waited 35 years for that moment.

"FOR LIFE AND TALENTS AND WEALTH AND FAME
ARE GIVEN TO MEN IN TRUST, AND EACH MUST WORK
WITH THE GIFTS HE HAS 'TIL HIS FLESH RETURNS TO DUST,
FOR THIS IS THE LAW WHICH GOVERNS ALL,
AND THIS IS THE COMMON TEST—
HE THAT SHALL COME TO THE BEST LIFE HAS
MUST GIVE TO THE WORLD HIS BEST. "

—Author Unknown

CONTENTS

ONE HEARTBEAT II

❝'EVEN AFTER THE REST OF THE BODY
HAS SHUT DOWN, THE HEART KEEPS ON BEATING.
WHEN IT IS THE ONLY THING REMAINING,
IT STILL IS TRYING TO KEEP ON GOING.'
AND IN THAT SPACE, IT IS NO LONGER
THE HEART, BUT THE SOUL.❞

—*Dr. Tom Kirksey and Bill Little*

FOREWORD

◀ Mack Brown and Darrell Royal

Five years ago, I had the pleasure of writing a foreword for two close friends of mine who had created what I had found to be a special book.

From the day Mack Brown took the job at Texas, he and I have been close friends. Mack has never been reluctant to share any information with me that pertained to the Texas football team. As a matter of fact, I have a standing offer of a seat on the airplane that our team uses to travel to our away games. He has included me, and he has included our lettermen, in everything he has done.

Bill Little has been a friend of mine and has helped me with my communications for many years. It's hard to express the value he has brought to me personally and to the University of Texas.

The original *One Heartbeat* was a heck of a book, because Bill is a great writer who is excellent at capturing a coach's thoughts, and Mack has a lot to say. Now, after the Texas Longhorns' national championship victory in the Rose Bowl, it is great that we get a chance to look at all that went into that moment in Pasadena. The added chapters of *One Heartbeat II* give us more of what was already a great story.

There are parts of the book that are touching, and there are parts that have just common sense advice for anybody. This book is for the young and the old, the teacher and the high school coach and the mom and dad, the players who've made it on the field and those who want to.

It's the kind of book you can read and re-read and take a chapter or two at a time and leave it by your bed. Each chapter gives a different insight into coaching and working with young people and just plain how to live life.

For every fan of college football, the Longhorns' win in the Rose Bowl was special. It is good to see that there are still guys like Mack in the coaching business who believe in winning, doing it the right way, and leaving a piece of themselves behind so that they will have mattered to somebody when they set their buckets down.

–Darrell Royal

1

NOTE TO THE READER

Shortly after Mack Brown came to Texas in 1998, we received several requests for him to write a book on his coaching philosophy. In 2000, in order to honor his dad and his granddad—both of whom were connected to the high school coaching profession—and to help young coaches, he agreed to do it.

The original *One Heartbeat* was the result of that endeavor.

With Texas's victory in the 2006 Rose Bowl—the 2005 BCS National Championship of college football—many publications sought to capture the story of the 2005 Longhorns.

In this second edition, *One Heartbeat II*, we tell the story of the Longhorns of the 21st century and of the path Brown, his staff, and their team took to the pinnacle of college football.

Because so many people found the philosophy of the original book helpful, we have chosen to keep that intact. Wrapped around the original *One Heartbeat* is the story—and Brown's own view—of the exciting journey; the decisions that were made and the people who made it so successful.

It begins where the first book ends, and it ends with the aftermath of the dramatic victory in Pasadena, where the Longhorns of Texas became college football's best.

—Bill Little

❝WHEN HE [HARVEY PENICK] DIED IN THE SPRING OF 1995, AUSTIN AND THE GOLF WORLD MOURNED.BUT THE GREAT TEACHER HAD LEFT BEHIND HIS MESSAGE OF LIFE FOR ALL TO READ AND UNDERSTAND: TAKE DEAD AIM.❞

—Bill Little

▲ THE MASTER TEACHER — Harvey Penick spent most of his life teaching golf and coaching at The University of Texas, but his fame grew with the publication of his *Little Red Book* with noted writer Bud Shrake. Penick's book produced the advice of "Take Dead Aim," which became the theme of the 2005 National Champion Texas Longhorn football team.

PREFACE
Take Dead Aim

In the beginning, it seemed an odd pairing. Here was a young football team in the early part of the 21st century, using a philosophy from a legendary golf teacher from the 1950s.

You would have been hard pressed to find a whole bunch of teenagers or twenty-somethings on the Texas Longhorn football team who had ever heard of Harvey Penick. Some may have known about former Longhorn golfers Ben Crenshaw, Tom Kite, or Justin Leonard. But unless they were tuning in to watch Tiger Woods, Phil Mickelson, or some of the recent former Longhorns such as David Gossett, the kids, it's a pretty good bet, weren't regularly watching the Golf Channel.

Yet when the University of Texas football staff was looking for a theme for the 2005 Longhorn football season, it was in that short window of the spring and summer when a few of the coaches hit the golf links in their spare time. And that is when the words of the master teacher became interwoven with the hopes and dreams of a football team.

Harvey Penick had carved his niche in Austin as a longtime golf coach for the Longhorns and as a teaching golf professional at Austin Country Club. He had followed the club from a course just north of the Texas campus to a location southeast of Austin near the Colorado River to its current location nestled along Lake Austin in the western part of the city.

He had been a friend of Longhorn football coach Darrell Royal from the time when Royal first came to Texas in 1956, and he and his staff were members of Austin Country Club. Harvey loved Texas football and attended Longhorn games as long as he was able.

When he died in the spring of 1995, Austin and the golf world mourned. But the great teacher had left behind his message of life for all to read and understand.

Harvey had thought it and taught it, but it was Bud Shrake who wrote it. Shrake, a fine sportswriter who made a grand transition to screenwriter and author, was working on an idea he had to turn Penick's teaching journal into a "how to" for golfers. He called it *Harvey Penick's Little Red Book,* and turned it into the bestselling sports book of all time.

It was subtitled, "Lessons and Teachings from a Lifetime in Golf," and on page forty-five, Shrake penned what Penick would call "the most important message in the book."

Take Dead Aim.

"When my student Betsy Rawls was in a playoff for the U. S. Women's Open championship, I sent her a one-sentence telegram. It said 'Take Dead Aim.' For golfers who might not understand Texas talk, let me put the advice in the telegram a different way: Once you address the golf ball, hitting it has got to be the most important thing in your life at that moment. Shut out all thoughts other than picking out a target and taking dead aim at it…refuse to allow any negative thought to enter your head, and swing away."

Over and over again, in the space of two pages, Shrake and Penick repeat the words.

"The expert player won't be surprised. The expert expects to hit the target. The only surprise here is that the expert sometimes allows disorganized thinking to make him or her become distracted from the primary object of the shot, which is to hit the target. I can't say it too many times. It's the most important advice in this book.

"*Take dead aim.*

"Make it a point to do it every time on every shot. Don't just do it from time to time, when you happen to remember.

"*Take dead aim.*"

Twelve games and twelve victories into the 2005 season, it was no longer important that none of the Longhorn players had a chance to know Harvey Penick, because it hadn't been about him.

It has been about his message.

From the start of fall drills in August, nearly every Longhorn player and staff member had worn the burnt-orange rubber bracelet with a Longhorn emblem and the words "Take Dead Aim" on it.

Since 2001, Texas had won almost all of its games, each year falling only a game or two shy of a perfect season. As Brown and the staff searched for a visible reminder of the importance of every game, "Take Dead Aim" seemed a way to stay focused, week after week.

And that was what had brought them, unbeaten and ranked number two in the country, to the City of Angels, on a magical ride in search of a dream.

For most of the season the college football universe had waited, anticipating the showdown that would come at the Rose Bowl in Pasadena. There, where ninety-five-thousand fans had crowded into the stately old stadium, when the bands stopped playing and the pregame festivities had ended, number two Texas and number one Southern Cal would play a football game for the national championship. It was, they said, a California postcard day in L.A.

When Mack Brown was hired at Texas in December of 1997, he took as his charge the task of putting Texas into the national championship game. Eight seasons later, here they were. But for the Texas Longhorn faithful, the wait had been far longer than Brown's tenure.

Darrell Royal had told Brown when he came that the University of Texas family was fragmented.

"It's like somebody has dropped a box of BBs," said Royal, "and they scattered all over the place. If this is gonna work for you, you are gonna have to get the BBs back in the box."

From his opening season in 1998, Brown had begun trying to collect the scattered pellets. That first season, Ricky Williams won the school's second Heisman Trophy, its first in over twenty years. The Cotton Bowl victory over Mississippi State was the Longhorns' first New Year's Day bowl victory in seventeen years.

The team won nine games, a benchmark from which Brown, his teams, and his staff would work. Then the 1999 Longhorn team earned a top-ten ranking, another step forward. And when Brown spoke at the press conference before the Big 12 Championship game against Nebraska, he talked about a "neighborhood" which included the elite of college football.

The Cornhuskers, to be sure, were in that group. Texas had stunned Nebraska in Lincoln the season before, snapping a forty-seven-game home winning streak. Nebraska and Florida State had been the dominant college football teams of the '90s.

So now, in the final year of that period, here were Brown and his upstart Longhorns challenging for the right to advance to a coveted Bowl Championship Series berth. Earlier in the year in Austin, UT had actually upset number three Nebraska, handing them their only loss.

When Brown spoke of "the neighborhood," he simply talked about the fact that the rebuilding Longhorns were "visiting the neighborhood." And then he said, "What we want to do is to buy a house there."

For a variety of reasons, that would not happen in 1999. Nebraska won the Big 12 Championship game, and in the first game of the new millennium, the 'Horns lost the Cotton Bowl game on January 1, 2000.

At the same time, the Longhorns' rival to the north, Oklahoma, was doing some rebuilding of its own. For over a decade, Oklahoma had also been absent from the board of college football's titans.

When the Big 12 was founded, teams of the Northern Division—Nebraska, Kansas State, and Colorado—had been in the mix for national honors.

But as the first decade of the league closed in 2005, the balance of power had shifted. After Brown's first two teams had defeated Oklahoma in '98 and '99, the Sooners had gone undefeated in 2000, surprising Florida State and winning the national championship. By the next season, Oklahoma and Texas were both back, and their annual October skirmish in Dallas seemed the breeding ground for the league's champion. But in a game where few things are certain, the only thing certain in the Big 12 was unpredictability.

Twice, in 2001 and 2003, Oklahoma seemed to have a lock on the league championship

after beating the Longhorns in October. But in a strange turn of events on the closing weekend of 2001 and in the championship game of 2003, that didn't happen.

The first time, Texas and Colorado suddenly found themselves in the Big 12 Championship game after the Buffaloes stunned Nebraska and Oklahoma State upset Oklahoma.

By the time Texas and Colorado kicked off in 2001, upsets at the very top of the collegiate polls had positioned the Longhorns on the threshold of a trip to Pasadena, this time to play Miami for the national championship. But four costly turnovers and injuries to their top lineman and running back left Texas frustrated, as number-seven-ranked Colorado edged the number-three-ranked Longhorns, 39-37.

The Big 12 had been started in 1996, and college football's elite conferences had created the Bowl Championship Series in 1997. The winners of six conferences—the Big 12, the Big Ten, the Pac-10, the ACC, the SEC, and the Big East—and two at-large selections would make up the eight teams who would play in the Rose, Fiesta, Orange, and Sugar Bowls. The national championship game would rotate among the four bowls.

Validation as one of the elite teams of college football seemed to hinge on an appearance in one of those four games. And no team in America was more "snakebit" than Texas when it came to getting into a BCS game. Texas had been the only team in the country ranked in the BCS's top fifteen every year from 1999 and 2003, yet the Longhorns still hadn't made it to one of the big games.

Just when it appeared the sixth-ranked Longhorns were a lock to play Ohio State in the Tostitos Fiesta Bowl in 2003, Oklahoma was upset by Kansas State for the Big 12 Championship. The victory gave the Wildcats the league's automatic bid into the BCS, and the Sooners, as an at-large selection, still maintained their number-one ranking despite the loss and played Louisiana State in the national championship game.

Even though they were shut out of the BCS games at the end of the season, Texas was establishing a consistency of excellence. Following the loss to Colorado at the end of the 2001 season, Texas saw only one obstacle on the path to ultimate success: Oklahoma. Other than a narrow loss at Texas Tech in 2002, the Sooners would be the only Big 12 team to beat the Longhorns over the next four seasons. The 'Horns had bowl victories over Washington in 2001 in the Holiday Bowl and over LSU in the 2003 Cotton Bowl.

Texas had gotten so close, yet still seemed destined to be the hard-luck guys of college football as far as the BCS was concerned. But in 2004, all of that changed.

A staff that had been a model of continuity since Brown came to Texas underwent a facelift. Veteran defensive coaches Carl Reese and Hardee McCrary both elected to leave, and receivers coach Darryl Drake took a job with the Chicago Bears of the NFL.

To replace them, Brown chose former NFL defensive coordinator Greg Robinson, former Arizona and Hawaii head coach Dick Tomey, and a young receivers coach from Washington named Bobby Kennedy.

The Robinson and Tomey hires surprised some college football observers. Robinson had been a successful coach with the Denver Broncos, and Tomey had been an outstanding head coach at both Hawaii and Arizona. However, Robinson hadn't coached college football in fourteen years, since he left UCLA for professional football, and the sixty-five-year-old Tomey was helping out with the San Francisco 49ers after leaving Arizona a season before.

Robinson was named co-defensive coordinator with secondary coach Duane Akina, and Tomey took the job of coaching defensive ends and serving as Assistant Head Coach. Brown knew they had good football pedigrees, and he got a huge bonus in the energy the two veteran coaches brought to the staff. Robinson, Akina, Tomey, and defensive-tackles coach Mike Tolleson were charged with rejuvenating the Longhorn defense.

On the other side of the ball, coordinator Greg Davis, line coach Mac McWhorter, receivers coach Bobby Kennedy, tight-end coach Bruce Chambers, and running-backs coach Mike Haywood were redesigning the Texas offense. It would feature a seasoned running back in Cedric Benson, a corps of rookie wide receivers, and a quarterback tandem of sophomore Vince Young and senior Chance Mock.

Young had won the starting job during the second half of the 2003 season, and as 2004 began he was already beginning to show flashes of the talent that had made him one of the state's top high-school recruits in 2002.

Benson was the workhorse of the offense, and he teamed with linebacker Derrick Johnson as the first Texas players in history to be named National Players of the Year at their positions in the same season.

The tone of the season was set in the second game of the year in Fayetteville, Arkansas. Young brought the Longhorns from behind and the defense came up with a dramatic turnover to seal a 22-20 victory over the Razorbacks.

The turning point for Young came five games later. After the team had a shaky offensive performance in a 28-20 win over Missouri, Brown and Davis got together with Young prior to the Longhorns' next game against Texas Tech. They showed him film of his best moments as a Longhorn, as well as reviewing some of his high-school video.

"This is the guy we want," they said. Then the three got together to ascertain a system that would work for the redshirt sophomore quarterback.

The dividends began to pay off the next week, with a 51-21 victory over Texas Tech in Lubbock. A 31-7 victory over Colorado at Boulder followed. Then came the game that Brown would later reflect on as the defining moment of the era.

Trailing Oklahoma State, 35-7, late in the first half, Texas managed a late score to cut the halftime margin to 35-14. In the locker room, Brown was upbeat with his team, and in a ploy that he borrowed from Darrell Royal, he wrote on the chalkboard: "42-35." Young electrified the crowd, the defense rose to the moment, and Texas went on to win, 56-35. The confidence builder would be needed badly the next week as the Longhorns found themselves trailing vast underdog Kansas late in the game. By then, Texas had moved to number six in the national rankings and was battling California and Utah for one of the two BCS at-large bids.

But all of that seemed a long way—in fact, eighteen yards—away, when Texas, trailing by three in the closing minute of the game, faced a fourth and eighteen near midfield. It was then that Vince Young first stepped up, and out, and into Longhorn immortality. He scrambled for twenty-five yards and the first down, then threw a twenty-one-yard touchdown pass to Tony Jeffrey with eleven seconds to play to win the game, 27-23.

The game had been saved, but the BCS berth was in doubt. By the rules of the Bowl Championship Series, a team from a non-BCS qualifying conference would get one of the two at-large bids if it ranked at least sixth in the final standings. Utah, a representative of the non-BCS Mountain West Conference, was a solid lock for sixth.

That left only one at-large bid, and it would fall to either Texas or California, a once-beaten Pac-10 team. The Bears held the fourth spot in both of the human polls used in 2004, the Associated Press writers' poll and the *ESPN/USA Today* coaches' poll. Texas, however, maintained a strong edge in the computers, which made up the third component of the BCS standings.

Each week as the BCS poll results were released, Texas edged closer and closer to Cal. After Texas defeated Texas A&M to end its regular season at 10-1, Brown publicly urged voters to consider his team. The Texas media-relations office produced a chart showing the performance in various categories of the top six teams in the BCS, reflecting the Longhorns' season compared to the others.

On the final day of the season, California traveled to Southern Mississippi to play a game that had been originally scheduled for early in the season, but was moved because of the threat of an impending hurricane. The Bears struggled against the Eagles, and following that game, coaches and writers cast their final votes.

DeLoss Dodds, the UT athletics director, had already been working with bowl representatives to secure a Texas appearance in the Rose Bowl against Michigan if they qualified for the BCS. Dodds and Brown were on a plane to New York when the results were announced. When they landed at New York's LaGuardia International Airport, Dodds turned on his cell phone and received a message.

"We're in," he said to Brown. "You're playing Michigan in the Rose Bowl."

From that moment, everything truly was "coming up roses" for the Longhorns. The Rose Parade theme of "Celebrate Family" fit everything that Texas football had become under Mack Brown. Now, for the first time, the hallowed tradition of the Rose Bowl and the storied tradition of Texas football were about to meet.

At first there was apprehension, because the Pac-10 Conference, one of the three owners of the bowl, had coveted a meeting between one of its own—the University of California—and Michigan. After all, the Golden Bears hadn't been to the Rose Bowl in over forty years. Some of the West Coast media had felt strongly that the Bears—not the Longhorns—should be playing in Pasadena, and they were quite vocal about it.

But the BCS had spoken, and this time, Texas finally caught the break it deserved.

The Longhorns had been to forty-three bowl games, but they had never played in the Rose Bowl, which had been exclusively a Big Ten-Pac-10 affair from the late 1940s until the bowl became affiliated with the BCS through its television partner, ABC.

As fate would have it, however, the union of the Longhorn program and the Rose Bowl people turned out to be a perfect match. Fast friendships formed quickly, and despite rains, which plagued Southern California the entire week of game preparations, 2005 dawned beautifully in Pasadena.

It was, after all, a conflux of three of the greatest traditions in all of college football, brought together for the first time. Texas had never played in the Rose Bowl, and Texas had never played the University of Michigan. Two of the legendary coaches of the college game, Darrell Royal of Texas and Bo Schembechler of Michigan, were on hand for the coin flip.

The ninety-three-thousand plus in the stands equally blended the burnt orange of Texas and the blue and gold of Michigan, and while the day did celebrate the history of the game, January 1, 2005, was about the young men who played it.

When Dusty Mangum kicked a thirty-seven-yard field goal on the game's final play for a 38-37 Longhorn victory, and quarterback Vince Young thrust himself on the national stage with an MVP performance, folks called it "the greatest bowl game of its era."

Prophetically, following the game, after someone acknowledged that the national championship game would be in Pasadena the next year, Young proclaimed to the crowd and a national television audience, "We'll be back."

With that, the Longhorns began their "Take Dead Aim" ride back to Pasadena, and it turns out that the "greatest bowl game of its era" was part of an era that would only last a year.

MB

It hardly seems possible that it has been five years since the first edition of One Heartbeat was published, just as the 2001 football season ended. Coming into the 2005 season, our team had won forty-three games and lost eight in the previous four seasons.

Our goal had been to win all the games. We were in the right neighborhood. But when you are so close, you have to try to figure out the minute points that will make that happen. That's hard to do. Very few teams do it. Very few coaches do it. It's so competitive that when you are in the top ten every year you don't want to throw out what's been getting you there, but you obviously need to tweak some things to finish better in those one or two games.

We were doing so many things right. To build a team, you have to look at its chemistry and combine its strengths and its concerns. We had built our program on character and family values and we had achieved a great deal of success.

The cornerstone of our house was a three-part premise of communication, trust, and respect. Our players were succeeding in the classroom and winning on the field, and that's the combination that a coach wants.

So we had to ask ourselves, "What is winning?" We determined that

11

the answer was "having fun while reaching the highest level possible within the rules."

Every year I ask our coaches and players to do a self-evaluation, and what I found was that we were putting so much pressure on ourselves, we were missing out on the fun. I believe a lot of that started with the Colorado game in the Big 12 Championship in 2001. The events at the end of the season, and in fact the day of the game, suddenly put us in the position where, if we won that game, we would have been playing for the national championship.

Suddenly, there was a tremendous amount of pressure on our team. From that point we went through a period where we were consistently good, but not great. Then there was the setback in 2003, when we had played well enough to earn a BCS berth against Ohio State in the Fiesta Bowl, but because Oklahoma lost to Kansas State, we were shut out. Then, we felt we didn't play well in our loss to Washington State in the Holiday Bowl.

That sequence of events really set our program back, but it made all of us want to work harder not to depend on someone else to get us to the right game. We wanted to control our own destiny.

As hard as the finish was of that 2003 season, it was the most critical element in the change. We changed our attitude. We came back from the Holiday Bowl determined to not ever feel that bad again. As a staff, we had hard conversations with each other. When we came to Texas, we thought that continuity on the staff was essential for success. We went from that philosophy to an approach that "it's really good for a long time, but then, at a place that's as high pressure as this place is, an influx of new energy and new ideas is needed."

Carl Reese and Hardee McCrary, two good defensive coaches who had been part of the staff from the beginning, had opportunities to leave, and they did. Carl retired to spend his time fishing in his home state of Missouri, and Hardee moved to our Longhorn Foundation staff so he could spend more time with his wife and kids.

We were tremendously fortunate to fill the vacancies with two veteran defensive coaches who brought a wealth of experience and a long history of success. Greg Robinson had won two Super Bowl rings when he was coaching the Denver Broncos, and Dick Tomey was a great friend who was the winningest coach at two different schools during his long career. They were both older guys who had been very successful at what they were doing on defense.

Fundamentally, we thought we could chase the ball harder, and we thought we could be more physical. But most of all, we needed some new energy.

And that is when we started trying to have more fun. We also used a new approach to "team building." At a staff retreat before the season, each of us coaches told our life's story to the rest of the staff. It got pretty emotional, and it was really powerful. Then we had each position coach tell his story to his players, and then the players had to share their life stories with their coach and teammates.

Each of us learned new things about one another and about ourselves. It was the beginning of a new kind of feeling about "team." You understand a guy better when you know what he's been through, and you fight for each other in a different way.

We also started emphasizing a "let's finish and let's keep playing" mentality. We started talking about "illusions"— understanding what is real, and realizing that if something happens, it's liable to change—for example, don't think the game's over just because you're behind in the fourth quarter. We did a better job of getting those things across to our team.

Over the next two-year period, after the Oklahoma loss and the Missouri game where we played so poorly on offense—at that point, our offense's darkest moments since we've been here—we pulled together and started being more about team, having more fun, and relaxing and enjoying it. And we found that one thing that everybody wants: the ability to come from behind in the fourth quarter and win a game. It's hard to get, and it's hard to keep; it's hard to know why you have it, and it's hard to know what it is when you have it. But it's the thing that helped us win two Rose Bowls.

The win over Michigan in the Rose Bowl brought tremendous enthusiasm to our program. It was great to see so many Texas people happy and to see our team so confident. But as we began preparing for the 2005 season, it was obvious that there was just one step that we hadn't taken. We had played in and won a high profile BCS game, and we had finished in the nation's top five.

As we sat around the table at our house, my wife, Sally, and I were talking about the upcoming season. "Our problem is," she said, "that when you start out the season as number two in the country behind Southern Cal, and you just won the Rose Bowl, your only expectation for success is that you go back. What about the opening game? Everybody's talking about Ohio State. Everybody's talking about Oklahoma and everybody's talking about the Rose Bowl. It's as if we have no other games."

Sally is really into golf, and she loved the teachings of the late Harvey Penick. Every golfer in Austin talks about Harvey. They remember the day they met him, what he said to them, how gentle he was with his teaching, but how powerful an effect his words had on them. Sally suggested we look at making a theme out of Harvey's most famous instruction, "Take Dead Aim." Harvey said to get rid of all the distractions around you and take dead aim at the pin. That is really what we were trying to do with our football team.

After the tragedies that have occurred in some schools around our country, we were sensitive to the possibility of someone missing the golf analogy and thinking about guns. So we tried to extend this idea not only to our team, but to the community and the state as well. We made it about a lot more than just football. It was about the players' academics, their families, their girlfriends; it was about giving someone their full attention when they were with that person. And hopefully, it was about practice on Tuesday, and not only a game on Saturday.

We created an archery target, with each ring representing a game. The bull's-eye was Reliant Stadium, where the Big 12 Championship game would be played. We created simple burnt orange wristbands with the words "Take Dead Aim" on them and gave them only to the team and the staff.

And as we began the journey that would take us to Pasadena, we were determined not to look ahead or look back. Each game and each moment required our full attention, and that is what "Take Dead Aim" came to mean to all of us.

I

ONE HEARTBEAT

PROLOGUE
One Heartbeat

❝TO BE SUCCESSFUL AS A TEAM,
YOU MUST BRING ALL THE PARTS TOGETHER
AND PLAY AS ONE HEARTBEAT.**❞**

—Darrell Royal

◀ ONE HEARTBEAT – The clinched fist has become symbolic of
coming together to play as one heartbeat, as shown here in
a post game celebration in the Longhorn locker room.

BL

I t was twilight at the house on Waters Edge, and the gentle breezes coming off
the lake left only a muted memory of the sweltering sun that had begun the
day. The juicy steaks catered by Ruth's Chris's had given way to a healthy helping of bread pudding as the seniors of the Texas football team indulged themselves one final time before the start of fall practice.

Mack and Sally Brown had made this a tradition, this senior dinner at their
home on Lake Austin before the start of each season. A couple of days earlier, the
incoming freshmen had sat in the same chairs by the same lake, but with young
and different dreams.

There is a moment that comes when you realize it's your last ride. For the
Texas Longhorn seniors, the dinner signals the start of their most significant year.
After three or four seasons of apprenticeship, it is now up to them to lead a foot-
ball team.

Darrell Royal knew all about those feelings as he rose to speak. It had been
over twenty years since he addressed his last football team, and at seventy-four
years old, it was good to see young faces there in front of him again. For too long
since he quit coaching in 1976, Royal had been distanced from the Texas football
program. For whatever reasons, those who had followed in his footsteps had failed
to take advantage of his vast knowledge and supreme interest. Since the moment
they had seen each other when Brown interviewed for the Texas job, Royal and
Brown had celebrated a bond of friendship.

From the beginning there were similarities.

Royal became a head coach at a young age, and he took the Texas job at age
thirty-two. Brown's first head coaching assignment came in 1983, when he was
thirty-two. While Royal's success as a head coach had been almost entirely at
Texas, Brown's tenure included the art of rebuilding. He gave Appalachian State
and Tulane their best seasons in years, and he took North Carolina from a 2-20
start to a 20-2 finish, with two top-ten rankings in his final seasons.

Royal's amazing success in the decade of the '60s, when his teams won three
national championships and came within eight points of three more, made a lasting
impression on Brown, who, as a kid growing up in Tennessee, spent his Saturdays

19

watching college football on television.

Both would have made great lawyers or doctors or ranchers or successful businessmen, but they were born to coach. The reasons both men did what they did sat before Royal that night in August of 1998—the kids who played the game.

That night, Royal talked a lot about what it took to win. Only the lapping of the water from the wake of a distant motorboat competed with his quiet, earnest voice.

He talked about values, about sacrificing individuality for team goals. He gave the seniors a premise about effort that soon would be mounted in big letters outside the locker room door: "What I gave, I have. What I kept, I lost."

There are many ways to describe teamwork. Folks talk about an engine hitting on all cylinders. In the tradition of the Old West, you'll find those who compare it to a team of horses, all strapped to each other and pulling together for the common good. Dog sleds in Alaska traverse the frozen north that way. Einstein said it is about momentum, that the value of the whole is greater than the sum of its individual parts.

But that night by the lake, Royal gave Mack Brown and his Texas football teams—that first one and those to come—a symbolism that would characterize team spirit and a plan for life:

"To be successful as a team," he said, looking straight into the eyes of the young men and raising his open palm and bringing it into a fist that shaped the muscle which pumps life into the body, "you must bring all the parts together and play as one heartbeat."

When people asked me to put some thoughts together in a book, I wanted to make sure the book would be something that could help people. In twenty-six years as a coach—seventeen as a head coach—a lot of people have helped me, and if I were to write a book, the reason would be to pay back all those who touched me.

It was kind of like that country song where the guy helps out the lady, and when she tries to pay him, he replies, "You don't owe me a thing. I've been there, too."

So, this book is a collection of stories and thoughts, and each has its own message. It's a collection of things that have happened to me and to our team, and it includes suggestions that have come to me from a lot of great people.

The strongest message of all, however, is the title.

The concept of *one heartbeat* comes straight from the soul of Coach Royal. It speaks not only about how you should play as a team—coming together for that thrust that sends life blood throughout a body—it talks about matters of the heart, about how you should treat people, win or lose. It's about leadership, pride, and character, winning games with class, having fun, and preparing for life after football.

Coach Royal's impact on college football in the '60s and '70s was incredible. The man won eleven league championships, three national championships and put together a thirty-game winning streak. He brought innovations that changed the game. It is hard to imagine that he quit coaching twenty-five years ago at the age of fifty-two. But he never quit loving the game, and he never quit caring about the kids who played it at Texas. All you have to do to realize this is go to a reunion of his players and see how much they appreciate and respect him.

He was one of the major reasons I took the job at Texas. Looking back, the friendship I have had with him is one of the most meaningful parts of this job. Seeing him with our players, watching him enjoy our staff and be a part of the return of our lettermen has been a gift.

In this book, I have a chance to share some advice from a lot of people who have helped me, like Gil Brandt of the Dallas Cowboys and Coach Paul Dietzel, who became my great friends. Guys like Chuck Neinas and Wright Waters saw me through some good times and some tough times. Head coaches Barry Switzer, Bobby Collins, and Jerry Stovall all had valuable advice for me as a young coach. David McWilliams and the late Mike Campbell helped our staff in so many ways when we came to Texas, and Fred Akers could not have been more supportive.

A big part of our success belongs to the high school coaches in Texas, North Carolina, and Louisiana. Eddie Joseph and his staff at the Texas High School Coaches Association, Charlie Adams of the North Carolina Coaches Association, and Tommy Henry of the Louisiana High School Coaches Association do a great job.

Part of that *one heartbeat* at Texas comes from the valued friends and supporters who are there, no matter what. These are people who don't try to run your business, but if you ask for their advice, they are there in, well, a heartbeat. It helps to be able to pick up the phone and bounce something off of them.

I can't talk about the Texas legacy without giving credit to the lettermen who built the hallowed Longhorn tradition on the field. Having Earl Campbell around our team, and counting on visitors such as Tommy Nobis, Bob Moses, Chris Gilbert, Roosevelt Leaks, James Street, Johnny Treadwell, and Rooster Andrews allows us to bring that Texas pride to our current players in a special way. Frank Denius, one of the most decorated heroes of D-Day and World War II, gives an example to our special teams, and to our team in general, about duty and honor. He's a modest man who comes to every practice, and few people realize that among his many gifts is the money with which the practice fields were built.

Coach Royal's message of the heart talked about all of those people and many, many more who will weave through the chapters of this book.

One Heartbeat is about team. It is a message to our assistant coaches and support staff to build a solid foundation, to teach our players how to win and to expect to win.

For the players, *one heartbeat* is a guidepost of life. It is a great example of what they can achieve in life, not only on the field, but beyond. It is a message of accountability, of trust, of faith in each other, and of faith in oneself. It is symbolic of all of the values I was taught as a kid.

We try to instill in our players the meaning of pride and the meaning of courage. When we leave the locker room on the way to the field at Royal-Texas Memorial Stadium, our players walk down a corridor which is lined with the plaques of Texas's all-Americans and academic all-Americans. At the end of the hall is a set of horns from a longhorn steer under a sign that says "Don't Mess With Texas." The players touch those horns to remind them of the pride with which those all-Americans played. Outside, they wait at the Steinmark scoreboard, named for Freddie Steinmark, the little safety on the national championship team of 1969. Freddie became a national symbol of courage when he lost his leg to cancer after the national championship game and then battled for life for a year and a half before losing the fight. As we wait in the tunnel to enter the field, we touch Freddie's picture. It represents the courage with which he lived his life. If you can feel that pride and that courage and you don't play hard when you hit that field, then you shouldn't be playing football for The University of Texas.

That commitment obviously works; our first twenty games at home, we were 18-2.

I treasure every minute I have with Coach Royal because he can take something complicated and make it simple. He has given counsel and opened doors for me that I could never have imagined. He has spent his life giving to others.

I guess that's why I agreed, as I turn fifty, to do this book. I wanted to give something back, too.

I learned a lot from the people in this book. Marc Pittman, who lost his son in a tragic truck accident, taught me about courage. Players like Ricky Williams and Hodges Mitchell taught me about being competitors and about being yourself. My players at North Carolina taught me about standing up for what you believe, and how to stand by what you believe until it works.

In my first season at Texas, after we beat Nebraska on the road to snap their forty-seven-game home winning streak, we called Coach Royal from the locker room. He told me his palms were sweating, and he was pacing, just as if he were coaching again. It was hard, as he relived that uneasy feeling that comes only to a coach's gut. But he also felt the joy of victory and the thrill of the game because it is in his blood.

And it manifests itself in *one heartbeat*.

DESTINY'S DESTINATION

"IT'S GOOD TO HAVE YOUR EYES ON
THE MOUNTAINTOP, BUT AS YOU'RE
GOING UP THAT MOUNTAIN,
WATCH WHERE YOU'RE WALKING."

—Mack Brown

1 Challenges

"THERE IS A LESSON IN EACH CHALLENGE AND WHILE YOU WON'T WIN ALL OF THEM, LEARNING TO HANDLE THEM AND TURN THEM INTO POSITIVES WILL MAKE YOUR LIFE A WHOLE LOT BETTER.**"**

—Mack Brown

◀ MEETING THE CHALLENGE - Special teams leader Beau Trahan
(18) is greeted by Mack Brown and Cleve Bryant. Trahan
represents the message of *One Heartbeat* and Challenges
as well as anyone on the team.

BL

To the farmer, it is a prayer for rain even when meteorologists say it won't. To the doctor and the nurse, it can be a delicate fight when the margin of life is very thin. The investor sees it as the gamble of when to buy or sell. A businessman worries about the bottom line and the people he's responsible for. The oilman searches for oil and the engineer strives to find better ways to do things—build smaller chips and taller buildings, safer bridges and better roads. The soldier, the policeman, and the fire fighter put themselves on the line for others. The teachers and state employees work every day with low pay, but with high goals to make a difference in people's lives. The moms and dads rear their kids, and the kids take on the formidable task of just being. The player tries to beat the opponent or the highest standard of the game itself.

Maybe it's about a journey, maybe it's about an adventure. This much is certain: destiny may really have a destination, but day-to-day living is about challenges.

Dr. Richard Coop, a professor of educational psychology who works with some of the greatest golfers in the world and teaches at the University of North Carolina, will tell you that the stakes may be different for each of us, but when it comes to taking care of business and managing our personal lives, everyone has challenges.

"If you wait until everything in your life is going perfectly in order to be happy, you won't be happy very often. Learning to accept the fact that you will have challenges almost daily is a very important aspect of having a satisfying and fulfilling life," Coop says. "I tell the golfers I work with to be prepared to handle at least three challenges each round. If there are more challenges one day, then borrow from tomorrow."

Dick Coop's philosophy touches businesses and teams, corporate executives and coaches, because companies and teams are made up of people, not computers.

And employees, just like players on a team, are looking for true leadership.

"Motivational techniques that are not consistent with how the leader lives his or her life will not work," says Coop. "They become gimmicks, because they are perceived as phony by the team, whether it is a football team or a business team or children in a family reacting to a parent."

After almost thirty years in the coaching profession, Mack Brown understands challenges. As a head coach, he took on those challenges at four diverse, yet similar, universities. Appalachian State offered a small-town atmosphere in the mountains of North Carolina, a wonderful place to live, and a good education. Tulane was known as a fine private educational institution located in New Orleans, one of America's unique cities. It had little recent football tradition in a state where the football power was the state school, Louisiana State University.

The University of North Carolina was known throughout the country as a college basketball mecca. Texas had a storied football tradition, but its football program had been inconsistent for fifteen years prior to Brown's arrival. Both Carolina and Texas were recognized nationally for their academic excellence and both Chapel Hill and Austin were rated among the best places to live in the United States.

At all four schools, it was critical, as Brown has so often said, "to win championships with nice kids who graduate." At each head coaching stop, Brown entered the arena where teams had struggled. Carolina and Texas were cases so typical of many found in the corporate world. The programs had flattened after significant success.

"His overall winning percentage will never reflect the kind of coach he is," says Coop. "He is a big picture person who is simultaneously very aware of the small details. Most people can do one or the other well, but not both. The ability to do both is what makes a great executive in any field."

Darrell Royal was perhaps as good an executive as there ever was in the world of college football.

In the summer of 2001, when people asked about the potential for the Texas team, Royal knew the answer. In the decade from 1961 through 1970, his teams won three national championships, but two losses and a tie kept them from three others.

"I tell people it will depend on how that oblong ball bounces—and it will bounce—in one or two critical games," Royal said. "Regardless how good you are or how much talent you have, there will come a time when you have to ante up if you want to play in big stakes games."

History underscores his reasoning. In 1963, Texas won its first national championship under Royal by coming from behind in the final minutes to defeat Texas A&M, 15-13. The Aggies had won only two games that season. In 1969, there was the famous rally to beat Arkansas, 15-14, in the "Game of the Century." Early in the 1970 season, a miraculous forty-five-yard scoring pass with only twelve seconds left beat UCLA, 20-17.

Writers have called those "defining moments".

Dr. Coop of Carolina would call them challenges.

Before the Oklahoma football game in 1999, Coach Royal told our team a story. It was about a guy named J. V. McEwing, who had gone to grade school with Coach in Hollis, Oklahoma. Every day as they walked home from school, there was this big kid who picked on J. V. Finally, J. V. had had enough. He challenged the ol' boy, and the guy whipped him. The next day, J. V. jumped on him again, and again the bigger guy seemed to have the better of it.

"I thought J. V. had lost the fight," Coach said, "but the next day, that big boy took another route home. We never saw him again on our path."

Red McCombs is one of the strongest men I know. If anybody understands challenges, it's Red. He started as a used car dealer with fifty dollars in his pocket, and today he owns the Minnesota Vikings and recently gave $50 million to our business school. He's had his personal challenges, and he helps people by being open and honest about the struggles he faced with alcohol and tobacco.

What J. V. McEwing and Red McCombs tell us is you need to understand the challenge and know what you have to do to overcome it.

Too often, we spend our time worrying about the wrong things. We're not effective if we spend 95 percent of our time worrying about 5 percent of our team. Concentrate on the right things, and pick your battles. We've all heard the expression that we are worrying about rat manure when there is elephant manure all around.

In a single football game, each team will run an average of seventy-five plays, but when it's all over, you'll find that five or six plays—call them challenges if you want—will determine who wins or loses. If you beat your opponent on those critical plays, you are likely to win the game.

My friends in the business world tell me that being a head coach is a lot like running a company. At each of the places I have coached, the environment was different and so was I.

I was young when I went to Appalachian State, and I remember well the first recruiting class we brought in. Appalachian is in the Smoky Mountains in Boone, North Carolina. It's a great place to live, and the atmosphere is completely collegiate. We brought in thirteen players—several from Florida—that first recruiting weekend, and we had a twenty-eight-inch snowstorm. I had just gotten there, so I didn't know we ever got that much snow. You can imagine how I felt when we sat the guys down to look at a recruiting video that the university had put together. It featured "winter sports fun" in Boone. There were lots of pictures of the snow, including some at football games.

One player after another met with me on Sunday and each just gazed out the window instead of paying attention to our conversation. Twelve of them clearly weren't coming. Finally, I met with a young man named John Settle, an outstanding running back who was being recruited by all the big schools. I had been surprised that he had even decided to visit.

He was the last recruit of the day, and I was prepared for another "no."

Reluctantly, I asked him, "What do you think?"

"I love it," he said, adding, "I have always watched those NFL games played up north and I have dreamed of playing football in the snow."

I looked to the sky and said a little, "Thank you, Lord," because I realized we had the first block in a solid foundation. John went on to become a 1,000-yard rusher two years in a row and was a big reason the Appalachian program got moving in the right direction. In the National Football League, John rushed for 1,000 yards for the Atlanta Falcons. He now coaches the running backs at Fresno State.

What I learned at Appalachian helped me in every job I've had.

You have to understand your product or your company or your university and recruit to it. Those are the kinds of challenges you can turn into positives. If you coach where it snows, recruit guys who can play and who like snow instead of those who complain about it. They are out there.

One day at North Carolina, I was really struggling with some personal issues and with our team. We weren't winning, and I had had about ten crises that day and it wasn't even lunch yet. I called my wife, Sally, and said, "I think I'm going to quit. I have just had it."

She said, "Well, don't do it right now. Let's meet for lunch and talk about it." She called Dick Coop, and the three of us met.

"If you want to quit, fine," they told me. "But wait a minute. Don't make any life-changing decisions like that if you are mad, tired, or confused."

As we talked, Dick gave me a game plan that still helps me today. He said to look at what you dislike about your job and at what you enjoy about it. Then figure out how to do more of what you enjoy and less of what you don't. For a head coach, that was tremendously valuable because I was trying to do everything. I wasn't turning loose of anything. From that day, I began delegating better. I gave the things I didn't enjoy to somebody else who would get them done. I realized I was doing things that zapped my energy, and they weren't helping anyone.

What was amazing was that I also realized that I was really feeling sorry for myself, and when you talk about challenges, I was way down on the list of guys with problems.

They tell me there is an exercise done in seminars where the participants write their problems up on a board. By the time the exercise is over, everybody wants to take his problems down because they seem so small in comparison.

After we lost Cole Pittman, our football player who was killed in a truck wreck in the spring of 2001, I said to his dad, Marc, "I don't see how you keep going."

"I don't have a choice," he told me. "If I could make it different, I would. But I can't."

Those are the kinds of challenges we struggle to handle. They test the human spirit. We may not want to deal with them, but they are there every day. And it's important for us to help each other understand.

Cole used to call his dad each night at 9:30. For months after his death, every night at 9:30 one of our players called him. They knew they couldn't replace Cole, but they wanted his dad to know they were there for him.

When I was nineteen years old, I had my fifth knee operation, and I knew my football career was over. As I lay in the hospital bed in Tallahassee, there was a curtain between the guy in the next bed and me. His legs had been injured in a train accident, and he was screaming all night that his legs hurt. When they came in to check his injuries, they pulled the curtain back; I could see his face and he was truly in pain.

Then, they pulled the covers back and I saw that he had no legs. He was delirious, and the nerve endings in his knee made him feel that his feet were hurting.

I never knew what happened to the man, but I do know that at that moment I realized that the challenge of my knee injury wasn't nearly as bad as I had thought it was.

I loved the game of football, and if I couldn't play the game, maybe there was something I could do in the game that would be of value to me, and therefore, to someone else. I tried to understand that there is a lesson in each challenge, and while you won't win all of them, learning to handle them and turn them into positives will make your life a whole lot better.

Blue Skies,
Burnt Orange Sunsets

❝AND SO IT WAS THAT ONE FATEFUL SATURDAY AFTERNOON
IN SEPTEMBER, UNDER A CAROLINA BLUE SKY AND
HEADED TOWARD A BURNT ORANGE SUNSET,
DESTINY RODE TWO DIFFERENT HORSES
FOR JOHN MACKOVIC AND MACK BROWN.**❞**

—Bill Little

◀ CAROLINA BLUE – The Brown family found a home in North Carolina. Here daughters Barbara and Katherine and Mack's mom, Katherine Brown, enjoy a Tar Heel trip to the Sun Bowl in 1994.

BL

Late in the first-ever Big 12 Conference championship game in 1996—a game John Mackovic and his Texas Longhorns were predicted to lose by three touchdowns—Mackovic and his quarterback, James Brown, decided to surprise the whole world. Texas was leading by just three points and was fewer than three minutes from a stunning upset over Nebraska. On what would forever be known as "fourth and inches," Mackovic told James Brown to run "Steelers roll left," which called for a quarterback option run or pass. No matter that he was deep in his own territory—James obliged. If Nebraska held, it would mean an almost certain Cornhusker score that would tie or win the game. As the defense stuffed the line to stop a plunge up the middle, James headed left. When he got to the spot where he would cut in for a first down that would keep the Texas drive alive, the quarterback saw a linebacker filling the hole.

Standing all alone, a few yards behind the defender, was tight end Derek Lewis. Brown straightened and lobbed a pass that Lewis caught. As he streaked toward the goal line and eventual victory, it seemed he was taking with him all the demons that had plagued John Mackovic in his time at Texas.

Far away in Chapel Hill, North Carolina, Mack Brown watched in agony as Lewis ran. His North Carolina Tar Heels, who had lost only to Florida State and Virginia that season, were poised to join the elite of college football if Nebraska won. If the Cornhuskers beat Texas, North Carolina was a good candidate for an at-large bid as one of the six teams in the Bowl Championship Series. With Texas's victory, the at-large bid went to previously unbeaten Nebraska.

Mackovic's riverboat gambler call was celebrated across the nation. Even though an injury-riddled Texas team lost to Penn State in the Fiesta Bowl, during the spring and summer of 1997, Mackovic's future appeared more secure than at any time during his Texas tenure. He was relaxed and confident as the Longhorns entered the fall ranked among the nation's elite. The euphoria surrounding football among the Longhorn faithful was back, and the showcase was to be a nationally televised game with UCLA on September 13.

If the inflated optimism was a bit premature in Austin, thirteen hundred miles away in Chapel Hill, Mack Brown knew he had the makings of a powerhouse football team. As his squad headed to Navy Field for its first practice of the fall, the Tar Heels were listed among the nation's preseason top ten.

The season before, his team had achieved ten victories and finished ranked in the nation's top ten. It was a far cry from the beginning in 1988, when Brown had taken over a program that had posted just one winning season in its last four years. The early years were hard and full of frustration, as Brown's teams managed only a 1-10 record each of his first two seasons. Yet that was only a faint memory that summer, for Brown's record over his last six years had put him among the nation's leading coaches.

Each season, the Tar Heels were getting closer to unseating Atlantic Coast Conference kingpin, Florida State. Knowledgeable national reporters recognized it, and Brown's loyal supporters in Carolina knew it, too. But the rich, storied tradition of North Carolina Blue was vested deep in its basketball program, and football was a sport to be appreciated only at a certain level. Any conversation about Carolina football usually migrated to a discussion of the potential of Dean Smith's basketball team, which was the linchpin of Carolina athletic success.

And so it was that one fateful Saturday afternoon in September, under a Carolina blue sky and headed toward a burnt orange sunset, destiny rode two different horses for John Mackovic and Mack Brown.

ABC television began the 1997 season with the theme "America's Greatest Road Show—College Football on ABC." On campuses across the nation, the production crews sought out students, faculty, and staff members to sing the jingle to begin the telecast.

In Austin before the UCLA game, a talented singer and former cheerleader, Emilie Williams, was the featured performer. She and another student convinced Mackovic that he should join in the sing-along, and when the camera flashed to the Texas coach saying "…College Football on ABC," it prompted announcer Brad Nessler to begin the telecast with the fateful words, "You can tell John Mackovic is feeling comfortable when you can get him to sing before a big intersectional college football game…."

But without James Brown, his experienced star quarterback who was injured in the opening game of the season, things began badly and got worse for Mackovic and the Longhorns. By halftime, UCLA led Texas, 38-0.

Meanwhile, in Chapel Hill, Mack Brown and his team prepared for a late afternoon televised game with Stanford. When the public address announcer gave the Texas-UCLA score, Brown and his quarterbacks coach, Cleve Bryant, who had coached with Mackovic at Texas and Illinois, were standing together during pregame warm-ups on the field.

"Naah," said Bryant. "That can't be right."

A couple of hours later, there was a lull in the action at Kenan Stadium in North Carolina. The public address announcer gave the final score: UCLA 66, Texas 3.

"I wouldn't want to be in Austin, Texas, tonight. I really hate that for those guys," said Bryant to Brown, who took but a second to digest the score, then turned back to his own game, which the Tar Heels won, 28-17.

In the press box, veteran North Carolina sports information director Rick

Brewer was handed scores of all big games to pass on to Dave Lohse, his assistant who handled the press box announcing duties.

Brewer, who understood Brown's love for the history and tradition of football and had often heard him speak of his admiration for former Texas coach Darrell Royal, slid the score to Lohse.

"I think we just lost our football coach," Brewer said.

There were other factors involved in Brewer's analysis. He knew of Brown's great friendship with former North Carolina athletics director John Swofford, who had moved on to become the commissioner of the ACC. Brewer knew that for Brown, trust and honesty were the qualities held in the highest regard in any relationship. He had had that with Swofford, but now, Carolina had a new administration.

Brewer also knew that Brown had taken Carolina about as far as he could take them. He had built the program from the dust of two 1-10 seasons into a solid structure on the national landscape.

"Mack had done everything he could do," said Brewer. "He never got the appreciation he should have. He built a tremendous football facility, and he left it for future generations. He didn't build it for Mack Brown, and he didn't take it with him when he left, yet there were still some people who were angry at him for leaving."

Weeks after that September afternoon, Brown and his wife, Sally, headed to lunch with Cleve Bryant and his wife, Jean. The Bryants had been in Austin while Cleve served as receivers coach for Mackovic during his first three years at Texas.

They drove down Franklin Street, turning at their good friend James Spurling's gas station, and headed out to The Loop, a little deli on Highway 15-501.

After the final game with Duke, Carolina was ranked number seven in the country, its only loss coming to number one-ranked Florida State, 20-3.

"DeLoss Dodds [University of Texas athletics director] has called about the Texas job," Brown said to Bryant. "Should I be interested in it?"

It took one sip from the sweetened iced tea for Bryant to answer.

"Definitely." Bryant began. "I can't think of a better fit for The University of Texas or for you. Your personality is exactly what they want, and you can recruit and coach at the level they need. You've given this university everything you can give them. You've taken them to a level where they've never been before in football."

The conversation continued, and Brown asked the Bryants if they would be willing to join them if Texas were interested in talking to Brown. Sally's concern was how Texas treated its student athletes on and off the football field.

Bryant had left the Mackovic staff following the 1994 season, but had maintained contact with some of his former colleagues who had been giving him ominous reports on the future of the current UT program.

As the final bites of the lunch were finished, Brown surmised that for several reasons a consensus of the "sandwich committee" might not even be an issue. First, Brown and his wife were very happy at North Carolina and had declined to even look at a lot of other coaching opportunities. Besides, Texas could hire just about anyone they wanted. The media was ripe with rumors that the Longhorn power structure had already picked a coach, and it wasn't Mack Brown.

MB

My main focus for the entire season of 1997 was to win the ACC and the national championship. It had nothing to do with The University of Texas. As with any high profile coaching job, I was aware of it, and Texas had an assistant coach who kept calling Cleve Bryant telling him things were finished for John Mackovic. Cleve stayed loyal to John and told the assistant coach to quit calling and to focus on winning at Texas.

At first, I was surprised. We had played Texas in the 1994 Sun Bowl, and I was impressed with the program John was building. I knew of their recent success, and everybody in the country was aware of their upset win over Nebraska. The UCLA loss was a shocker, and Texas never seemed to recover. Then they ended the season at 4-7, after being rated very high in preseason. But that was a long way from my mind at the end of that season.

What I wanted most, for our school and our team, was a berth in the Bowl Alliance. At that time, the alliance included the six teams playing in the Sugar, Fiesta, and Orange Bowls. Since the ACC champion automatically got a bid, I knew if we beat Florida State we could possibly play for the national championship. Even with a loss, with a 10-1 record, I felt as though we deserved one of the two at-large spots.

Our kids had earned that right.

We had just finished our football facility, and we were excited about moving into our offices that December. Recruiting was going well. We already had seventeen top commitments for the 1998 signing period.

Sally's business continued to do very well. Her real estate development company was one of the most successful in Chapel Hill. She had just purchased over five hundred acres to develop in that area. Our kids were growing up with strong Carolina ties. Matt was at Western Carolina, Katherine was a student at North Carolina, and Barbara and Chris were both talking about going to school there as well.

In order for us to make a change, it would have had to be the perfect situation. And in literally a matter of days, that situation arose.

John Mackovic was fired November 30, the day after the Texas-Texas A&M game. At about the same time, I learned from John Swofford that the Bowl Alliance committee would be choosing two other at-large teams, and our team would be returning to the Gator Bowl for the second straight year, despite being ranked in the nation's top eight all season long. Rick Catlett, executive director of the Gator Bowl, and the Jacksonville people do a great job, but our kids deserved a Bowl Championship Series bid. For the second year in a row, we had been left out, despite having one of the nation's best teams.

One of the questions the BCS asks schools considered for at-large bids is whether the schools are willing to guarantee the purchase of a large block of tickets. The other schools under consideration did that; we did not. I believe our athletic administration should have fought harder for us. Our team had done everything it could do on the field. They'd played their hearts out before losing to number one-ranked Florida State, and that loss should not have cost us a chance to play in a tier one bowl.

Knowing how disappointed I was, Chuck Neinas, the former head of the College Football Association and a dear friend, called after John Mackovic's reassignment and asked if I would be interested in the job. As Sally and I talked about it, our first impression was that anyone who coaches football would be interested in coaching at The University of Texas. But from all we had heard, we felt the university was going in a different direction and had another coach in mind. And we were very happy where we were.

On Monday, as the speculation surrounding the Texas job went national, the media asked me after bowl practice if I was happy at North Carolina. My answer was very honest. It was "yes".

"Well," they asked, "are you planning on staying here?"

I said, "I'm planning on staying here a long time."

And that was the truth.

When I got a call from DeLoss Dodds, my feelings didn't suddenly change. Sally and I were planning on staying at North Carolina. When we agreed to talk to them, we decided they had to really want us and we had to like what we heard. All of that happened. It happened very quickly.

There was a lot of irony in the whole situation. In 1986, when I was head coach at Tulane, Chuck Neinas and I were having dinner. We were talking about the good jobs in college football, and I knew Chuck and DeLoss were close friends dating back to their Big 8 days.

"I'll tell you what," I said, "if you get me the Texas job one day, I'll give you my first year of radio and television money." He made me write it down on a cocktail napkin and sign it. We laughed about it, but I never thought it might come true.

There wasn't a lot of discussion about the Texas job in our house until DeLoss called. In fact, we had a lot of anxiety about whether or not we should even discuss the job.

I decided to meet with the athletics director and the chancellor at North Carolina and ask for a ten-year contract and a salary that would match that of our basketball coach, Bill Guthridge. I had two years left on my contract, and I didn't even know how much money Bill was making. Bill was a great coach and a great friend and deserved whatever they were paying him, but I thought it was important that the ten-year football coach make as much as the first-year basketball coach.

The North Carolina administration told me to interview with Texas and perhaps they would match their offer. I told them I didn't feel comfortable with that scenario. It wasn't fair to Texas or the UNC fans and players. Besides, I believe you should pay a person what you think he's worth, not what somebody else thinks he's worth. But the chancellor and the athletics director insisted that I talk to Texas before renegotiating with them. I thought that was a little strange, but that's what we all decided to do.

We were not interested in traveling to Austin to talk about the job, but Sally and I were going to the ACC Awards banquet in Atlanta. We had ten players on the all-Conference team (Dré Bly, Greg Ellis, Vonnie Holliday, Kivuusama Mays, Jeff Saturday, Robert Williams, Omar Brown, Alge Krumpler, Jonathan Linton and Brian Simmons), so it was a special time for us. A lot of those seniors had decided to stay for a fifth year, and we wanted to be there for their awards banquet. Those kids had won twenty-one games over their last two seasons. They were part of a special class. We loved those kids very much.

So we said if the Texas people wanted to meet us in Atlanta, we'd talk to them.

I really thought we'd just talk, then go home and see if there was enough interest from our standpoint and from theirs to continue discussions. Chuck had told us the plan was to see if there was enough interest on both sides to schedule a formal interview the following week in New York during the week of the College Football Hall of Fame. More than anything, we felt as if we'd be back in Chapel Hill for the rest of our lives.

When we got up on Wednesday, Tom Hicks, owner of the Texas Rangers and the Dallas Stars, and the Board of Regents representative on the Texas screening committee, was quoted in *USA Today* as saying, "We are looking for a guy who could win the national championship."

Sally said, "Well, here's your first question: are you that guy?"

In the early discussions with DeLoss, Tom, and Chuck Neinas, we had a great two hours. Sally and I were very relaxed and were having a lot of fun. There was no pressure in the meeting. We both enjoyed talking with Tom and DeLoss, and Sally and I love and trust Chuck. Both Chuck and John Swofford had told me DeLoss was one of the best athletics directors in the country. DeLoss said, "We have some other people downstairs, and we'd like for you to eat lunch with us."

I thought we'd head to the coffee shop, but instead we walked into a meeting room where the entire screening committee was waiting. It was an impressive group. Besides DeLoss and Tom, there were Dallas business developer Mike Myers, who represented the Ex-Students Association, and Mack Rankin, Jr., who was chairman of the Longhorn Foundation Advisory Committee. Dr. Waneen Spirduso, head of the kinesiology department, was chairperson of the Athletics Council, and law professor Charles Alan Wright was well-known nationally for all of his work with the NCAA. Butch Worley, Texas's Senior Associate Athletic Director, was DeLoss's staff liaison.

There were four former Texas football players on the committee—Alfred Jackson, Corby Robertson, Bob Moses, and Doug English—and the guy I wanted to see most, Coach Darrell Royal.

Sally and I talked for another hour or so with the committee. At lunch, I had a great chance to visit with Coach Royal, who seemed sincerely interested in my taking the job. The fact that he cared so much really touched and impressed me. But then, who wouldn't be impressed with Coach Royal? Coach and I were sharing stories and Sally was talking to Doug English and Mike Myers about development when DeLoss suggested we go back upstairs.

We said fine, because we were getting ready to return to Chapel Hill, and they were scheduled to talk to another coach.

When we got back to the suite at the Four Seasons, DeLoss said, "We want you and Sally to come to Austin; we want you to run our football program."

We were overwhelmed, because we were not in any position to make a decision. We hadn't even had a chance to talk privately. Obviously, we wanted to find out more about the position, but I sure didn't want to be interested unless the committee was unanimous, because we knew the Texas job would be a tough one.

For a lot of reasons, Texas had not been consistent for a number of years. Sally and I didn't want to leave a place we loved that was comfortable to go to a situation where there were too many unknowns.

We had thought the meeting was going to be more of a "Let's sit down, visit, and see if there is anything for the future." Then, suddenly, they were offering me the job. They even wanted us to go back to Austin with them right then.

There was no way we could do that. They offered to fly us back to Chapel Hill in a private jet, but we told them we'd fly home on our own. It was an overwhelming offer, but we wanted to talk to our family, our team, and our staff.

We had a lot to talk about, a lot of things to consider.

Going To Texas

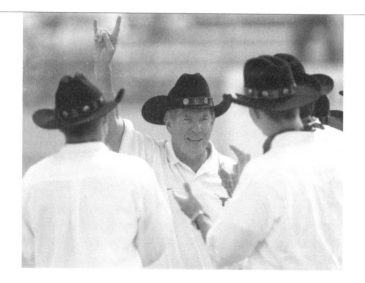

❝ IT IS IMPORTANT TO UNDERSTAND THAT MACK BROWN COMPLETELY BLEW THE COMMITTEE AWAY. IT WAS NOT A CASE OF ONE GUY DOING SOMETHING WRONG, IT WAS SIMPLY THAT MACK WAS EVERYTHING THAT WAS RIGHT. ❞

—Darrell Royal

◀ HOOK 'EM 'HORNS - With gifts of a Texas flag which flew over the State Capitol the day he was hired and a cowboy hat presented by a student service organization, Longhorns celebrated the arrival of their new head coach.

BL

I n the posh Four Seasons Hotel, the battle of Atlanta had begun. Only this time, it would not be a struggle fought with cannons, but rather it would be a tug-of-war of the heart. It had been significant that Mack and Sally Brown had come together to the interview. They were a package deal.

On the flight back to the regional airport serving Raleigh, Durham, and Chapel Hill, Mack Brown was a man torn between what he knew people would tell him he should do, and what deep inside he knew he had to do.

At North Carolina, he had the best situation a man could want. He had established a strong program, he had achieved job security, and Sally had built a successful business. Yet the North Carolina administration was sending mixed messages. With only a few years left on Brown's contract, rather than being proactive and renegotiating, they had encouraged him to talk with Texas.

And there were voices of a childhood inside him telling him to follow his heart.

When the Browns emerged from the final meeting with Dodds and returned to the committee, Darrell Royal was standing outside the room. The coaching legend looked at his younger friend and knew what Brown's decision would be. Royal put his arms around Brown and hugged him.

Inside the conference room, the committee was resolved.

"Before we left Austin," said former Longhorn star Doug English, "we determined we would look at every coach in the country. Each of us said the qualities we were seeking in a coach. We put them all together, and the guy who emerged as the best candidate was Mack Brown. We said, 'If this guy is anything close to what we think he is, he is the one.' He was all that and more."

For Royal, the trip to Atlanta was a pilgrimage to find the one person he believed could lead the Texas program back to the level where it had once been. At seventy-three, the man who one year before had received the honor of having his name added to Texas Memorial Stadium, knew this might be his last search committee if this one didn't work. Twenty-one years before, he had had his heart broken when a committee, searching for Royal's successor, bypassed his recommendation of his good friend Mike Campbell in favor of Fred Akers.

Ten years later, Royal had supported the hiring of former Longhorn captain

David McWilliams and had watched in agony as McWilliams's program failed.

Royal knew that DeLoss Dodds and Tom Hicks had met that Wednesday morning in Chicago with another Division I head coach, the man the media had proclaimed as the favorite and a lock for the job. He knew the plan was for the committee to leave Atlanta and go interview the other candidate in St. Louis.

But the entire screening committee had been captivated with meeting Brown. There was clearly a contrast in the style of the two men, both of whom had been successful at their respective institutions.

"It is important to understand," Royal would say later, "that Mack Brown completely blew the committee away. It was not a case of one guy doing something wrong, it was simply that Mack was everything that was right."

After a caucus with the screening committee, Dodds made the appropriate calls to the other candidates to tell them Brown had been offered the job.

As the two limousines carrying the Texas contingent and the Browns prepared to go their separate ways, Dodds looked at Royal as the two were about to get into the car. "Go over there," Dodds said, "and make him look you in the eye one last time. He trusts you. This is really a hard decision for him. We don't want to lose him."

The last thing Mack Brown saw as the car left the Four Seasons was the steel blue eyes of Darrell Royal.

"I've always felt," says Butch Worley, who was riding with Dodds and Royal, "that that moment may have been the thing that made the difference. It would have been easy for Mack to stay at North Carolina, but I knew if we had one thing in our favor, it was his respect for Coach Royal."

That night, the other candidate withdrew his name from consideration.

But Mack and Sally Brown still had a lot of thinking to do. On the way to the airport, he tried, as had been their plan, to call his athletics director, Dick Baddour, who was with the North Carolina basketball team in Chicago at a preseason tournament.

Worley, who handled the details of the coach search for Dodds, had reached Baddour as he was boarding a plane to accompany the Tar Heels to the tournament.

When he arrived in Chicago, Baddour called Worley back.

"Dick," said Worley, "I'm sure you know why I'm calling. We'd like to request permission to talk to Mack Brown about our head coaching vacancy."

"How long do you think the process will take?" asked Baddour.

"Forty-eight hours," said Worley.

There was a long silence on the other end of the phone.

"You're kidding," Baddour said.

"No," said Worley. "If this is not a fit for us and a fit for him, we'll move on. We're not going to keep anybody hanging."

There was another long silence, and then Baddour said, "Okay."

Worley figured Baddour would be on the next plane back to Chapel Hill, trying to keep Brown. Instead, he never left Chicago.

On the way to the airport in Atlanta, Brown repeatedly tried to call Baddour, but there was no answer on his cell phone.

They say timing in life is everything, and in December of 1997, it was working in Texas's favor.

Looking back, I think Sally and I were both overwhelmed as we left the Four Seasons and headed for the airport. On the way to Atlanta, Sally said she felt there was a good chance they'd want to interview us, but she thought that after the first meeting in Atlanta, we'd go home and determine whether we wanted to go to New York to be interviewed. We discussed how far we would want to go with it because we wanted to be fair to the North Carolina people who had been so good to us.

If, when we left that meeting they had said, "Well, we're not sure...we'll get back with you," we would have gone home and said, "There's no 'getting back.'" If they had said, "We're really interested, but we have two more people to talk to," we probably still would have pulled out because we weren't hunting for a job.

Then DeLoss walked up and offered me the job, and Coach Royal told me I needed to take it.

We had tried to reach Dick Baddour before we left, and when we landed in North Carolina, we turned on the radio to the basketball game. Woody Durham and Mick Mickson were calling the game, and the Tar Heels were leading.

One of them broke in, saying, "There is a report out of Austin that Mack Brown has taken the Texas job." Sally and I just looked at each other.

There was no doubt we were very interested, and I'm sure the committee felt that. But we had players, coaches, and families to talk to. There were a lot of people involved in a decision like this. We called DeLoss from our car and asked his permission to say that we had been offered the job. He said, "That's fine, but you need to take it."

I still couldn't reach Dick Baddour. When we got home we had media representatives banging on the door and reports all over radio and television, and we were dealing with a dead cell phone. Finally, we called a friend in the media who called Woody and Mick to tell them the situation. They got Dick Baddour to call me. I told him I had been offered the job and was leaning toward taking it, but that I had a lot of things to consider. We agreed to meet the next day.

Midnight marked the beginning of the longest day of our lives together. We already had a team meeting scheduled at 3:00 P.M. to talk about bowl preparations. There was no chance for sleep, between the media and the internal questions we struggled with. I was overloaded. On the one hand, the Texas job was one I had looked at as a young coach and said, "If Texas ever calls, I definitely have to talk to them." On the other hand, we had built so much at North Carolina.

Then it hit me that I was sitting here miserable because of the pressures I was putting on myself. There was pressure on Sally because this had become her home. There was pressure on me because I felt that I couldn't leave the players at North Carolina. But I had to separate the reality of the situation from my feelings for people.

41

The North Carolina program was in much better shape than we found it. Sally and I were both really proud that we had helped build one of the finest football facilities in the country. The realization that we might not be moving into that building was painful, but it wasn't about us. The building was a tribute to the legacy of the North Carolina football program.

The only other nagging guilt I felt was that I wished we had beaten Florida State and won the ACC Championship. When I took the job, FSU wasn't in the league. They definitely changed the deal in that league. We finished second a lot, but second is not good enough. That's the one thing we didn't accomplish, and I really regret that.

I had lost my dad and my granddad during that last year, and I wished somehow I could talk to them. The next day Sally brought that up.

"What would your grandfather and your dad say if they were still alive and sitting here with us?" she asked.

I knew that in both cases, they would kick my rear end if I didn't take the Texas job.

With morning came a blur of meetings and conversations. I spent most of the day with the staff, Sally, and Dick Coop.

I remember putting on a Carolina blue and gray sweater Sally had bought for me in Italy. We talked to our children, Dick Coop, and our staff the entire morning. Everyone was really supportive. Dick Baddour came over to our house around one o'clock that afternoon. The university offered me the package I had asked for, but Baddour made it clear that it would create a real hardship on the department if I took it. He also said, "If you want football to be equal to basketball, you should go to Texas."

Texas had offered $750,000. I was making $375,000 a year, with just two years remaining and no buyout clause. Bill Guthridge, Carolina's basketball coach, was making $1 million, with a five-year contract. Baddour said if they paid me the same salary, it would bankrupt the department. Sally and I felt as if Baddour, who had been a friend, was being sincere. He told us the chancellor had said to offer a ten-year contract, and the extension was the most important bargaining point to me, as I had only a few years left on my contract. He did add that he didn't feel the Board of Trustees would approve the long-term deal.

At that point, Sally and I felt that the new athletics director wanted to hire his own football coach and put his own stamp on the program. We both thought that was fair. Only Sally, Dick Baddour, and I were in the house at that time. As much as Sally wanted to stay in Chapel Hill, after talking to Dick a final time, she said, "I don't think we have a choice."

This wasn't about Bill Guthridge and me or football versus basketball. This was about whether the North Carolina football program was going to get the respect it had earned and whether the administration really wanted us to stay.

After Baddour left, Sally suggested one more thing that was critical in the decision process. She suggested I try to picture myself at the Texas press conference, accepting the job, and if it was a very proud moment in my professional life, then we should probably go. It was tremendously unselfish of her. I was so involved in the decision, I didn't realize how badly Sally really wanted to stay.

I wasn't very fair to DeLoss or to Texas that morning, because I kept them sitting and waiting all day wondering what we were going to do. Finally, at 2:30 P.M., I called him. Fifteen minutes later, I had my final meeting with Dick Baddour.

Then, at three o'clock, I went to the office to talk to the team. At that point in my career, it was the hardest thing I had ever done professionally. Members of the media were trying to grab me, and all I wanted to do was talk to my team. Sally couldn't go; it was just too hard for her. She had gotten so close to those kids. The toughest part was that I had told them I would be there for them, and in a matter of days, things had changed. It served no purpose to place blame on anybody. Those players were still going to be there, and if they were going to be angry, it was better for them to be angry at me than at North Carolina.

I tried to think of all the things I wanted them to hear, but in retrospect, they weren't going to hear anything. I can't remember everything I said. I was teary. I had a sciatic nerve problem and couldn't stand upright, so I had to lean over on my side. I do remember saying, "We brought you to a great school, and I hope you appreciate that fact." I also said, "I love you very much." I warned them that some people would be very critical of me and would try to get the players to say bad things. A few gave in to the negative, but most of the guys were very positive. When I finished, they gave me a standing ovation and there were a lot of hugs.

An hour later, we were on Tom Hicks's private jet to Texas. Our son Chris was in the back of the plane with his feet propped up. The flight attendant offered him food and a series of videotapes to watch on television.

"I don't know how the rest of this job's gonna be," he said, "but it's starting out really well."

When we arrived at the airport in Austin, I was still wearing that blue and gray sweater. We went straight to the stadium, where the Texas team was waiting. I remember thinking how anxious the kids looked.

I told them, "I know how you feel. You just lost your coach, and Sally and I just lost our team, so we're in this together."

I also said I didn't believe in "rebuilding years." We owed it to the seniors to make 1998 a good year. I wasn't sure how we would do it, or who we would do it with, but as we headed to a 10:00 P.M dinner with university officials, I knew that together, we would find a way.

At the end of a long day, I realized that there was truth in something Sally had said: We weren't leaving North Carolina, our home that we loved so much.

We were going to Texas.

The New Frontier

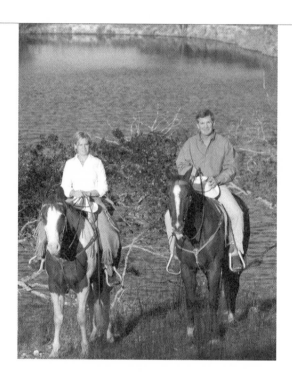

❝DO YOUR OWN THING AND BUILD ON
WHAT YOU CAN DO, NOT ON WHAT
SOMEBODY ELSE DIDN'T DO.❞

—Mack Brown

◀ RIDING THE RANGE – The Brown ranch near Austin provides
an off-season haven for Mack and Sally Brown, who enjoy
horseback riding and fishing in the Texas Hill Country.

BL

Had it only been twenty-four hours? Mack and Sally Brown could only
wonder, and they sought a moment of solitude as their elevator ascended
to the 21st floor of the Bank One Building and stepped into the polished
oak corridor of the Headliners Club in downtown Austin.

It was Wednesday, December 3, 1997. The night before, they had landed at
the regional airport in the research triangle of North Carolina and flipped on the
radio to a Tar Heel basketball game. Now, here they were, thirteen hundred miles
and a lifetime away in the Texas Hill Country.

They were tired, emotionally drained, and probably suffering a severe case of
"buyer's remorse"—the moment when the purchaser of a dream house thinks
frantically that maybe he or she should cancel the whole thing.

The visit with the Longhorn football team was like a balm to a wound. In
Mack Brown's home town of Cookeville, Tennessee, it would be like "new folks
movin' in." New friends, new opportunities. Only now and then did the Columbia
blue knit on Mack's sweater remind them of all they had left behind.

It was after ten o'clock when Mack and Sally arrived at dinner, and neither
could remember when they had last eaten. The dinner was practically a command
performance, attended by a select collection of university officials whose sole
purpose was to meet the Browns and make them feel welcome.

It was after midnight when they finally arrived at their suite at the Four Seasons
Hotel. Sixteen floors below, flickering lights reflected on Town Lake. A slight
December chill had set in, and for a moment from the balcony, Mack and Sally
Brown shivered in wonder and disbelief.

They awakened the next morning to newspaper headlines proclaiming Brown
as the new Texas head football coach, only the fifth man in the last forty years to
occupy the position many said was a harder job than being governor of the state.

A media conference was scheduled at 3:30 P.M. in the Burnt Orange Room of
the Frank C. Erwin Center, but first, Brown had meetings with UT administrators
and a lunch with the selection committee and members of the Men's Intercollegiate
Athletics Council.

At lunch, Brown felt like a college student pulling an all-nighter while cramming

45

for a final exam. He used every minute of the time to talk to Darrell Royal and others about Texas football traditions.

When Royal had first come to Texas forty years before, he had called on a friend to help him with public speaking. The friend gave him a poem to read about an old man who built a bridge for those who would follow him. Now, as Royal talked to Brown, Royal spoke about rebuilding bridges that, for many reasons, had fallen into disrepair.

Mack and Sally Brown walked into the packed room with the blazing camera lights bouncing burnt orange over television screens from New York to Chapel Hill and live to every station in Austin. The new head coach was ready. He worked from his notes and from his heart, and he accepted the head coaching job at the largest university in the country.

Then he posed for a picture that would become a symbol of his tenure at Texas—shaking hands in front of a burnt orange TEXAS banner with his new best friend, Darrell Royal.

Sometime in the next hours, euphoria gave way to reality. Mack had a job to do if he intended to turn the 4-7 Texas team into a winner, as he had done with rebuilding efforts at Appalachian State, Tulane, and North Carolina. It was time to get to work.

MB

The number one thing you can do when you take over a program is to meet with your team and to encourage them. You need to begin building communication, trust, and respect. The Texas team had been beaten up by the media and the fans, and they were really down. I wasn't so sure how "up" I was on the way to Austin, but before we went to dinner with anybody, I wanted to see those kids.

The next thing to do is get in touch with the kids who were being recruited by the previous staff and try to be honest with them. If they were promised a scholarship, I believe it's a coach's responsibility to live up to that commitment. By the same token, we had seventeen verbal commitments from outstanding players who had said they would come join us at North Carolina.

We called every one of those players and asked them to stay firm with that commitment to Carolina. They had chosen a university, not a football coach, and they had done it for all the right reasons. We had only one young man—he had lost his stepdad, so he stayed closer to home to be near his mom—who changed his mind and didn't sign with North Carolina. I feel very strongly that if you recruit young men and then you change jobs, you shouldn't recruit them for your new school, unless the other school was already recruiting them in the first place. We had no crossovers between North Carolina and Texas.

Coach Royal encouraged me to call Eddie Joseph of the Texas High School Coaches Association on the way to the press conference. He knew how important that relationship would be for our staff, and he knew how much I respected high school coaches. I also called Joe Jamail, the Houston attorney for whom the field at Royal-Texas Memorial Stadium is named, just to introduce myself and to let him know I was honored that I'd be coaching on the field that carries his name.

We were in an incredible whirlwind as far as timing was concerned. We had ended our season at North Carolina on November 22 with a 50-14 win over Duke and were awaiting a Sunday, December 7, decision of the Bowl Championship Series that would determine a bowl bid for the Tar Heels. I already knew the news was not good. I had learned on Tuesday before the BCS announcement on Sunday that Carolina would not be chosen, and I was crushed for our players and the UNC fans.

John Mackovic had been reassigned on Saturday, November 30, and on Thursday, December 4, I was the new coach.

Your first priority as a new head coach, after taking care of the kids, is to put together a staff. You don't have to hire everybody right away, but you had better get a core of trusted people who can help you build.

The most important part of building a successful program starts with hiring a great staff, and it doesn't make any difference whether you are talking about coaching or business. The same principles apply; surround yourself with good people.

Hire guys who love coaching and who love young people. You must have great communication to function well as a staff. You cannot expect to have unity on a team if you don't have it on your staff. You need to understand your people, take advantage of their strengths, and develop well-defined job descriptions. Above all, you must have the complete trust of your coaches and their families. They must be the right fit for your school. They need to be a match for the university and for the region.

It is also very important for the new coach to meet, as soon as possible, with the assistant coaches who were on the previous staff. This is a tough business, and these are good men with families who need to know if they will fit your system, or whether they need to be looking for a job somewhere else. That is one of the toughest things for me as a head coach. I have been lucky; I never have been fired, but I have a lot of great friends who have been, and it is a hard thing. That was especially true at Texas. It was important to be honest with them.

I had a pretty good idea of the guys I wanted on my staff, but I wanted the Texas assistants to know I would help them find spots if I could. They were open about the problems they'd faced. I didn't want them to give us an evaluation of the players who were here. When a new coach comes in, it is important for kids to have a new start. I didn't want to cloud that start with any preconceived notions.

Sometimes hiring a coach from the previous staff puts him in a very uncomfortable position because of his loyalty to the coach who is leaving. After a head coach is fired, the assistants are often mad at the school, the athletics director, and a lot of people for making the change. They may be down on the players. Although I've done it both ways, I've found in most cases it is better for everyone to get a fresh start.

I met with the Texas assistants on Friday, then set up a meeting with Ricky Williams, who was in the process of deciding whether he should leave school and turn pro. Obviously, Ricky became our number one recruit.

Saturday, some of the members of our North Carolina staff came to visit. I had hoped that one of our assistants would get the head job there. I am proud of the fact that at every job I have left, one of my assistants succeeded me as head coach. At Appalachian it was Sparky Woods, and at Tulane it was Greg Davis. When that happens some of the staff have a chance to stay there. Any time a head coach makes a decision about a job, he can't help but think of his staff. Coach Royal told me that was the toughest part of his decision to quit coaching. He worried about what would happen to his assistants.

Cleve Bryant had told me he was interested in moving into administration while we were still at North Carolina. I asked him if he would come to Texas with me and become our associate athletics director for football operations if he was not considered for the UNC head coaching position. He had done a great job with two different coaching stints at North Carolina, and I thought he at least deserved an interview. When that didn't happen, it wasn't hard to convince Cleve and Jean to come since they'd been here in the early years with John Mackovic's staff.

Cleve is a great administrator and will soon become one of the top athletics directors in our business. Jean, who handles our life skills program, is every bit as good as Cleve. They love the kids and are great for our business.

Greg Davis, our offensive coordinator at Carolina, is a Texas native, and he was an obvious choice to come as well. Tim Brewster, who had done a tremendous job with recruiting and coaching our tight ends, is one of the most loyal people I've ever known, and he wanted to come. Carl Torbush, our defensive coordinator, was very good and could have come also. With those four as the start, we began building a staff.

After a while, Carl Torbush was named head coach at North Carolina, and several of the older staff members stayed with him, which I completely understood. Most of them had begun to put down roots there. North Carolina was invited to the Gator Bowl, and Greg Davis and Tim Brewster agreed to go back and help Carl coach that game. Cleve stayed in Austin to help us recruit because we were so far behind.

I asked Dick Baddour if I could come back and coach the game, but he apparently thought it was better to have Carl do it. Nobody told me directly, and even though I learned from reading the paper that I wouldn't get to coach the game, I did understand. One of the loneliest days I've spent was that New Year's Day when Sally and I sat alone in an apartment in Austin and watched our team win.

Sally went back to Carolina to take care of her business after the holidays. Cleve and I moved into an apartment together and worked non-stop on recruiting players and a staff. It was critical that we get Jeff Madden, who handled Carolina's strength and conditioning, to join us, and we did that. Jeff is a major part of our staff.

The North Carolina players missed Jeff more than they missed me. He is an incredible person. He has a gift of knowing when to drive a player hard and when to hug him. He had been at Colorado during their national championship season of 1991, and he has a list of all-Americans and Olympians in all sports who he has trained. Nobody in the country does a better job in strength and conditioning training, and bringing him to Texas was as important as anything we did.

The separation between a coach who takes a new job and his family back home is hard. There were probably times when Sally wanted me to just come back and forget the whole thing. A coach has his work, but his wife is left with issues. She's the one who's left to sell and close a home, buy a new house, and handle all of the things related to the physical move.

It is important for a coach to be sensitive to that. We get wrapped up in our problems, and we don't want to listen to theirs. Trust me. Take the time to listen. In our case, it was especially hard on Sally, because she was leaving what she had spent seventeen years of her life building. When you leave one job for another, there are folks who won't be happy you left. That's not a bad thing. There are only a few ways to leave a job: you leave of your own accord, you get fired, or you die. I prefer the first, and all I could do was hope that in time, people would appreciate what we had been able to accomplish at Carolina.

Some people in Chapel Hill were so rude and critical of me to Sally that she couldn't even go to the grocery store without being harassed. It is a real shame that the actions of a few people can hurt so much. We had, and still have, many friends in Chapel Hill. They may not even have known how hard it was for Sally.

Attitudes were as positive in Austin for the beginning of a new era as they were negative in Chapel Hill about our leaving. I received all the positive feedback, and Sally was overloaded with the bad. I strongly suggest that when a coach leaves for a new job, he move his entire family immediately. Sometimes people are just not fair to your family. Changing jobs in coaching is like changing jobs in any other profession. The interview process is very visible and people get emotional about their school. Leaving a school is like going through a divorce. Don't anticipate anything less and protect your family.

In college, when there is a coaching change, it usually comes after the season and in the middle of recruiting. You have to start running. You are automatically behind in recruiting, and the time is very short between the time you hire your staff and national signing day for recruits in early February. Because of the experience of the staff we hired, we put together

49

a good recruiting class, despite getting a late start. Our biggest victory came early when Ricky Williams announced in January that he would return for his senior season. His decision gave us instant credibility with recruits.

A few days after we arrived in Austin, I was at a basketball game with then-Governor George W. Bush. I was asked to say a few words at a time out. I hate to speak to 16,000 people. It is so impersonal, and I didn't know what to say. So I asked the governor for advice.

"Just tell them, 'I'm proud to be the coach at The University of Texas in the great State of Texas.'" I said exactly that, and the crowd cheered for five minutes. The man knows his politics.

I also learned of the generosity of Texans. I had seen a small note card with a beautiful scene of Longhorns and cowboys with a rain cloud in the distance. It was called *Gathering Storm* and it was painted by Ragan Gennusa, a former player for Coach Royal who has become an outstanding wildlife artist.

I inquired about getting a poster of the painting. Ragan had other ideas.

He painted a new picture of Longhorns with the cloud in the background. He called it *Longhorn Storm*. He showed it to Red McCombs. Red has been tremendously successful, and he really cares about The University of Texas. Red paid $23,000 for the painting and put it on permanent loan in our football offices. He also had the posters we wanted made and gave them to Coach Royal and me to distribute as we pleased.

When signing day came, there was another round of celebrations with the Texas folks. Sally and I headed down to Palmer Auditorium in Austin for what I thought would be a small gathering of Texas fans the night after signing day. A crowd of 3,500 showed up. It was like a giant pep rally.

In my speech, I told them they could help us succeed by "being positive and by being patient."

When I walked off the stage, I asked Sally what she thought.

"It was really good," she said. "But that part about being patient? I think that went right past them."

Looking back, I can say we couldn't have had better support. We have the greatest fans in the world, and it is important to remember that with twenty million people in the state of Texas, there will be some who don't like you. But if it's a handful out of twenty million, that's not very many. Whatever you do, it's important to consider the source of any criticism when you evaluate how you are doing. Remember to stay focused on your goals and dreams, and don't let a few negative people waste your time or energy.

As soon as recruiting was over, we went around the state talking to Longhorn Foundation gatherings, and later in the spring we had a series of golf tournaments. Everywhere we spoke, we had great crowds.

We talked about the future, and we didn't dwell on the past. A new coach and staff should NEVER criticize, publicly or privately, the guys who were there before them. They are not there to defend themselves. It serves no purpose to beat them up. Do your own thing and build on what you can do, not what somebody else didn't do.

John Mackovic and his staff did some very good things at Texas. They left us with some great players, and John had worked hard to begin the facility reconstruction.

The university had decided to go in a new direction, and in the spring of 1998, it was up to us to take the program there.

There were so many people who helped us get started. David McWilliams, who had been a player, assistant coach, and head coach at Texas, became a friend and an invaluable resource. David took over as head of our letter winners association and gave me great advice about what to do and where to go to meet the people who would really help us.

But the one guy who made the biggest impact on our staff that spring was Mike Campbell, who had been Coach Royal's top assistant and friend for years.

Mike was known throughout the coaching profession as a defensive genius. Even after he was out of coaching, he used to break down films, not only to watch Texas, but to help his good friend Spike Dykes, who was head coach at Texas Tech.

When Joe Jamail agreed to sponsor our lettermen's golf tournament at our first reunion, he wanted it named for Mike Campbell, and Mike and his wife, Mary, were both very much a part of that early time.

Mike came to every practice that he could that spring, and he always had a piece of witty advice.

The first day we were out there, we were running an inside drill where we worked on running and stopping runs up the middle of the defense. We knew we had a lot of work to do on the fundamentals of the team if we wanted to get back to the kind of defensive football Mike Campbell believed in playing.

I asked him what he thought that first day.

"Well," he said with that southern drawl of his, "I'm glad I was watching, because they sure weren't hitting anybody hard enough for me to hear it."

We lost Coach Campbell to cancer that summer, and we all miss him. We figure he's looking down and smiling when our defense makes a solid stop, and he can hear the hit way up there where he is. We will always be thankful that he touched our lives in such a positive way.

We came together as a team and as a staff that spring, and though we were a long way from where we wanted to be, we were on our way.

STORIES OF THE HEART

"FOR IT IS IN MATTERS OF THE HEART WHERE
COURAGE AND WILL, LOVE AND COMPASSION—ALL OF
THE ATTRIBUTES OF CARING AND DETERMINATION—RESIDE.
IT IS THERE WHERE DREAMS TAKE HOLD. IT IS THERE WHERE
BROTHERHOOD AND SISTERHOOD AND THE MAGIC
OF TEAMWORK GERMINATE."

—Bill Little

The Curve In The Road

❝THEY'RE WORKING, WHILE I'M MISSING YOU
THOSE HEALING HANDS OF TIME
IN TIME MY TEARS WILL WASH THE HURT
FROM THIS HEART OF MINE.**❞**

—Willie Nelson

◀ THE STORY OF NUMBER 44 – The death of Longhorn Cole Pittman *(44)* in the spring of 2001 brought togetherness to the Texas team, which mourned his loss but celebrated his life. His touching story reached far beyond the circle of the team.

BL

W hat happened to Cole Pittman in the seconds before his vehicle went airborne over a creek in deep East Texas will probably never be known. They do not have "black boxes"—those devices that tell us what went on in the final moments before a commercial airline crash—in Chevy trucks.

He could have swerved to avoid another vehicle or an animal. He could simply have been distracted as he approached the sharp curve, or he could have gone to sleep with the cruise control on, sending the truck careening down an embankment and into the creek bank across the water.

Whatever happened, at 7:45 on a morning in late February, as dawn came on U. S. 79 near Bryan, Texas, twenty-one-year-old Cole Pittman died.

On a day when he would meet the media to talk about his team's spring practice, Mack Brown's life was about to change forever. In twenty-nine years as a coach, he had never had a player die while on his team.

A little over a year before, Mack and Sally Brown had taken the lead as The University of Texas reached out to its rival, Texas A&M, in the face of the Aggies' own tragedy. When twelve young people died working on A&M's bonfire—the spirit symbol which annually burned before the Texas-Texas A&M game—Brown cried. With the help of the Longhorn team and staff, the Browns organized a blood drive for the survivors of the tragedy. He and Sally sent flowers to the funerals of those killed.

At a memorial service on the Texas campus honoring those killed in College Station, Brown had delivered a moving speech to the gathering of students and friends from both universities. He remembered the moment he had learned of the accident and the sympathy he had felt when he heard that parents who were trying to call their kids to see if they were okay couldn't get through because the telephone lines were jammed. In his speech, he talked about the parents of those killed—how they must feel—and he prayed that his kids would all outlive him.

Brown had reached out to the Texas A&M community after talking with his friend, Aggie legend John David Crow, who himself had lost a son in an accident. Darrell Royal, who had lost two children in separate vehicle accidents, had told

55

Brown you never get over losing a child. Now, unknown to him as he went about his efforts preparing for spring training, a young member of his extended family was gone.

Monday morning, February 26, 2001, had begun with a staff meeting, with much of the discussion centering on the upcoming spring drills, which were to begin the next day. At the headquarters of the Texas Department of Public Safety in Austin, Lance Coleman was preparing for a training session. Coleman, an instructor for the DPS, had become a part of the Texas program as a security escort for the team during the Ricky Williams era. He had traveled with the team on road trips, and his counterparts in the DPS in Bryan had shared similar duties with Texas A&M.

Late in the morning, Coleman got a call from the Bryan office. There had been a truck accident, with a fatality. DPS officers were working on identification, and so far, they had found a Big 12 South Division championship ring and a Cotton Bowl watch. The truck had Louisiana license plates registered to Marc Pittman. Trying not to alarm anyone, Coleman called the Texas football office and asked them to try to locate Cole Pittman.

As Brown and assistants Greg Davis and Carl Reese headed to Bellmont Hall for a media conference, Coleman came to the campus. At the conference, Reese talked about how Pittman could be a factor with his move to defensive tackle. A Florida State player had died during workouts that same day. Members of the media asked Brown if he had ever had a player die, and he said no, and he rapped his knuckles on the wooden table for good luck.

When he came back from the media conference, Coleman was waiting for Brown. There had been positive identification. It is tradition for the Texas DPS to send someone in person to notify a family of a fatality, and the Louisiana State Troopers, who have that same tradition, were on their way to talk to Marc Pittman.

His dad's urgent voice on a phone message machine, pleading for Cole to call home immediately, sent Cole's new fiancée, soccer player Caren Lyons, searching for his truck in the student parking lot. An assistant trainer in the women's athletics department found Lyons in tears walking through the Moncrief-Neuhaus building. The assistant trainer took her to Randa Ryan, the women's staff counselor.

Minutes after Coleman shared the news with Brown, his assistant, Kasey Johnson, answered the phone in the head coach's office. It was Marc Pittman.

"Tell me it's not true," he pleaded. "Tell me what they are saying is not true."

"All I can say," said Brown, "is that they are saying it is true."

Then he closed his door and tried as best he could to listen a lot and to say something that would matter to a man hurt with immeasurable pain.

When Brown came out of his office, his eyes were red and he looked drained, but his work was just beginning. He had only a few minutes to decide what to say to his football team, which was downstairs waiting for a meeting about spring training.

W hen we recruit a player, we promise his parents we will take care of their son. In fact, that was a conversation that Darryl Drake, our assistant who had recruited Cole, had had with Cole's dad. Of all of us, I think Darryl and I took Cole's death the hardest.

Sally had said it best when we first learned of his death.

"I wish I could have died in his place," she said. "I'm in my forties and I've lived a good life. It's not fair for a young person to die at twenty-one with so much life left to live."

Nothing about this time seemed fair. I knew one of the hardest things I would have to do would be to tell the team, but it was something that I had to do. When I got to the team meeting room, Sally and Jean Bryant were there, along with the staff and players. We had made arrangements to have Fellowship of Christian Athletes representatives and certified counselors available for the players.

We took Phillip Geiggar and Stevie Lee, two players who played with Cole in high school, out of the room to be told privately. We should have taken Chance Mock, who was probably Cole's best friend.

When I got in the room, I remember pulling up a chair on the stage and just sitting down to talk to the team. One of the hardest things about it was looking into the faces of the players. They were all so excited about the start of spring practice, and I had something to tell them that was about to shatter that excitement.

When you have a team of 120 guys, some will know each other better than others. I had to recognize there were players who barely knew Cole, and there were others who were very, very close to him. Everybody talks about a team being a family, and that afternoon, I felt that more than ever.

In the next few days, we saw some amazing things.

The Pittman family decided to have Cole's funeral in Shreveport on Wednesday. The athletics department planned a memorial service for Thursday in Austin. There was an outpouring of support, both inside and outside our department. Cleve Bryant mobilized airplanes to take some of our players and staff members to Shreveport. Red McCombs and Duer Wagner of Fort Worth provided planes. Ron Paynter, general manager of the Marriott at the Capitol and the folks at the Austin Hilton provided hotel rooms. Many other people offered to help. We got hundreds of floral arrangements, messages, and phone calls.

I was amazed at Cole's Dad, who spoke at the funeral. The Evangel Christian Academy football team, where Cole played in high school as a member of the First Assembly of God Church in Shreveport, announced they would name a new field house for Cole. They also said they planned to erect a statue of Cole in uniform, with a Longhorn and the Evangel logo on either side of the helmet.

The Pittman family showed us a lot about the love of a family and their faith. Cole's minister, Denne Duron, who was also the director of the school and a coach at Evangel, gave us a lot to think about when he asked us to consider, "How many Saturdays do you have left?"

I started counting, figuring—well, I'm forty-nine and my granddad lived to be ninety-one.

"Not one of us knows," he said. "Last Saturday may have been your last. You'd better make each moment count."

In Austin, the memorial service was attended by all of our student athletes. Before the service, we walked as a team through the stadium, where Cole's picture was on the JumboTron. Cole's dad asked the players not to forget Cole or their family. We all turned to Cole's picture above the stadium and sang "The Eyes of Texas."

In September, we dedicated our North Carolina game to Cole, and we had a pregame ceremony to honor him and the Pittmans.

Willie Nelson, the famous country singer, is a good friend of Coach Royal's, and Coach had given me the words to Willie's song, "The Healing Hands of Time." Freddie Powers, who had written songs for Willie and for Merle Haggard, sang it at the memorial service in UT's Bass Concert Hall. Gerald Mann, the preacher at the 9,000 member Riverbend Church in Austin, gave the message. Two of our players, Matt Trissell and Ahmad Brooks, spoke. I can't remember exactly what I said, but I know a big part of it was that Marc and Judy Pittman had shown us the way to be better parents because of the relationship they had with their son.

The most powerful moment came when they played a video tribute to Cole, and his Dad spoke. Every one of us could feel his pain, but we also felt his power. He's a big man with an even bigger heart.

Dr. Mann told us Cole's life should be remembered in the quality, not the quantity, of years. He told us the only way to deal with grief was to replace it with gratitude. Be thankful for each other and for the short but wonderful time Cole was with us.

We made plans to keep Cole's locker exactly as it was for the duration of his scholarship. No player, unless it is Cole's brother, could wear the number 44 while Cole would have been here. The players chose to wear the initials CP on their helmets as a tribute to Cole during the 2001 season. The athletics department established a scholarship in his name.

As I watched the Pittmans, I realized that all of us can learn from their family. I like to think I became a better father because of what I saw over those very difficult few days. I call my kids more and say "I love you" a whole lot more.

One of the most valuable parts of the healing process for me—besides the support from Sally—came from the contacts I had from fellow coaches. I learned how many others in our profession had lost a player at one time or another. We had a press briefing the day after Cole died to allow our players to share their thoughts with the media. The coaches gave us many different ideas on what to do about practice, and we just decided it was best to get back to work as soon as we could.

Throughout the year, our team is on a schedule, which involves their training, classroom work, and study halls. We had been off schedule, and counselors told us the best thing we could do was to get back on schedule.

We had been given a lot of advice about how to handle Cole's death. I chose to take some time on the first day of practice, and we spent twenty minutes sharing our thoughts.

I made up my mind that I would never say, "We need to move on," because we won't ever really do that. We will never forget Cole Pittman, and he and his family will always have a place in our hearts. It is important, however, to move forward, taking a little piece of Cole with us, and that is what we tried to do.

We had a high school coaches' clinic scheduled the weekend after Cole's death, and because of the schedules of one thousand coaches, we made plans to go ahead with it. It was a good thing, because so many coaches came up and shared their stories with me. In grief, we need each other. Cole's family lived with the thought that the only way they would make it through was with the help of faith, family, and friends.

After the funeral in Shreveport on Wednesday, I woke up Thursday morning tired, and I dreaded the days ahead. As I was dressing to go to the memorial service, Sally gave me some very important advice that helped me sort some meaning out of the whole experience. I was talking about all of the emotions and the pain I had seen and felt.

"This is the toughest time to be a coach," I said.

"No," she replied, "Your kids need you now. It's the best time to be a coach."

The Deaf Kid

❝HE WAS TOTALLY LOCKED ON ME. IT WAS AS IF HE
COULD SEE WAY DOWN DEEP INSIDE, AND I COULD
DO THE SAME WITH HIM. I REMEMBER THINKING
IF, AS A COACH, YOU CAN TOUCH
ONE KID LIKE THAT, IT'S WORTH IT.**❞**

—Mack Brown

◀ LITTLE MAN BIG - Brad Hermes *(40)* proudly displays the "Hook 'em 'Horns," sign after a Longhorn game in 2001. Brad played on a kickoff in each of the first two games of the season, standing tall despite his 5' 8" frame. A senior with a 3.8 grade point average, he is on track to graduate with honors.

BL

I t was the fever that had done it, when he was just a year and a half old. But years of reading lips, learning to sign, and adjusting to a hearing aid that brought "environmental sounds," such as a knock at the door or the honking of a car horn, had given him the confidence to believe in himself. We are taught as children that if we work hard and do the right things, we can accomplish almost anything. He had overcome so very much in his eighteen years of living. It would have been easy to run from this one. The idea of making a college football team, let alone the Texas Longhorns, had to be a stretch.

Sure, he had played sports in Denton, and was good at them. The fact that he was deaf hadn't stopped him yet. He was proud of who he was; he wasn't about to apologize for it.

Being deaf is not a curse; for some, it is a fact. Brad, like so many who have lost their hearing, recoiled at the label of "hearing impaired, " which some consider to be politically correct.

Mack Brown, the coach he wanted to play for, tells people to take a negative and turn it into a positive.

Brad Hermes knew better than most what that meant. Now, as he walked into the cavernous Dr. Nasser Al Rashid Strength and Conditioning Room, he reminded himself to be brave.

Perhaps there was something serendipitous about the circumstances. Here was this brave young man believing that he could beat the odds. Dr. Nasser Al Rashid, the man who gave the money to make the Texas strength facility the finest in the world, would have understood.

Forty or so years before, Dr. Rashid was a young foreign student who dared leave his homeland to come to Texas for a college education. He fell in love with the Longhorns and what they stood for, then he returned to his native Saudi Arabia to become one of the most successful businessmen in the world. He used his engineering degree to help build the infrastructure of his country and used his wealth to, among other things, build a hospital in Saudi Arabia.

He would be proud of Brad Hermes.

Because NCAA regulations allow only eighty-five players to receive scholarship aid, college football teams are made up of three general categories: recruited athletes who are on scholarship; "invited" walk-ons, young men who the coaches know something about because of their high school careers, but don't have room for in the scholarship quota; and the "true" walk-ons, students at the school who just want to try to make the team.

That's what Bradford Hermes was trying to do when he walked into the weight room that day. From the baby who had lost his hearing, he had grown to a compact 5'8" fighter who would play big. Yet, as he stood there looking at Jeff Madden, he thought he had met the biggest man in the world. The puppy had not only met the Big Dog; he had met "Maddog."

Jeff Madden came to Texas with Mack Brown, and now, as Assistant Athletics Director for Strength and Conditioning, he is charged with creating a team in the best possible physical condition. He also serves as coach of the spirit, and he helps mold the character of the team and its players. It is Madden who handles team discipline, and woe be to him who, through his shortcomings and failure to "do right," arrives in the Dog House.

In the workout that day, Madden saw enough. He knew that Brad Hermes might never play a down for the Longhorns, but he believed Brad should have a chance to play the game he loved. While others may have worried about his hearing and his size, Madden saw only one thing—his heart. But having a deaf player would present challenges not on the field or with the players, but administratively.

For Brad to be on the team, the football program had to provide an interpreter for every practice, every meeting, and every trip. The program would have to pay an hourly rate of over twenty dollars an hour for the signer. In the university's Office of Aid for Students with Disabilities, they found their man. Only thing was, she was a woman.

Lynn Blazek had grown up with deaf parents, so she learned her communication skills early. She also grew up a huge football fan. So when the job was posted, she said, "I'm there."

In Madden's grueling off-season program, it didn't take long for Brad Hermes to win acceptance from his teammates. In the heat of the Austin summer, when the sun bakes a dreaded sand pit that the players run in to increase speed and stamina, the solid winner of the drill was a little guy from Denton. He may not have heard the cheers from the players, but he could see them in their eyes and feel them deep inside, where God had made him one of his perfect children.

MB

It was the week after the Oklahoma game in 2000, and I was mad and embarrassed because we played poorly and lost badly. We were practicing for a tough road game at Colorado I felt we had to win. As Sally would tell anybody, I don't deal well with defeat. I didn't go out to eat that week, and I was so hard on the assistant coaches that they didn't want to be around me. At the end of every practice, I always gather the team in a semi-circle for a final meeting. I make a point of standing facing the sun, so that the players won't have to look into the sun as they listen to what I have to say.

That day, I was really frustrated, and I remember thinking, "Why do I keep doing this?" Sometimes in those meetings after a hard practice, it is tough to maintain the kids' attention. We have a standing rule that the players are to pay complete attention to whomever is speaking. I don't want jerseys being taken off or glances at other guys or any kind of distractions. So I pay a lot of attention to eyes.

Brad Hermes is always in front, so if his interpreter isn't there, he can read my lips. This was one of those days. As I pushed myself through my comments, I happened to glance down at his eyes. He was totally locked on me. It was as if he could see way down deep inside, and I could do the same with him. I remember thinking if, as a coach, you can touch one kid like that, it's worth it.

His eyes reminded me of something else. I could see the eyes of my sweet daughter, Barbara, who has 90 percent hearing loss in one ear. If for no other reason, Brad deserves a chance for Barbara and all those like her.

When I finished my talk after the practice and headed to speak to the media, I felt better, not about losing, but about life in general, and why I coach and believe in kids.

A few days later, I was watching practice. Roy Williams, who has a chance to be as good a receiver as there has been in the game, was running a pass pattern against Brad, who was playing defensive back. I wondered how Brad would know to stop when the drill was over. He is an aggressive kid, but I guess the dad in me was being overprotective. I didn't want to see him get hurt.

The action went the other way from Roy and Brad, and the whistle blew. As the play stopped, Roy Williams, who stands a good 6' 4", is eight inches taller and a lot bigger than Brad, reached out and gently caught him, wrapping him in a quick hug before he patted him on the rear and headed back to the huddle.

It was clear he wasn't being easy on Brad; what mattered was that Roy cared about him and respected him.

Every now and then, when I need a "pick-up" at practice, I'll check out our young, talented receivers like Roy, B. J. Johnson, Sloan Thomas, Tony Jeffrey, and Kyle Shanahan and watch them with their teammate. It says a lot about them and a lot about Brad.

When Jeff Madden first came to me about Brad, I worried about him getting hurt, about how he would be accepted, and about the general issues of having an extra person like a signer in all of our meetings. Jeff said that anything new like that would feel different, but he believed that is how people grew.

One day last fall, I brought Brad over with Lynn and asked him about playing in a game. In practice, I knew his teammates challenged him, but they protected him after the play had stopped. I wanted to know how it would actually work if I got him into a game. "How will you know to stop, since you can't hear the whistle?" I asked.

"Coach," he said through Lynn. "When they stop, I'll stop. But I'll keep going until then."

In our last scrimmage before the 2001 season, Brad made a big tackle late in the practice. When the team met in the center of the field, we added one of the "Ohhh, Texas!" cheers for Brad. He beamed and cupped his hand to his ear, as if to say, "Let me hear it again." Everybody laughed. Then, at the end of our opening game against New Mexico State, Brad got into the game on a kickoff. It had to be one of the proudest moments of that kid's life.

We've all grown with Brad, and when he got on the field, sure, he was proud. But his coaches and his teammates were proud of him and for him.

Here's To You, Joe DiMaggio

❝THERE IS GREAT WINNING TRADITION AT TEXAS.
THAT'S WHAT I ALWAYS LOVED ABOUT THE YANKEES.
YOU EITHER LOVED OR HATED THE YANKEES. EVERYBODY HAD
AN OPINION ABOUT THEM. UT FOOTBALL IS THE SAME WAY.
THE YANKEES WON, AND THEY DID IT WITH CLASS.
THEY WERE MY ROLE MODELS AT A TIME WHEN
OUR COUNTRY NEEDED SOME HEROES.**❞**

—Mack Brown

◀ THE COOKEVILLE CAVALIERS – Baseball was a big part of
growing up as a Brown brother. Mack was shortstop and
pitcher on his high school team and is a lifelong fan of the
New York Yankees.

BL

The bright December sun warmed the window of the cab, competing
mightily with the brisk winter wind as the van sped along the expressway by
the river. The short drive from the posh downtown hotel to the historic
stadium in the Bronx was more than a morning jaunt across New York City
for Mack Brown. It was a nostalgic trip to a little-boy place in his soul.

As long as he could remember, he had liked the Yankees. Growing up in
Cookeville, Tennessee, he had dreamed of being Mickey Mantle or Roger Maris.
He was ten years old when Maris broke Babe Ruth's home run record by hitting 61
in 1961, but in all of those years, he had never seen Yankee Stadium. This day, in
his third year at Texas, on a day when Sally was shopping and he could bring along
his cell phone to answer any recruiting question that might come up, he decided to
indulge himself.

There wasn't time for a tour, just for a look. Even so, the media office of the
Yankees prepared a backpack kit which included a book, a Christmas tree ornament,
and a tan "gimmee" cap with the "NY" emblem emblazoned on the front.

The stadium may have been new to Brown, but the emblem wasn't. His first
coaching job came as a teenager. His dad and granddad owned a sporting goods
store called Brown & Watson's Sporting Goods, and while he was playing Connie
Mack League baseball himself, Mack coached the store's Little League team to a
championship.

As Brown waited in the reception area for a guide to take him into the stadium,
a Japanese couple on their honeymoon came into the room. They spoke no English,
yet they clearly shared their country's fascination with the game of baseball. Each
posed in front of the giant Christmas tree decorated with Yankee baseballs and tiny
caps and little blue bears. Brown reached out, took the camera, and put the two
together in front of the tree for a Kodak moment. He shot the picture, then pointed
to the centerpiece of the reception area—a life-size photo of Yankee legend Joe
DiMaggio batting.

Brown had no idea if the young couple would even know who Joltin' Joe was,
but he offered to take their picture in front of the mural anyway.

"Ah, Joe DiMaagsho," said the young man in broken English, and then he and his new bride smiled widely as Brown flashed the camera.

The young couple had no way of knowing the man taking their picture was pretty famous in his own business, but it didn't matter. Darrell Royal says the mark of a man is how he treats people who can never do anything for him, or how he treats them when no one is watching.

In a few moments, the guide came and ushered Brown into the stadium. He walked in at field level, just above section 24. The Yankee dugout was just in front of him, and the famous right field wall seemed closer than it did on those radio broadcasts or on the black and white television shots from the early '60s. The ornamental façade was there, and out beyond the center field wall was Monument Park, where plaques commemorate the game's immortals.

The Japanese couple had long since left, and the cabbie was waiting when Brown left section 24. In fifteen minutes, he was back in the heart of the city, where the Christmas shoppers filled the stores on Fifth Avenue.

It was a long way from Brown and Watson's Sporting Goods, but in his heart, it wasn't very far at all.

MB

The Wilson Sporting Goods plant was across the street from the sporting goods store, and they made all of the equipment for the Yankees. In the store we had full uniforms of Mickey Mantle, Roger Maris, and Yogi Berra on display. When I was at North Carolina, Yogi's granddaughter was one of our student athletes, and I got to meet him. I still have all of his books. I loved the HBO movie about Maris and Mantle because I clearly remember that year.

As a kid, we had just one television set. I don't remember ever watching television unless there was a game on. We weren't on the telephone either because we were too busy playing sports. In the summer, Dad would have us baling hay or working on the farm or at the sporting goods store in the mornings. Then we played sports all afternoon long and sometimes we played until after dark. We got up the next day and did the same thing over again. Sports just consumed our whole lives.

We had a 10:00 P.M. curfew. The girls could usually stay out until 10:30 or 11:00 o'clock. I told one of my dates I had a stomach ache so I wouldn't have to tell her I had to take her in early because my Dad made me be in by 10:00 o'clock.

Baseball taught me a lot of lessons. I can remember Dad getting onto me about taking a third strike in Little League baseball. If you've already got two strikes on you, you don't have the luxury of waiting for the perfect pitch. He told me, "If you're not going to have enough guts to swing the bat when you're up there, you might as well stay out of the game."

Dad was really tough, but he loved us. He was quiet, but he talked to me a lot in his later life. He died while talking to me about the number of National Football League prospects from North Carolina as compared

67

with those at Tennessee. Dad was always bragging on his son to his buddies who were Volunteer fans.

My grandmother was a very strong lady whom I loved dearly. I can remember her saying that there are very few Mickey Mantles or Roger Marises, but there are a whole lot of lawyers and doctors, so you should be a lawyer or a doctor. She said we—my brothers Watson, Mel, and I—should get away from the sports, that we needed to read and study. She was constantly saying, "Enjoy sports, but don't get consumed with sports like your dad and your grandfather."

My granddad was one of the nicest, most even-keeled people you would ever meet, but my grandmother was pretty tough, so we didn't ever question what Grandmother said. She was an artist, and Sally and I kept all of her paintings and we display them proudly in our house.

But when we were fishing, or in another room of the house, Granddad would say, "You're not going to be successful unless you're enjoying what you do. So if you enjoy football, go for it. If you don't want to coach, don't do it." I knew he always felt the best parts of his life were when he was coaching. Granddad was the guy that you'd slip off with, and he'd let you talk and he'd ask you questions. Granddad made everybody feel as if they were special. Even if he didn't know who they were, they all thought he did.

My mom is just like my granddad. She loves people and makes everybody feel special. She's at ease with everybody. At the Culligan Holiday Bowl, she hung out with our friend, the singer Larry Gatlin, and his son-in-law. They talked football and politics and even struck up conversations with some Oregon fans. She is the best mom anyone could ever wish for.

Every time I go fishing, I think about my granddad. I kept all of his fishing gear, too. It's important to keep family stuff; it keeps a piece of the person with you always.

It is important to ask older people questions, especially family members. We won't have them forever. We don't realize that when we are young. We think they will be here forever.

When I went to college, I thought I wanted to be an attorney, but the more I got into football I realized that I had to coach. I wanted to go to a school where sports were important. And I wanted to win all the games.

We got so close to winning them all at North Carolina, and when we came to Texas we made it clear that winning a national championship was our goal. There is great winning tradition at Texas. That's what I always loved about the Yankees. You either loved or hated the Yankees. Everybody had an opinion about them. UT football is the same way. The Yankees won, and they did it with class. They were my role models at a time when our country needed some heroes.

I'm glad I took the time to go out to the stadium. Someday, when the schedule fits, I'd like to go to a game there.

For now, I'll just wear the cap when I go fishing, and I'll think of my granddad.

When Dreams Are Lost

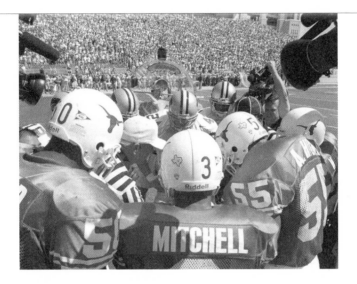

❝ THE RESPONSIBILITY OF A COACH IS TO PREPARE
KIDS FOR LIFE AFTER FOOTBALL. AS BADLY AS I HURT
FOR HODGES MITCHELL THAT NIGHT IN SAN DIEGO,
I APPRECIATED THE FACT THAT OUR PROGRAM WORKS
VERY HARD TO MAKE SURE KIDS HAVE OPTIONS. **❞**

—Mack Brown

◀ THE LITTLEST LONGHORN – Hodges Mitchell *(3)* was small in
stature, but played with as much heart as any Longhorn
ever. In the Longhorns' Culligan Holiday Bowl game with
Oregon, a knee injury ended his college career and
challenged him to face the possibility of life without football.

BL

I t was a simple play. "R-19" called for the tailback to sweep left.
   Hodges Mitchell was a special player to Mack Brown. In fact, he was
   special to the Texas team of 2000. At various times during the season, certain
   players combined to contribute the skill, the brawn, and the brains of the
team. Hodges Mitchell was always the heart.

Hodges's dad had played football with Brown at Florida State, and he was an
ironic link to the Texas staff and the staff Brown had at North Carolina. Brown had
tried to recruit Mitchell to be a Tar Heel, but he determined it was too far from his
Dallas home, so Brown advised him to go to Texas and become a Longhorn.

The next season, Brown found himself at Texas, too.

Now, three years later, Mitchell was a leader on Brown's Longhorn team that
was ranked number twelve in the country and playing eighth-ranked Oregon in
the Culligan Holiday Bowl. The Longhorns had led, 21-14, at the half and were
trying to answer a Duck touchdown that had tied the score at 21-21.

It was early in the third quarter, the 45th play of the game, and Mitchell, the
tailback, was on pace for a 100-yard game. He took the handoff and headed north.
It was the last play he would ever run at Texas. A missed read by a lineman caused
the fullback to block the wrong man, and the Oregon cornerback had a wide open
shot at Mitchell. He planted his helmet squarely on Hodges's right knee.

At the left hash mark, five yards deep into the Texas backfield, Mitchell
crumpled. All the major ligaments in his right knee had been ripped apart.

Football trainer Tom McVan sprinted onto the field, followed quickly by the
Texas team doctors. In the press box, offensive coordinator Greg Davis was stunned,
but he knew the game had to go on. It was his job to figure out what play to call
next and where to go after losing a critical part of the offense.

McVan and the others tried quickly to calm Mitchell, who was screaming
hysterically from the pain. Nothing worked. As he tried to determine the source of
the pain, McVan remembers a calm, quiet voice in the midst of the now-silent
stadium.

"You're going to be okay," the voice said. "You're in the best hands possible.
They're going to take care of you."

Mitchell looked up through the glare of the lights and saw his head coach. Mack Brown hadn't waited for a signal from his medical crew. He knew knee injuries. He'd had five knee surgeries himself. Maybe the moment took him back to a kickoff return against Alabama when he was at Vanderbilt. Maybe it was the final blow in a game with Houston when he was at Florida State. He knew the pain more than most. He knew that Hodges Mitchell might never play football again.

Brown walked back off the field as Mitchell was carried off on a gurney, and he thought about how sad it was for Mitchell, who had played so hard for all of his time at Texas, in the twilight of a dream which was leading toward a budding NFL career.

As hard as it was in that moment, seconds before he put the headset back on to hear Davis call the next play, Mack Brown was proud of his young player because he knew Hodges had prepared himself for that moment when the cheering fades.

And Brown is living proof that there is life after an athletic career stopped short by an injury.

MB

In the spring of 2000, Lynn Swann, the former Southern Cal great and Pittsburgh Steeler Hall of Famer, came to talk with our team. He helped them with a lot of things. Since he works for ABC Sports, he talked about how to deal with the media. He put up charts showing how players should take care of their money, even if they sign for a lot with a professional team.

Every time we have a chance to have someone like that talk with the team, we do. The kids know these stars and really look up to all they've accomplished as athletes and positive role models.

Another guy who had particular impact—and it really fits when I think of Hodges Mitchell—is Bo Jackson.

Bo was a superstar. He won the Heisman Trophy while at Auburn and was one of those gifted players who was playing at the Major League level in baseball and as a top star in the NFL as well. And then, in one game, a blow to his hip changed everything.

We are fortunate in Austin because a lot of famous people are interested in Longhorn football. Whenever a person like Bo Jackson wants to come to practice, Cleve Bryant sets it up.

When Hodges was hit in the Holiday Bowl, I knew it was bad. There is no question his injury had tremendous impact on our team. As young as we were, we had a lot of kids who looked to him for guidance and leadership. I can only imagine what they thought when he was lying there. All of us hurt for him.

I knew the doctors needed him quiet so they could determine the injury and stabilize his leg. That was the first priority. All the time we were on the field, I knew he was gone for the game. The positive thing about Hodges was that he was prepared for life after football, if that was what that moment meant. At the same time, you don't tell a kid that

71

then. It's not fair to take away dreams when players are hurting enough from the physical pain.

I guess a part of me did think about "what might have been." I was never as talented as Hodges, but I was like every other guy who plays any sport. Kids grow up believing they can be Big League stars in baseball or in basketball or in football, and that's a good thing. I was no different. I thought I was invincible before I got hit on that play against Alabama. I didn't have surgery then. I just wore a cast for what seemed like the rest of the year.

I remember two things about the trip back to the sidelines while the trainers wheeled Hodges off to the dressing room. The first was how sad it was for a young man who had given so much to our school to be seriously hurt in his very last game as a Longhorn, and I realized it was an injury that might end his football career.

The second thing that went through my mind was, as tough as this is for him emotionally, it was good that Hodges had taken care of his business in the classroom. We spend a lot of time—and we have a great staff to do it—working with our players on their academics. I have always said we are in the entertainment business on the weekend, but the education business during the week.

That was what Bo Jackson had talked about to our team at the end of practice that chilly evening in November. He talked about his NFL career and how he thought he had it made until one play changed everything. The lesson he left for the kids was being enacted right there in Qualcomm Stadium for our own players.

Hodges Mitchell had almost a 3.0 grade point average, and he is as well rounded and well liked as any player I have ever had. For his dream, I hoped that he would come back from the injury. He certainly deserved that chance. There is no way to minimize the impact of a potential career-ending injury on a young player. Athletes who suffer these need a lot of support.

It is important, however, for kids to realize that life isn't always what we plan it to be. Despite our highest hopes, things don't always work out. That's why, when we recruit players, we try to be totally honest with them. I will never promise a player that he will start as a freshman or that he'll win all the time. We've been very fortunate to have a lot of our kids play in the NFL in recent years, but if you are good enough to make that league, you'd better figure out what you are going to do when you get out. Consider your options at the time, and go forward with a plan for a future.

The responsibility of a coach is to prepare kids for life after football. As badly as I hurt for Hodges Mitchell that night in San Diego, I appreciated the fact that our program works very hard to make sure kids have options if serious injuries come.

That's what I told him that night, and even though he might not have heard me, I think he will understand in time. He does know that I will always respect, admire, and love all that he stands for on the field and in his life.

The Ricky Factor

❝RICKY TAUGHT US ALL SOMETHING. HE GAVE ME
A DIFFERENT PERSPECTIVE ON PEOPLE. HE TAUGHT US ALL
TO GET PAST WHAT A PERSON MAY LOOK LIKE,
EVEN IF IT IS A LITTLE DIFFERENT. HE TAUGHT US
THAT WE ARE NEVER TOO OLD TO LEARN.**❞**

—Mack Brown

L ife is not about what you do to impress others; life is about what you do for others. It is not about what you look like, but who you are.

The silver-haired lady came home from the store in December of 1997 and told her husband, "I just met Ricky Williams." She went on to tell the story of how she was looking for something in the supermarket, and she couldn't find it. A young African American man wearing dreadlocks offered to help her. She knew who he was—he was the only bright spot in a season gone bad that had seen the Longhorns finish at 4-7 and fire a coach. She knew he had led the nation in rushing, but he had no idea who she was. Impressed with his kindness, she told her husband about it.

Her name was Edith Royal, the wife of Darrell Royal.

Ricky Williams was raised in San Diego by his mother, Sandy, and the story of the loving bond with his two beautiful sisters, Cassie and Nisey, is well-told. He used his bonus money as a baseball player to help bring them to Austin and pay for their education. All three plan to earn their college degrees.

The wonderful part of the story is that Ricky Williams, who was such a shining example to us all, never set out to make a statement. And in following that course, he made a huge statement.

When Ricky Williams chose to wear his hair the way he did, it wasn't to be a rebel; it was because he liked it that way. He loved the entertainer Bob Marley and originally wore dreads in his honor. The "statement" was simple. Do not judge a man by his clothes or his hair...judge him by his heart.

As the snow glistened on the mountain peaks in Steamboat Springs, Colorado, in that spring of 1998, the phone rang at Doak Walker's house. The balloting for the Doak Walker Award, given to the nation's top running back, was underway. Walker had never met any of the candidates, but he had seen pictures of Williams. On the other end of the phone was Edith Royal's husband, Darrell.

"Doak," he said, "I need to talk to you about Ricky Williams. He may look a little different than what you are used to. I know that it would be easy for some people to make a judgment without ever finding out who he really is, but he is a very special person, and I think when you get to know him, you will like him. I am going to vote for him, not only because he is the best running back in the country, but because I like what I see of him as a person."

The touching friendship that developed between Ricky, the budding superstar with the dreadlocks, and Doak, the football legend, was very real. Doak Walker had been the greatest football player in Southern Methodist University history, and when the Ponies moved their games to the Cotton Bowl stadium, folks nicknamed it the House that Doak Built. A week after Walker died of complications from a skiing accident, Texas played Oklahoma in the Cotton Bowl. Williams, in Walker's honor, chose to change from his usual number 34 to Walker's number 37. He led Texas to victory. A couple of months later, as he helped Texas beat Mississippi State in the Cotton Bowl game, Williams gained over two hundred yards, with his last collegiate touchdown run coming from thirty-seven yards away.

Williams was the first player ever to win the Doak Walker Award twice. He won the Heisman by the largest margin in its history. He combined an impish smile with amazing physical ability. He had honed his God-given body into a power machine. Watching him play, it was easy to expect a lot.

And with Ricky, you always got more than you expected.

MB

Every college coach's goal should be to have great players who are nice kids who will graduate. But in my wildest dreams, I couldn't have imagined Ricky Williams.

In December of 1997, we had just finished a great run at North Carolina, and when Sally and I decided to come to Texas, part of the reason was its great tradition. As a kid, I grew up admiring Coach Royal, but most of what I knew about the Texas program in 1997 came from a couple of trusted friends and assistants. Cleve Bryant and our offensive coordinator, Greg Davis, had coached in the state. I knew the wealth of talent produced by Texas high schools, and I knew John Mackovic had recruited some good players.

When our team isn't playing, I am just like any other football fan. I watch every game I can on television. For years, Thanksgiving meant the Texas-Texas A&M game and, if we weren't playing, I always watched that game like everyone else in the nation. When Texas and Texas A&M played in 1997 on the Friday after Thanksgiving, I tuned in. Because of heavy rains, a lot of the video portion of the telecast was interrupted. From what I saw of it, Texas made a good run at the Aggies. The Longhorns had a big running back named Ricky Williams who had gained a lot of yards. I could tell he was good; I just didn't know how good.

And I didn't know that I was about to find out.

From the time it was announced that we were coming to Texas, Ricky had one month to decide whether he would return for his senior year or opt to enter the NFL draft. I had to do a lot of things in that month. We had to put together a staff, and we had to recruit. We had a football team that didn't feel very good about itself. They had been beaten up badly, going from two straight Alliance Bowl bids to a 4-7 season and losing their football coach.

We had to re-recruit this team and their families. Transition can be really tough. Coaches change, schemes change. Every single thing we had to do dealt with communication, trust, and respect.

After the first team meeting, I asked all of the players to come up and speak. When we finished, I realized there was one that I did not meet.

"Was Ricky here?" I asked.

The answer was yes.

I am a positive person, but I didn't think it was a good sign that I didn't see him after the team session.

The next day I set up a meeting with him.

It was a little stiff at first. I told him my experience with players who had gone to the NFL early. He wanted to know what kind of offense we would run and who his coach would be. I took it as a good sign that he wanted to know if I thought we could win next year. It was clear that being part of a team—one that succeeded—was important to him. He asked if I would make the team disciplined enough to win.

I began to see something of Ricky Williams right then that excited me. He didn't ask me if he could set records or win the Heisman Trophy. He wanted to know how our team would play defense and if we had a chance to be good.

Sally came with us to lunch, and Ricky really liked her. She wasn't a football fan when we married, but she was a people person, and Ricky liked that. They have a great connection.

I have always believed that players' appearances should be important to them, because every time they are photographed or appear in public or on television it is the same as a job interview. Like it or not, the public is wary of folks who look different, and Ricky looked different. But I quickly found out Ricky wasn't wearing his hair in dreadlocks to make a statement. He just liked his hair in dreadlocks. His hair became his trademark, and it wasn't likely that Ricky would need to interview for jobs.

A lot of people were telling Ricky to take the money and leave school. So as our relationship grew, I was greatly complimented when he asked me a critical question.

"Should I do what everybody tells me I should do, or should I do what I want to do?" he asked.

I tried to turn that question into a positive for Ricky.

"Few people in life ever get to do what they really want to do," I said. "If you need the money right now, then you should go. If you don't, then do whatever it is that you really want to do."

When Ricky announced that he was staying at Texas, he sent a message to every kid that staying in school to get an education is important. He told them that there is value in friendships and being part of a team and a community that genuinely cares about you. His message was that it is okay to have fun, even if you take a risk on not earning big money. Ricky had already proved he was unselfish. For his first two years he played fullback, because that's where the team needed him. A lot of top players are too self-centered to do that. Now his message was that he wanted to finish right at Texas. He needed to get the 4-7 taste out of his mouth.

We now had the best running back in the country, and he turned out to be a coach's dream. Ricky did everything we asked him to do. He was on time, he was a team player, he behaved as a model football player.

We were coming off of a 4-7 season, and for Ricky to achieve records and national honors, we had to have a team that would win. So we made Ricky's national success a team goal. Greg Davis and our offensive staff did a brilliant job of devising an offense that would move the football and still get Ricky his yards. We were one of only two teams in the country that rushed for 250 yards per game and passed for 250 yards per game. It might be the best job I have ever seen of an offensive staff balancing the race for the Heisman with winning.

Ricky was a great asset to our defense because our offense was able to control the ball. Carl Reese and the staff took what had been a struggling defense in 1997 and made it stronger. A lot of guys stepped up to help Ricky offensively. Major Applewhite stepped in and led the team at quarterback after Richard Walton got hurt. Kwame Cavil and Wane McGarity opened the game up as receivers, and Ricky Brown, our fullback, played an important role by blocking for Williams. Derek Lewis provided leadership at tight end, and the offensive line had a great year.

It is important to me that Ricky and our team succeeded by doing things the right way. We never left him in a game just to get numbers, and we never did anything contrived to promote him.

He won the Heisman on the football field. From the minute he decided to stay in school, he was a national figure and the preseason favorite for most national honors. It was important that he be accessible to the national media, and our sports information staff helped him with that. John Bianco, who handled the player media relations, did a great job of making Ricky accessible without allowing him to become abused. Ricky and John were like brothers. I admire the way they handled a lot of pressure and time management issues.

As good a football player as Ricky was for us, he is an even better person. He taught us all something about people. I am not sure I would have been able to coach a Ricky Williams when I first became a head coach as a young man. It is important for a coach to understand today's players. Kids and styles are different today. There are more single parent homes, so we as coaches often have to be cop, counselor, friend, and father figure. That's why the makeup of our staff is so important. A head coach is only as good as the people who work with him. It takes a diverse staff with the ability to communicate and build trust.

As a coach, I gain the most from seeing young people reach their dreams.

I have been fortunate to coach a lot of great players. Ricky Williams may be the best college player I have ever seen, let alone coached. He is tremendously talented, he is bright, and he is an intense competitor. He has shared his success with his teammates, and perhaps the neatest thing I heard from our team that year came from our fullback, Ricky Brown, whose role was primarily as a blocker for Williams.

When somebody asked him his goal for that season, he simply said, "I want to do my job well enough so that Ricky can win the Heisman Trophy." Ricky Brown got hit twice every play—by the defensive player in front of him and by Ricky Williams from behind.

Ricky Williams rushed for more yards than anybody in the history of NCAA Division I-A football, and he has set more than forty school or NCAA records.

Balancing his success with our team success was a challenge, but it was one of the most gratifying times in my coaching career. When he won the Heisman, he asked that we place a tiny replica of the trophy on each player's Cotton Bowl ring. He actually wanted us to take the whole team to New York for the dinner, but the NCAA wouldn't allow that. So the team got together and watched the presentation on television, and Ricky signed the *Sports Illustrated* cover photo of his record run only for his teammates and the coaches.

Ricky taught us all something. He gave me a different perspective on people. He taught us all to get past what a person may look like, even if it is a little different. He taught us all that we are never too old to learn.

Family Ties

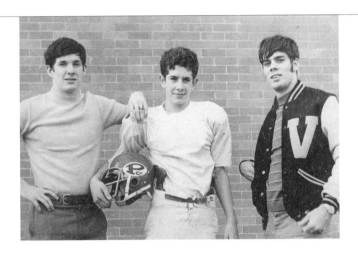

“PRIDE IS AN INTERESTING QUALITY.
IT IS LIKE BERMUDA GRASS IN A HOT OKLAHOMA SUMMER.
YOU CAN BRUISE IT AND YOU CAN WOUND IT,
BUT YOU CAN'T KILL IT.**”**

—Bill Little

◀ BROTHERS THREE - Brothers Mack *(left)* and Watson *(right)*
pose with youngest sibling, Mel, when they were in college
and he was in high school. Mack and Watson followed
their granddad into the coaching profession.

.... BL

The first thing Mack Brown noticed about Oklahoma football was its pride.
Its roots were deep, as deep as the mesquite which reaches down in the red
clay of the land for its life source; as deep as the pools of oil which kept the
state from starving through years of drought and depression.
The winds that ravaged the state's once fertile farmlands, along with the
depression which ravaged the nation's economy, hadn't left Oklahomans with very
many reasons to feel good about themselves. Then Bud Wilkinson started building
Oklahoma football. By the mid-fifties, he had made the Sooners the winningest
team in college football. The only thing that slowed Wilkinson as he headed into
the sixties was the success of his former pupil, Darrell Royal, down in Texas.

Mack Brown was twelve years old in 1963, when number two-ranked Texas
defeated number one-ranked Oklahoma, 28-7, in the classic game they played
annually in Dallas. By the time he was in college, Texas was winning national
championships and running up a thirty-game winning streak—the best in the
country since Oklahoma's forty-seven-game run under Wilkinson in the fifties.

The Sooners weren't gone from the national college football landscape for
long, and while the program may have had many off-the-field storms it was
none theless hugely successful on the playing field.

Pride is an interesting quality. It is like bermuda grass in a hot Oklahoma
summer. You can bruise it and you can wound it, but you can't kill it. Through
everything that's happened to Oklahoma football, good and bad, the pride has
always remained.

Mack Brown knew all of this, and twice he was courted by the Sooners to be
a football coach. The first time, he decided to give up his first head coaching job
after only one season to accept the offensive coordinator's position at Oklahoma.
As Barry Switzer's offensive coordinator in 1984, Brown helped Oklahoma develop
its best passing attack in years as he coached quarterbacks Danny Bradley, who
became a first team all-Big 8 selection, and Troy Aikman, who later transferred
to UCLA before going on to become one of the NFL's great quarterbacks.

After the Sooners won a Big 8 championship and a berth in the Orange Bowl,
Brown left Oklahoma to become the head coach at Tulane.

Ten years later, in one of the two jobs he seriously considered taking while at North Carolina, Brown was courted once again by the Sooners. He had made many friends during his stay in Oklahoma, and the athletics director, Donnie Duncan, was one of his closest friends.

When OU approached him about the job, Brown realized that pride was not the only human quality which had to come into play in this decision. Brown's brother, Watson, had been the offensive coordinator for Gary Gibbs, who had just been dismissed as the Oklahoma head coach. Watson updated Mack daily on the situation and encouraged his younger brother to go after the job. Even though Watson had head coaching experience, he told Mack he had no chance to replace Gibbs. But things change quickly in coaching searches and when Mack got to Oklahoma for his interview, he learned that there was some speculation that Watson himself still might be a candidate for the job.

Suddenly, pride ran smack-dab into loyalty and family, and there was no question which was going to win that contest.

MB

ome people have found it unusual that I took a head coaching job at Appalachian State for a year, then left to become an assistant again. I had been an assistant at Southern Mississippi, Memphis State, Iowa State, and Louisiana State University. When Steve Sloan and Bill Battle became head coaches before they were thirty, I got this thing in my mind that I wanted to be a head coach before I was thirty. It became really important to me, and I was not mature enough or smart enough to figure out that it would be better to take a job where you could win, rather than just take a job.

Appalachian State had a great athletics director in Jim Garner, who is now in charge of a fifteen-state area as regional director for the Fellowship of Christian Athletes, and I hated to leave. I still love Appalachian and the people in the mountains of North Carolina. Sally and I even kept a house on a beautiful lake there and we go back every summer. Hugh Morton, who owns Grandfather Mountain, built the lake, and he and his wife Julia remain friends. But the Oklahoma opportunity was one I couldn't pass up. I was making $38,500 as the head coach at Appalachian, and Oklahoma was paying more than $100,000 for the offensive coordinator's position. I learned so much at ASU. It was a good experience, and I will always be thankful for my first opportunity as head coach. I worked with some solid people there. Sparky Woods, our offensive coordinator, was successful following me as the head coach, and Jerry Moore continues to do well there today. I check their scores and pull for Appalachian State each week.

Everywhere I've coached I have had a goal to leave the program in better shape than it was when I got there. Our staff did that at Appalachian State.

I really appreciated my time at Oklahoma. The people there were wonderful to me. At Appalachian we were in the North Carolina mountains, one of the prettiest places in the country. The tallest thing in Norman, Oklahoma, was the football stadium. But that's a good thing. Somebody once told me it's not bad to live and coach where the football stadium is the biggest building in town.

Coach Switzer knew as much about getting a team to win as anybody I have ever been around. We had good players, but he also had a way of keeping them loose and getting them ready for the games we had to win.

He made it very clear from the start that the most important game in Oklahoma is the Texas game. I had been an assistant at Iowa State in the old Big 8, and I thought winning the league was important—and it was, but not nearly as important as that game that takes place the second weekend in October.

I learned a lot from Barry Switzer. He was one of the most unusual guys I have ever known. Some thought he was cocky, but he just wanted his players to have an attitude. If you believe you're the best, you will generally play like you are.

In the trip back from being a head coach to a coordinator, I was able to learn some things that made me better prepared when the next head coaching opportunity arrived. When the chance to go to New Orleans and coach at Tulane came up, I felt it was the right move to make.

When I left Norman, I couldn't have imagined that ten years later I might have the chance to go back. But the opportunity brought about one of the toughest decisions of my life.

By 1994, we had just finished our seventh season at North Carolina. I had no closer friend than Donnie Duncan, who was the athletics director at Oklahoma. Donnie had been my head coach at Iowa State, and was like a brother to me. My brother Watson had been a head coach at Austin Peay, Cincinnati, Rice, and Vanderbilt and had come from working as Jackie Sherrill's offensive coordinator at Mississippi State to help Gary Gibbs at OU. After some struggling, it looked as though Gary was going to save his program at OU. He had earned a bowl bid, but it turned out that wasn't enough. He hadn't beaten Texas. Barry was right; that's the game that matters the most. Gary is an outstanding coach, but anyone would have trouble following a legend like Barry Switzer.

Sally and I had been married a short time, and she was new to football. But she wasn't new to people. After I got a call about the Oklahoma job, Watson and I talked every day. He assured me from the start that he didn't think he had a chance to get the head coaching job. We even talked about what it would be like to coach together after all the years. But by the time we got to Norman for the interview, things had changed. Watson had gotten word from an influential source that he had a chance of getting the job.

My brothers and I were close growing up. Watson was a very talented player. I wanted to be like him, and that's why I followed him to Vanderbilt.

We thought we could team together to build a winner there, but it didn't work out that way. I was disappointed in the way Watson had been treated there, so I transferred to Florida State.

Being in competition with him was never fun. He and I coached against each other three times, and it nearly killed our mom. There's a lot of caring in our family. The three games weren't worth the hurt feelings. I hope we never play each other again.

There was no question of Oklahoma's commitment to football. Whoever is coaching there will always have a great chance to succeed. The OU tradition is rich in winning, and I would have been very excited to work for Donnie. They would have more than doubled the salary I was making at North Carolina. I knew a lot of people there, and they were very supportive. It meant a lot that they wanted me to consider coming to Norman.

The decision would have been a tough one, because we were just coming into those really good years at North Carolina, and things were going well for Sally's business.

As we left the Oklahoma interview, Sally and I talked about things other than football. I didn't ever want to hurt Watson's chance for the job. I had a great job, and I wanted him to get another head coaching position. He had fought uphill in some tough situations, and the OU job would give him a chance to show everyone just how good a head coach he really is.

I will always appreciate the time I spent in Oklahoma and the friends I have there. After Sally and I talked about the situation, I called Donnie and withdrew my name from consideration. I dreaded making that call very much, because I respect Donnie and appreciate his friendship. He had supported me for the job, and I put him in a tough spot when I backed out.

They named Howard Schnellenberger to replace Gary Gibbs, and, as it turned out, Watson didn't stay on that staff. He is now doing well as the head coach at Alabama-Birmingham. We talk at least once a week, and it is great to have somebody that you love and trust who will tell you the truth, whether you want to hear it or not.

I never looked back. I did what I thought was right at the time. As long as Watson was a candidate for the job, it wasn't worth it for me to be interested in it.

It's like Sally said, "There will be other jobs. You only have two brothers." I love both of my brothers very much. And I wasn't about to hurt one of them over a football job.

A Look At Leadership

❝THIS STORY TELLS MORE THAN ANYTHING ELSE
THE IMPORTANCE OF RECRUITING THE RIGHT KIND OF KIDS.
YOU HAVE TO RESPECT AND BELIEVE IN EACH OTHER,
TRUST EACH OTHER, AND BE WILLING TO SPEAK FRANKLY.
THEY ASKED FOR WHAT THEY WANTED, AND I WAS PROUD
OF THEM FOR THAT, EVEN IF IT WAS CONTRARY
TO A STANCE I HAD JUST TAKEN.**❞**

—Mack Brown

◀ A FATHER'S GUIDANCE - In his early days at North Carolina, Mack Brown faced some tough decisions on guidance and discipline, and many of his views of leadership came from his father, Melvin Brown, Sr.

F
or the nation's oldest state university, it was, simply put, the biggest student crisis since the Vietnam War. For Mack Brown's football program it was a turning point.

It was not without irony that a matter totally removed from football brought Brown and his North Carolina football team to a crossroads. This was a university chartered in 1789 and located where several colonial roads converged.

The late Charles Kuralt, a 1955 graduate of North Carolina, once said of his alma mater, "Our love for this place is based on the fact that it is, as it was meant to be, the University of the people."

In the fall of 1992, the people were speaking.

On the gridiron, the Tar Heel football team had won its first two games, and with an upcoming game with Army, had a great chance to start the season 3-0 for the first time in ten years. The fifth year of Mack Brown's stay at Carolina could well be pivotal. His first two teams had gone 1-10 and 1-10, then after seasons of 6-4-1 and 7-4, 1992 appeared promising. A victory over the Cadets of West Point on September 17 would give the Tar Heels a foothold on a chance for their first bowl appearance since 1986, Dick Crum's last year as coach.

On Wednesday, he had had one of his few nights out since the crumbling of his eighteen-year marriage—a pleasant dinner with a local real estate developer named Sally Jessee, set up by a mutual friend.

But at the university, angry voices rose from the picturesque campus where such notables ranging from our 11th president, James K. Polk, to actors Andy Griffith and Jack Palance, learned their trades. It was at Carolina that Michael Jordan proved that man could fly, and across the campus from the protests, Mia Hamm was making a name for herself on the soccer field.

The issue, in the view of the students, was a promise made and a promise broken.

The storm centered around the building of a Black Cultural Center, a learning center, gathering place, and historical reference point about African American contributions to North Carolina culture.

The center had been promised to the students in 1984, and in 1988 the

85

university's board of regents allocated $2.5 million for the facility. But it never was built. The debate centered along interesting lines, with people on both sides calling the other "racist". The university's position, championed by chancellor Paul Hardin, was that building a free-standing facility was segregating, rather than integrating.

When the university cut the $2.5 million down to $500,000 for expansion of the existing Black Cultural Center—a small office in the student union building—six hundred students marched to Hardin's office in the spring of 1992. Several, including some football players, were arrested. Throughout the summer, efforts of several committees, including the Black Awareness Council, which had several players as members, failed to break the deadlock.

By the week of the Army game, the students had given Hardin a deadline of November 13 to take the proposal for a free-standing center to the board of trustees or face undefined "direct action." A newspaper of the day pretty well summed up the dilemma facing Brown.

"In the middle of the football season, Black athletes have emerged as leaders in one of the most intense debates to arise on the Carolina campus since the Vietnam War protests of the late 1960s and early 1970s...."

Friday night before the Saturday game in Kenan Stadium, the protest groups planned a rally at the Smith Center, where film director Spike Lee and militant spokesperson Kahlid X were to appear. The Reverend Jesse Jackson, who had been on campus for the spring protest, also was scheduled to appear.

And a number of Brown's football players wanted to go.

MB

I have always told our players that they were students first, and I have encouraged them to be involved in student activities. The only thing I ever asked of them in that regard is that they speak their opinion as simply that—their opinion—and always express it in a first class manner. We had 123 guys on that football team, and each had his own opinion. I didn't feel it was a distraction as long as our players spoke on any subject as individuals and not as representatives of the football team.

I asked them to understand the other side and to express their feelings showing complete respect for other people. I'm not for demonstrations and shouting. I think you accomplish far more by sitting down and talking with each other.

Looking back, this issue probably created the most visible group of leaders our team had had up to that point at North Carolina, and it helped us pull through a time when we were in trouble. After four years, our team was finally beginning to get better, but the issue was threatening to tear our campus apart. Some of the kids felt the university had promised them a Black Cultural Center, and now they weren't going to give it to them. I'm sure that's not the way the university saw it, but I took up for the kids, which I will always do. I understand frustration with the system. There were tough issues on both sides.

When it comes to our players, I try really hard to separate the deed from the person. I might not like what somebody did, but I still like them as a person. I do not hold a grudge. We make decisions and move forward.

I'd only met Sally one time, but it didn't take long to figure out that she supported the kids, too.

Spike Lee and—rumors had it—Jesse Jackson were coming to town to look at the situation and to make sure the kids' side was heard. They were having a rally Friday night at the Smith Center and they asked our team to be present.

Obviously, I had a date with our team Friday night at the Marriott Hotel. That's where we stayed and went through our pregame meetings the night before a game. Most NCAA Division I-A teams, on the night before the game, move off campus and keep their team together at a hotel, with a full schedule planned for them.

When the request to attend the rally came, some of the guys said, "We want to go." I took a hard line. I stood up and said, "We've got a team function on Friday night, and anybody who's not there is off scholarship." I said, "If we have ten guys left, we'll play with ten. But that's the deal."

The four captains, three of whom were African American, came to me after the meeting and said, "Coach, we want you to think about something."

I stopped and listened.

"We know you're concerned about the game, but you've been great about the Black Cultural Center. There are three guys that are really involved. One of them's going to play Saturday, and the other two are hurt. We want you to consider letting them go to the function with a coach. They can watch it, be involved, speak if they need to, and be back by curfew at 10:30. Then they can tell the team what happened. It won't be a distraction, and we'll let it go from there. If you don't let them go, it's not an issue. We'll do whatever you want."

This story tells more than anything else the importance of recruiting the right kind of kids. You have to respect and believe in each other, trust each other, and be willing to speak frankly. They asked for what they wanted, and I was proud of them for that, even if it was contrary to a stance I had just taken. We were all trying to communicate. I decided I would sleep on it. It was a tough decision.

The next day I brought the three kids in, plus the four captains.

"I'm going to let you go, but I want you to handle yourself with class. I want you to be back by 10:30, and Coach [Donnie] Thompson is going with you."

There was an uneasy silence in the room. Then Jonathan Perry stood up and looked at the three players.

"You heard the man," said Jonathan. "He said you could go, and he said he's going to let you handle it. You need to handle it with class, and you need to be back by 10:30."

"Now, understand this: number one, he doesn't think you should go.

He's doing this because we asked him to. Number two, he doesn't believe in the way you are handling it, because that's not his style. And number three, if you ever bring it up again after Friday night, I'm gonna personally whip your ass."

The other three captains agreed. One of them said, "Nah, Jonathan, you won't have to personally whip their ass. You'll have some help."

It was the last time we ever had an issue. That team won nine games and beat Mississippi State in the Peach Bowl. That was the beginning of our bowl run at North Carolina.

This was leadership. It was a story of handling a challenge—a crisis—and bridging it to a positive. These players stood up for strongly held beliefs and were willing to respectfully disagree with their coach. They accepted and supported one another's differences of opinions. My job was to listen, and as long as it didn't hurt the team, to respect their stand.

This could have ruined those kids' lives, and it could have gotten me out of coaching. I could have kicked a bunch of kids off the team. Instead, together we took what could have been a divisive issue, and we used it to unify our team.

The next week, the *Chapel Hill News* ran the following story:

"A planned proposal by a leader of a group of black university athletes may break the impasse over a free-standing Black Cultural Center. The leader, Tim Smith [one of the players who went that night] of the Black Alliance Council, was drafting a proposal to the chancellor of the University of North Carolina asking for a committee to develop architectural plans and program offerings for a free-standing building. The plan is the first sign of compromise on the part of students who had given Chancellor Paul Hardin a November 13 deadline…."

All of those kids have gone on to be successful. Corey Holliday is currently working in the football office at North Carolina, Tommy Thigpin is the secondary coach at Bowling Green University, Jonathan Perry lives in Atlanta and is a lawyer and a sports agent, and Randall Parsons is the manager of a major hardware store. Jimmy Hitchcock, another team member who attended the meeting, is a starting defensive back for the Carolina Panthers.

Sally and I married a year later.

In the spring of 2001, the University of North Carolina broke ground in a grove of trees near Kenan Stadium for a free-standing Black Cultural Center.

As co-chairperson of a committee which raised some of the funds, Sally flew back for the celebration, filled with pride that we had a small hand in fulfilling a promise to a bunch of young people.

Be Careful What You Ask For

❝THE LOVE OF THE GAME AND OF THE KIDS
EXISTS FOR BOTH THE HEAD COACH AND THE ASSISTANT,
BUT CLEVE BRYANT SAID THE TOUGHEST THING FOR HIM
WHEN HE BECAME AN ADMINISTRATOR WAS THAT
ASSISTANT COACHES USUALLY HAVE A MUCH CLOSER
RELATIONSHIP WITH THE KIDS, SIMPLY BECAUSE OF
THE TIME THEY GET TO SPEND WITH THEM. **❞**

—Mack Brown

◄ FROM A COACH TO A FRIEND – That's the path that Cleve Bryant *(with Longhorn star Ricky Williams)* followed when he left on-the-field coaching to become the Longhorns' Associate Athletics Director for Football Operations. Maintaining his relationship with the student athletes was of paramount importance for Bryant as he moved into his new administrative role.

BL

I t was a scene straight out of Americana: a rustic old ball park whose 1930s wooden plank seats were juxtaposed within a pop foul of Interstate 10 in far east San Antonio.

Father's Day afternoon had brought out the best in Sunday-go-to-meeting clothes, as the home team Yankees hosted a bunch of youngsters from up the road in Austin.

Mr. Miller, the public address announcer, had complete control of the crowd. That is, after a brief encounter with Sister Rosalie down in the fourth row behind home plate.

As Mr. Miller was telling the folks, "There's nothing like a cold beer and a good ball game on a beautiful Sunday afternoon," he announced that due to travel arrangements for the visitors, the second game of the doubleheader would be shortened to seven innings.

The large woman in the fourth row rose immediately, put both hands on her hips, and in her loudest voice proclaimed, "I want to play nine innings!"

Mr. Miller paused for a second, yielding to the power of the voice without a microphone, then said, "Sister Rosalie has requested that the second game of our doubleheader be nine innings. Therefore, the second game of our doubleheader will be nine innings."

The giant lady sat, and the game proceeded with Mr. Miller resuming his banter with the fifty or so fans in their coats and ties and Sunday best.

In the seventh inning of the first game, the Yankees had a rally going. They had runners at first and second with nobody out, and all ol' Jimmie Johnson had to do was lay down a bunt to advance the runners. He squared his shoulders and popped the ball in the air toward the Austin pitcher. Displaying the quickness of youth, the hurler bent forward and scooped up the ball at his shoe tops.

He whirled around and looked at second, where the runner was scrambling back. He decided not to throw there. By the time the pitcher looked at first, the runner had safely returned there. A chance at a sure double play had been missed in the hesitation.

"Well," said Mr. Miller over the microphone. "He got what he wanted, but he lost what he had."

Mr. Miller had to leave later in the day to go check on his sick aunt, and all the audience prayed for him and those in his family. But for those who were there that afternoon, he left an undeniable truth: Too often in life, in getting what we want, we give up something far more valuable.

We get what we want, but we lose what we had.

--- **MB**

There is no message I could give young coaches stronger than "Be careful what you ask for...you might get it."

And it might not be what you wanted after all. When we are young in this profession, most of us dream about becoming a head coach, but it is really important to look at the moves we take to get there.

The award-winning video documentary that Hollywood producer Rich Hull did about Coach Royal shows an interesting exchange between Coach and Miss Edith, his wife. They're talking about places they've been.

"Not a lot of wives would put up with moving eight times in eight years," says Coach Royal. "We went from North Carolina...to Tulsa," says Miss Edith.

"Starkville, Mississippi..."

"Canada..."

"Back to Mississippi..."

"Then we went to Washington...."

"And then we came to Texas."

I asked Coach about that one time, and he told me, "You always have to know where you want to get. I took some jobs along the way—just to learn—where I didn't necessarily want to stay, but I knew they were moves that would help me."

My granddad could have coached anywhere at any level, but he found his joy with those high school kids in Cookeville, Tennessee. And he lived a good life because of it.

Many of us aren't willing to take the time Coach Royal did to get the job we dream of. I have had friends jump at what turned out to be a bad job. I know many guys who are not bad coaches, they have just had bad jobs where they had no chance to succeed.

When Notre Dame hired Gerry Faust, he was one of the most successful high school coaches in America, and when the folks at Notre Dame called, he was interested enough in what things would be like at the next level that he took the job. In his autobiography, *The Golden Dream*, Coach Faust admits he was naïve and made many mistakes. He felt he could have done a better job putting together his first coaching staff. He changed Notre Dame's offense without considering carefully the type of players he had inherited. He failed to adjust to his talent. The Notre Dame job seemed the perfect dream, but he had had a great life as a high school coach. He got what he wanted, but he gave up what he had.

My brother Watson has taken some tough jobs, but now some good things are happening for him and he's having success at the University of Alabama-Birmingham.

When you want to be a head coach, you have to decide the path you want to take. I've chosen Appalachian State, Tulane, North Carolina, and Texas—schools that want good students. They have to act right. They have to be able to speak properly in public. It's also harder to win at those schools. The pool of athletes that will fit your program is smaller. But some institutions and coaches don't care about academics or even the kids themselves. They are just obsessed with winning.

I have chosen to be where people understand and care about graduation. I want them to know about the value of being an academic all-American. At North Carolina and Texas, it's harder to maintain a high grade point average than it is at many other schools.

Some schools have special programs designed for athletes. The four schools where I've coached put the players in the mainstream of the academic curriculum. At Texas, there is a strong commitment to the quality of education. Coaches who work here need to believe in that. It is our job to give our kids a chance to succeed. But you need to understand the deal going in. In college, you get to decide what kind of kids you want to work with. The high school coach doesn't recruit. He has a responsibility to take the kids he has and make a difference in their lives.

I tell my assistants all the time that if they want a head coaching job, I'll help them get it, but I advise them to take a long look and make sure it is the right opportunity for them. If you are good enough in this profession, in time you'll have a bunch of chances to advance. Don't jump at the first one. Just take the best one. It is not worth being a head coach unless you can have success. Losing is too tough. The money looks good, but the short money is not worth the long-term scars and pain of losing.

I was lucky because I probably wasn't ready to be a head coach when I went to Appalachian State, but it worked out because Jim Garner was a great athletics director for me. Tom Bohannon, who is now a vice-president at Baylor, was a super faculty representative, plus, we had a good staff. It was a tough decision to leave and go back to being an assistant at Oklahoma, but it turned out to be the right thing to do. I learned so much from both the Appalachian and Oklahoma situations. Both stops were valuable in my development as a coach and as a person.

When Sally and I were faced with the tough decision of whether to take the Texas job, we had to consider what our long-term goals were, and where they could be best accomplished. When we came to Texas, it was with the ultimate goal of bringing that program back and winning a national championship. That's what we want to do, and that's why we decided to move from a place where we thought we would finish our careers.

There are only a handful of schools where you have a chance to have continued success at the highest level, and if that's your goal, you must try to achieve it. Understand as you make your decision that nothing is ever as great as you think or as tough as you fear, but reality is somewhere between the two.

Our friend, Roy Spence, is one of the founding partners in the advertising/public relations firm GSD&M. When the partners graduated from The University of Texas, they had a desire to stay in Austin. So they started from scratch and created one of the most successful businesses in the country. They set the goal of where they wanted to live and what they wanted to do, and they figured out how to make it happen. It would be easy to see where they are today and to miss the fact that they had to pay a price to get there. Roy works as hard as anyone I know. He has paid for his success.

The most important thing for a coach to realize is where his strengths are. Being a head coach is far different from being an assistant. Greg Davis, who has been both, says an assistant makes suggestions, but a head coach has to make decisions.

My life changed a lot when I became a head coach, and the hardest time ever was when, at the age of thirty-three, I was both the head coach and athletics director at Tulane. It was also tough when we started at North Carolina, but it changed even more when we got to Texas. I finally understood something Johnny Majors said when people asked him the difference between coaching at Tennessee, where he was, and at Pittsburgh, where he had been.

"At Pittsburgh, you're the football coach in the fall," he said. "At Tennessee, you're the coach year 'round."

I never stop being the head football coach at Texas. I have been in a diner in the mountains of North Carolina and had someone come up to me and ask, "Who's going to play quarterback, Major or Chris?" They even know their first names. Skycaps and waitresses want to know the same things. I love being a head coach, but there are things I miss today about being an assistant.

The love of the game and of the kids exists for both the head coach and the assistant, but Cleve Bryant said the toughest thing for him when he became an administrator was that assistant coaches usually have a much closer relationship with the kids, simply because of the time they get to spend with them. Cleve was a great coach, but he felt the time was right to check out administration. When DeLoss Dodds hired me, he said he wanted the experience for the kids to be great. As our associate athletics director for football operations, Cleve has expanded his duties in order to work directly with the players so that he could remain close to them.

We've got a bunch of guys on our staff who can be outstanding head coaches, if that's what they choose to do. Salaries play a big part in the decision. Everett Withers, who played for me at Appalachian State and was our secondary coach for three years, left college coaching because of a tremendous salary opportunity in the NFL. He made what he considered the right choice for his career. He was making $110,000 as an assistant for us, and will make at least $200,000 a year on a guaranteed three-year contract with the Tennessee Titans.

Coaches today need to look at opportunities for annuities and retirement packages. Because college assistants usually don't stay in one place a long time, they don't have a chance to become vested in retirement programs. For high school coaches, the Texas Teacher Retirement System is excellent if they stay in the secondary school system. The University of Texas gave our coaches a retirement plan to help their families as they get older. At Texas, they demand a lot, but they take great care of you. That's fair.

My advice is to weigh every decision and look at what works and what doesn't work. And the bottom line is to realize what really matters to you.

Mike Campbell is the best example I can think of. As Coach Royal's assistant, he turned down a lot of head jobs to stay at Texas. Then, when the Texas job opened, he was bypassed for the job. There were a lot of hurt feelings.

When I met Mike Campbell, I found a guy who was not bitter and who still fervently loved the game of football. More important, when he died, hundreds of his former players came back to honor him.

In the end, I think a whole bunch of us would trade that love and respect for all of the head jobs there are.

That's the other thing my granddad taught me: Be thankful for what you have. We've all heard the saying, "Enjoy the journey...don't worry about the destination." It sounds corny, but it is true.

What Love Has To Do With It

❝ YOU LOVE EACH OTHER, AND WE LIKE EACH OTHER.
WE NEED A MOM AND DAD, SO WHY DON'T YOU GUYS
JUST GET MARRIED? **❞**

—Barbara Brown

◀ THE BROWNS AT HOME – The Brown family portrait their
first year at Texas in front of their house on Waters Edge.
Left to right are Katherine, Chris, Mack and Sally, Matt,
and Barbara.

BL

The philosopher Kahlil Gibran wrote in his popular book *The Prophet*, this advice on marriage: "And stand together, yet not too near together: For the pillars of the temple stand apart, and the oak tree and the cypress grow not in each other's shadow."

Kahlil Gibran must have known about the football coach and the land developer.

Mack Brown was in his fifth year as the head coach at North Carolina, and it had not been a smooth ride. Somewhere in the middle of rebuilding the Carolina football program his eighteen-year marriage ended, and as a single father he was trying to raise two daughters and produce a winning football team.

The last thing he was looking for was a woman in his life.

Sally Jessee was a single mom with two sons and a highly successful real estate development company.

The last thing on her mind was a football coach.

But Art Chansky, a former sportswriter who shared a friendship with both Sally Jessee and Mack Brown, as well as an office in the same Franklin Street complex as Sally, was the eternal optimist. He had tried for a good portion of the summer to set up a lunch date with his two friends.

Finally, on Wednesday, the 16th of September, 1992, Mack Brown and Sally Jessee agreed to meet for dinner.

Seven years before, Sally, with sons Matt and Chris, had sold a small horse farm and had had to borrow money to begin her career as a single woman working in a man's world. Now she was a member of a bank board.

After his divorce, Mack Brown had immersed himself more than ever in the game he coached and in the lives of his two young daughters, Katherine and Barbara. He was a single father, trying hard to rear two little girls. He knew nothing of politics and couldn't tell you whether the sitting president was a republican or a democrat, and he really didn't care. Year five of the North Carolina football program offered a glimpse of light at the end of what had been a pretty dark tunnel.

So, at a diner not too far from Sally's office on Franklin Street and a short distance from Kenan Stadium, Mack Brown met Sally Jessee, and the two fell in love.

Sally remembers that Mack helped an old man—a stranger—with his tray of food. Mack remembered a soft-spoken confidence in the resiliency of a pair of sparkling eyes.

As the year progressed, Mack's football team earned a berth in the Peach Bowl in Atlanta, and Sally agreed to go.

One year later, eleven-year-old Barbara Brown called a team meeting with Mack and Sally. "I am moving in with Sally," she said. "Why don't you marry her now?"

Loosely translated, it went something like this: "You love each other, and we like each other. We need a mom and dad, so why don't you guys just get married?"

It wasn't exactly the Brady Bunch, but it was close.

Quietly on a Monday—an off-day after victories over USC and Ohio—Sally Jessee became Sally Brown on a quick trip to Dillon, South Carolina.

The marriage cost sixty dollars and took about sixty seconds. There was a ten-dollar tee shirt for sale that said, "I got hitched in Dillon," but Mack and Sally decided not to get one. On the way home, they stopped for a wedding dinner at Burger King, and then hurried home so Mack could watch films on Maryland, Carolina's next opponent. He had a new reason to want to win.

Mack told his team, amid hoorahs and congratulations. Sally's secret was outed at a meeting of the Public-Private Partners Board, a group of university officials and private business people formed to promote a thriving atmosphere in the Triangle.

When the media questioned her, the answer was simple: "There is nothing to divulge. We're married. We're happy. That's all there is to it."

With that, Sally Brown became a coach's wife. Mack and Sally, knowing the hardships of the profession and the number of marriages that fail or are unhappy in it, determined they would find a way to do it differently.

Where some wives sat at home lonely with nothing to do, Sally was active in her own career. Where some became embittered with their husband's job, Sally embraced it. She didn't have to know the difference between a draw play and a blitz, she only had to know that the game was played with kids.

"Miss Sally," as she became known to players at North Carolina and Texas, became a treasured friend to the young men on Brown's team. Sally is an intensely private person in a public world, and her nurturing became a balm to the players. She didn't care what their time was in the forty-yard dash or how much weight they could lift. She learned about their parents and their girlfriends and what was good and bad in their lives. She has set a tremendous example for coaches' wives everywhere. She found a way to be a vital part of the program, while continuing with her own career and outside interests.

That same kind of caring permeated the staff's families. Nurturing comes naturally to Sally Brown.

Her kids are grown now, but Sally's larger family, that family of big kids who play football, continues to grow.

Those who specialize in landscaping in the beautiful Texas Hill Country understand about the oak tree and the rose. The majestic live oaks, with their spreading branches, provide shade for Texas landscapes, but the rosebush needs sun in order to bloom. The oaks need pruning to maintain proper growth. When the oak is trimmed, it lets in the sun to the rose bush.

The oak flourishes.
And so does the rose.
The secret is to keep growing, but give each other a chance for that sunlight.

MB

A good friend once told me he knew his marriage was in trouble not too long after he had been named head coach and athletics director at his alma mater. He came home late one night. It had been a long day of practice, and he was trying to juggle his life and two jobs. He remembered crawling into bed, and his wife was sobbing. She finally summoned the courage to ask, "Are you…having an affair?" He sat straight up in bed.

"No," he said. "First of all, I'm too visible. Second, I'm too busy. Third, I'm too tired."

There was a pause for a minute. Then she got angry and said, "But you didn't say you loved me."

He obviously didn't answer the question very well. Too many of us get so busy and so tired, we forget to do that.

If you are going to be married in the coaching profession, folks will tell you you'd better have an understanding wife, but I would add that you'd better be understanding yourself.

Both the coach and the spouse need to understand the deal. This is a very tough profession. It is hard not to live your job twenty-four hours a day, and the spouse who marries a coach shouldn't go in with the idea that she's going to change him. There will be lots and lots of hours away from home, and because we live and die with victories and losses, there are a lot of emotional highs and lows in this profession.

During my first marriage, I believed my job came first. I worked hard at it because I wanted to succeed. I believed that was the way to provide for my family and raise my kids. I needed the support of my wife in the hard times, and I thought I was a good husband, but Sally has taught me a lot about being a good partner.

The number one complaint when coaches' wives leave is, "He was never there." It is true we have a job that is different from most others. We work long hours during the season, long hours during recruiting, long hours in the spring. Now, even our summers are changing with recruiting patterns.

As a coach, you're responsible for 125 kids and their families and you can have problems any time of the day. When a young coach walks into his house after a long day and he's met with his four kids' problems and his wife's problems, there is no doubt that some nights he feels like he's had it. He's heard everybody's problems, and he feels he's got to solve them.

So, after he's had five kids in his office all day with problems, and he comes home to find his daughter missed curfew and his wife says,

"Handle this," he says, "You've got to be kidding."

With Sally's help, we try to make our staff a big family. Sally has a suite at the game and includes our coaches' wives. Once a year, we take the wives on a plane trip with the team to a game. On bowl trips, we include all the coaches' families and provide them with comfortable living quarters. Sally plans activities for the wives on the trips and during the year.

Most of all, we encourage our wives to get involved with our players. Sally brings a different perspective than I can bring. There are times when she has insight on a recruit or on a player's problems that changes their lives. She is as close to our players as a staff member could be.

Loneliness is a bitter thing. It can poison a person, and it can destroy a marriage. It is good when a spouse—the wife or husband of a coach or of a business executive—creates interests beyond his or her spouse's career.

When we moved to Austin and Sally sold her company, we bought a ranch in the Texas Hill country because I wanted her to have horses once again. Besides being very much a part of our team, she has done charity work and has been closely involved with Helping Hand Home, an organization which helps abused children.

We make an effort to go to lunch together as often as we can, even during the season. It is important to take time off, just for ourselves. Coaches work long hours, and there needs to be a time when they can get away from the job completely. We kept a cabin on a forty-acre lake in the mountains of North Carolina, and every summer we take a couple of weeks and go there by ourselves.

I still take a lot of my job home with me. I don't think a coach can ever avoid that. But you can't get so channeled in your work that you forget to communicate with your partner. Sally and I have been married long enough that she understands when I am down after a loss, but she's also got a tremendous gift of cutting through things I see as big deals.

Once, after a particularly tough loss, she told me, "Think of it this way: of all the teams in America that played today, 50 percent of them lost." She knew I wasn't going to get over it, but it certainly helped to see it from a different perspective.

I've thought many times about that tee shirt that was on sale in Dillon, and I wish we'd gotten one. That was the only decision we made that day that was not good.

Molding The Clay

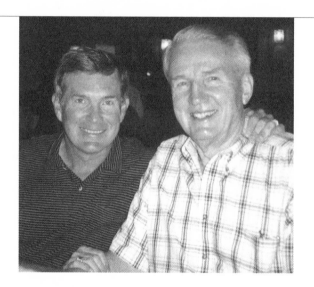

❝MORE THAN ANYTHING, HE'S A PERSON WHO,
REGARDLESS OF YOUR IMPORTANCE, NEVER FORGETS YOU.
IT DOESN'T MAKE ANY DIFFERENCE IF YOU'RE
THE JANITOR IN HIS FIRST JOB AT APPALACHIAN STATE
OR THE PRESIDENT OF THE UNIVERSITY OF TEXAS.
HE TRULY CARES ABOUT PEOPLE.**❞**

—Gil Brandt

BL

he large scenic cruiser lumbered toward home through the mountains of North Carolina. The trees, a montage of brilliant colors, flashed by the windows like a technicolor strawberry-peach swirl. The sunset shot beams like sunbursts across the landscape, displaying autumn as could only be done in the Smokies.

In the two seats of the front row, class was in session.

The pupil was Mack Brown, one of the youngest head coaches in the country. At thirty-two, he was in his first head coaching job, at Appalachian State. He was listening intently to his fellow rider, whose assignment that trip had been to be the color analyst on the radio broadcast on the Mountaineer Network.

The teacher earned fifty dollars a game for his efforts, a paltry sum considering the knowledge he brought. What he gave Mack Brown in those visits, as the credit card commercial says, was priceless.

Thirty-five years before, he had set the college football world on its ear.

Paul Dietzel was only thirty when his LSU Tigers won the national college football championship in 1958. In the next three decades, he had made a decision from the heart by returning to coach the U. S. Military Academy, where he had learned his football under the legendary Red Blaik. He served as athletics director at Indiana, where he had to manage a football coach named Lee Corso and a basketball coach named Bobby Knight. He was head coach and athletics director at South Carolina, where he wrote the school's alma mater and redesigned the mascot. He returned to LSU as athletics director and finally retired to the Carolina mountains where he would become an artist.

There was much to learn from Dietzel, whose suave, debonair style had once made him the darling of college football. To keep his hand in the game he loved, he signed on to talk on the radio about college football. His wife, Ann, said if he'd take a full-time job instead of doing the color on the Appalachian broadcasts, she would have a chance to see more of him. There was nothing part-time about Dietzel when it came to football.

He was an important mentor in a series of men for whom Brown had worked and from whom he had learned.

101

Brown's education in football began with his high school coach, Bucky Pitts, and progressed through the jobs he held. Brown's first coaching position, as a wide receivers coach at Southern Mississippi, brought him three years with Bobby Collins from 1975 through 1977. Richard Williamson, now the wide receivers coach with the Carolina Panthers, was head coach at Memphis State during Brown's stay in 1978. Donnie Duncan was the head coach at Iowa State when Brown was there from 1979 through 1980.

Williamson had played for Paul "Bear" Bryant at Alabama and coached with him, as well as with Frank Broyles at Arkansas. Duncan had been on the Oklahoma staff as assistant head coach for six years during some of the Sooners' most successful years. Jerry Stovall, who was a great player at LSU, was the coach and Dietzel the athletics director during Brown's stay with the Tigers in Baton Rouge in 1982.

Everywhere he went, Brown helped produce winners. Collins was extremely successful at Southern Mississippi, where he coached before moving to SMU and creating some of the best teams in Mustang history. Duncan's tenure at Iowa State was the school's best in the last half of the 20th century. At LSU, Stovall was named national Coach of the Year as the Tigers rebounded from a previous 4-7 season to finish 8-2-1 behind Brown's offense, finally losing to a great Nebraska team, 21-20, in the Orange Bowl.

Jim Garner was the athletics director at Appalachian who gave Brown his first shot as a head coach, where he produced a 6-5 record in his one season of 1983. It was the first winning season for the Mountaineers in four years.

The Oklahoma Sooners of 1984, with Brown as the offensive coordinator, rode the best passing attack of Barry Switzer's tenure, finishing 9-2-1, winning the Big 8, and vying for the national championship.

"Throughout my twenty-seven years of coaching at the college level," Switzer would say later while he was head coach of the Dallas Cowboys, "Mack was clearly the most talented offensive coach that I was associated with. You could tell early on that he was the complete package, and that he was going to be a very successful head coach. What he accomplished was no surprise to me."

At Tulane, Brown became his own boss as coach and athletics director, but he got great help from Wright Waters, who was an athletic administrator and is now head of the Sunbelt Conference. At North Carolina and Texas, he worked with two of the most respected administrators in all of college athletics—John Swofford at Carolina and DeLoss Dodds at Texas.

With each association, Brown built a friendship, and he showed the respect of a willing learner whose purpose was to experience life and to learn from it, to listen to advice and to profit from it.

"I've known Mack ever since he was a young graduate assistant coach," says Gil Brandt, who, as player personnel director, helped build the Dallas Cowboys dynasty under Tom Landry. "He's got great character, great intelligence...he understands organization...he's a very good football coach. He delegates authority well. More than anything, he's a person who, regardless of your importance, never forgets you. It doesn't make any difference if you're the janitor in his first job at Appalachian State or the president of The University of Texas. He truly cares about people."

Brandt talks of Brown's "boundless energy."

"Every place he's been, his teams have been successful. The apple didn't fall far from the tree. You can go back to Cookeville, Tennessee, today, and everybody talks about the Brown brothers. His mother is one of the loveliest people in the whole world, and his wife, Sally, is one of the great ladies of all time."

Brown views himself as a collection of all those he has known, including Brandt, who remains a valued friend.

MB

I t would be impossible to list the people and the friends who have helped shape my life, but to be helpful to young coaches, I'd like to direct this chapter toward the opportunities they have to learn from those they work for. Many of the things that worked for me as a head coach, I picked up from the men I am about to talk about.

I was a young coach, fresh out of Florida State, when I met Bobby Collins.

He taught me the fundamentals of football. He grew up with the old Mississippi State system, with a Tennessee background in the kicking game. Bobby Collins was as sound and simple and tough as any football coach I've ever been around. He had an obsession with the kicking game. He just retired as a fund-raiser at Southern Miss.

I learned a lot about people and dealing with players from Donnie Duncan, and I learned how to keep your head up, even though you were fighting pretty long odds. Donnie's a great example, too, of how paths cross many times in this business. Who would have ever thought that he would be an athletics director at Oklahoma, and later the Associate Commissioner of the Big 12? Ours is a friendship that has lasted a lifetime, yet as close as we are, he understands his job as well as mine. He did reprimand me for a questionable comment I made about the officials.

Jerry Stovall was an all-American and an NFL first round draft choice at LSU. He had a tough job, trying to follow in the footsteps of guys like Paul Dietzel and Charley McClendon. He was a tireless worker and was extremely positive. He worked so hard at recruiting. He was very organized. He knew every kid, wrote every note, dotted every *i* and crossed every *t*. He was a great recruiter because of his work ethic and his organizational skills.

It was really important to him to have recruiting meetings every morning. The year I was at LSU, we signed twenty-seven of the top twenty-eight players in the state. It is a shame he didn't get a chance to coach them. He was released from his alma mater the year after he was national Coach of the Year. This is a tough business.

Coach Dietzel was an entrepreneur at the highest level. Here's a guy who won the national championship at LSU when he was thirty years old. He was from upper Ohio, but he fit in at Baton Rouge. He changed the whole concept of substitutions in football. At a time when players traditionally played both offense and defense—single platoon football—he devised a defensive team and an offensive team to back up his first unit. He developed three teams, and the legend of the Chinese Bandit defense is still alive and well in Baton Rouge today. He was always thinking, and, without question, he left his imprint on college football.

Then he wanted to go to Army and take Red Blaik's place during the Vietnam War because he thought it was a great place to lead young men. In fact, he brought a good football team to Austin and played Texas in 1964 in what turned out to be the first night game Army ever played. He had a quarterback named Rollie Stichweh, who would have been the best quarterback at a military academy at the time if Navy hadn't had a guy named Roger Staubach.

After he left Army, he became the athletics director and head football coach at South Carolina, where he developed the facilities and did a whole bunch of other good things. Coach Dietzel has always been way ahead of the game. Forty years after he won that national championship, at age seventy-seven, he is an artist. He ran for mayor of Banner Elk, North Carolina, and at the same time was teaching skiing up in the mountains. He's one of the most positive human beings I've ever seen.

Jim Garner was a guy who never met a stranger. Nothing was ever a problem. Every day that you walked in, if something was really bad, he'd say, "Come here, and let's figure out how to fix this." He never said, "God, this is awful." Today he's working with the FCA and continues that positive attitude.

As I've said, I learned a lot from Barry Switzer in the way he developed a relationship with the kids. He approached recruiting the same way he did everything else. He dealt with it and moved on. He always said he was a "five play guy" when it came to recruiting. If he watched five plays of game film and he couldn't figure out which player he was supposed to be watching, he turned the film off. He said "If he's not good enough for me to know who he is in five plays, I'll be damned if I am going to sit here all day tryin' to find him." He knew how to give his team confidence, and he knew how to put things in perspective.

When I first went to Oklahoma, I wondered why we didn't do "quick cals," those coordinated calisthenics that teams do before games. Bear Bryant and everybody in the South all did "quick cals" together. It was important for team unity and all that.

I asked Coach Switzer why we didn't do that. "I thought everybody does that," I said.

He said, "Why is it important to work on something that looks pretty before a game but that you will never use during the game? You're asking me to get our team to squat like they are using the bathroom and to try to all hit their heads at the same time. That has no purpose. You have to be really careful how many things you make important to them because they have to know what's important in winning. If too many things are important, they won't be able to separate them." Some people said Barry was a great recruiter, but just an average coach. Nothing has ever been farther from the truth.

John Swofford understood the challenges we faced at North Carolina, and he did everything he could to allow the football program to rise to the standard set by the basketball program. He made sure it was always done with class and integrity.

DeLoss Dodds has given us everything we have asked for at Texas. He has often joked that he gave us "an unlimited budget, and you exceeded it." But he's made it possible for us to hire and keep the best staff in America. The last piece in the puzzle of an extremely successful administrative career at Texas for DeLoss was returning this program to a national contender in football. He's done everything he could to make that happen. DeLoss, as well as Jim Garner and John Swofford, would do anything within the rules to help kids.

When I look back at all of the guys I have worked for, I am thankful for the time I had to spend with each of them. Each gave me something I have been able to put to good use in my life, with our staffs, and with our teams. It is a great lesson for a young coach to realize that he doesn't know everything, and it's not a crime to take ideas from those who have been there a long time.

We are like pieces of clay, and each person who touches us makes an impression.

Dedication Day

❝THE MOST IMPORTANT PART ABOUT DEDICATION DAY
IS THAT IT GIVES ALL OF US A CHANCE TO THINK ABOUT
THE PEOPLE WE NEED TO BE THANKFUL FOR AND TO
COMPETE THAT DAY IN THEIR HONOR.**❞**

—Mack Brown

◀ SALUTE TO A LEGEND – Dedication Day is always special for Mack Brown, but none was more special than the day he dedicated the 2000 Iowa State game to Tom Landry, the longtime coach of the Dallas Cowboys. Landry, a Texas-ex, died not too long after the Longhorn victory. Brown had presented him with a "T" ring during his illness.

A freak injury on the practice field in West Texas, an unfortunate collision of headgear with a shoulder pad, had left Joe Beene clinging to life in a Dallas hospital.

Roy Williams knew Beene. He had practiced against him every day of his senior season at Odessa Permian. He was a "scout team" player, the kind of dedicated young man who often sees little action in games, but is a vital part of a team's success. Boxers get better because of sparring partners. Players get better because their own teammates challenge them to improve, to succeed. Joe Beene had made Roy Williams better.

Once a year, Mack Brown selects a game for his team to use as a "Dedication Game." In a meeting on the Thursday before the game, Brown suggests that each player select someone who has made a difference in his life, and that he dedicate his play in that game to them. The idea is to give them a symbolic "game ball" for what they have meant to the player.

In 1999, Brown himself had pledged his Dedication Day ball to the legendary Tom Landry, a former Longhorn who gained his fame as coach of the Dallas Cowboys. Landry was hospitalized for the illness that would eventually kill him.

For Brown, that dedication had special meaning. Landry was a coaching icon for him, dating back to his teenage years. After Brown became a coach, Landry and Gil Brandt always reached out to college coaches with a golf tournament they hosted in Dallas.

Roy Williams was one of the most talented freshman receivers in America in the season of 2000. Early in his senior season at Permian, he and his teammates learned that their backfield coach, Bucky Jones, was dying.

"Before we took the field, Coach Jones broke down and told us he loved us. He knew he was going to die, and was suffering from cancer," wrote Williams in an article for the school paper, *The Permian Press*.

Jones lived through the season, but as December came, Williams and the other players were left with only faint hope for his survival.

"He had cancer in his liver that had spread into his body. The doctors gave him some 'miracle medicine'. They said if it worked he would live to see February,"

107

wrote Williams. "I guess the medicine didn't work, because on Christmas Eve, Coach Jones left us. He went on home, home to glory. His funeral was on December 26. Coach Jones wanted to be cremated, so he was. Some of his ashes were tossed upon the practice field where the quarterbacks warmed up.

"I have dedicated my college career to Coach because he told me that I could make it. He also told me that he had never coached anyone like me. When the chips are down, I just think of ol' Coach," Williams concluded.

A thousand miles away from Odessa, on the cold plains of Kansas, Roy Williams thought of his coach and his former teammate. The Kansas Jayhawks, significant underdogs, had jumped to a 14-0 lead over Texas. A defensive back had stepped in front of Williams and taken an interception all the way back for the second score. The player made the mistake of "talking smack" to Williams after the play.

The old Jim Croce song says you don't spit into the wind or tug on Superman's cape, and that day, they could have added that you shouldn't mess with a determined future superstar.

Roy Williams finished the day with four catches for 180 yards and two touchdowns, and Texas won, 51-16.

When he woke from his coma in the Dallas hospital, Joe Beene would learn something special.

Roy Williams had played that day in cold Kansas for him.

MB

One of the most important things we can do is to say thank you to those who have made a difference in our lives. Every Thanksgiving we have a meal together where all of the players get up and say what they are thankful for. I remember having tears in my eyes the first year we were here; Major Applewhite—our redshirt freshman quarterback who got to play because of an injury to Richard Walton, our senior quarterback—stood up and said he was grateful for Richard's support and friendship. I appreciated him giving Richard credit, because of all of the talk about our quarterbacks at Texas—whether Chris Simms or Major Applewhite or Major Applewhite or Chris Simms should play—Richard Walton was the one who never got to live his dream. A broken finger gave Major a chance to play, and Richard never got back in.

Each time we have that service, similar things happen. It is a private time that is just within the team. I want our players to know that it is important to tell people how much they have meant to you. Every day I'm thankful for what my grandparents and my dad meant to me when they were alive. And there is no way to ever say enough thanks to my mom. She's always been my biggest fan, and I love her dearly. All of us have people like that in our lives, and we need to take the time to thank them.

We started the Dedication Game to do that. Jeff Madden told me that Bill McCartney did it when he was at Colorado, and I really liked the idea.

I put a lot of thought into which game to choose. It is amazing how many times the game has a special meaning, as it did that year for Roy Williams. The same was true in the case of Coach Landry. He had meant so much to me as a coach and to everybody who loves the game of football. Even though he didn't have a lot of time to come back and visit, he was a former Longhorn player, and that always meant a lot to him. I wanted to make sure he got that game ball, and that he knew we cared. Not only did we give him that game ball, we also gave him one of the "T" rings that Coach Royal had made such an honored tradition. The ring goes to a football letterman who earns a degree, and it's the most cherished possession most of them have from their college days. It seemed to touch Coach Landry when we gave it to him.

In choosing a game, I always try to pick one where we could be flat and need to play with extra emotion. There are two reasons for that. First, when I ask the players to dedicate the game, they put added pressure on themselves. When you dedicate something to somebody, you want to come through for them. I don't want to see our kids disappointed because they promised something and then didn't produce. The other part of why we do it is so we won't let down and overlook our opponent. One of the things I have learned is that there are no easy games at Texas. Everybody we play, particularly in the Big 12, competes against us as if they are playing for the national championship. That also goes for Rice, Houston, and Arkansas, who we have played in non-conference games. You have to be ready to play every Saturday.

The most important part about Dedication Day is that it gives all of us a chance to think about the people we need to be thankful for, and to compete that day in their honor.

I try to take the time after our Thursday practice to talk to the team about that. I want them to understand the blessings they have had because somebody cared about them. Each player makes his own selection, and we break into position meetings so they can talk more about it. Then, we ask them to call the person before and after the game.

Most select a relative or a close friend. The person doesn't have to be living. It just needs to be somebody that the kid wants to honor. Then they write down who they've chosen and why. That information is personal. I never ask them to share it unless they volunteer, so it's not a test of picking something "right." The most important thing is to focus on something beyond the game and to realize that without that person, their lives would be different.

That's why I chose Tom Landry that year. In the years we have done this, I have had a chance for a lot of Dedication Days. That one was particularly important because it was a small way for me to say thank you to a guy I grew up admiring.

I don't know if I coached better that day, but I know I tried.

STORIES OF THE MIND

**❝BE POSITIVE IN EVERYTHING YOU DO.
DON'T TALK ABOUT THE NEGATIVES.
YOU CAN EAT YOUR LIFE UP BEING NEGATIVE.
THE OLD STATEMENT ABOUT THE GLASS
BEING HALF-FULL OR HALF-EMPTY HAS MERIT,
AS FAR AS I AM CONCERNED.❞**

—Mack Brown

The High School Coach

❝THERE IS NO WAY TO PUT A VALUE ON WHAT
HIGH SCHOOL COACHES DO FOR KIDS OR ON
HOW HARD THEIR JOB IS. THEY ARE, LIKE OTHER TEACHERS,
VASTLY UNDERPAID, BUT VERY IMPORTANT
TO THE FUTURE OF OUR SOCIETY. **❞**

—Mack Brown

◀ THE COACH – Jelly Watson was the winningest high school coach in middle Tennessee history, and his legacy lives on in his grandsons, Mack and Watson, who continue in the coaching profession. His advice was sound, and his example set a standard Mack strives to live up to today.

BL

I t has become a rite of spring in Austin—the caps and the jackets and the shirts in the bright school colors, with the logos proudly signifying the schools they represent. They come in all shapes and sizes, all ages and skin colors. They are from in-state and out-of-state and they have come to study Mack Brown and his coaching staff.

These are high school coaches, and they are welcome on the Frank Denius Fields, where the Longhorns hold their NCAA-allowed fifteen spring practice sessions.

More than one thousand will attend the annual high school clinic put on by Brown and his staff, featuring speakers that rank among the nation's best coaches. They will listen to talk about pass patterns and practice routines, plays and game plans. They will swap stories and ideas, as Brown and his staff host them for a day or a week, whichever fits their schedule.

From the day he was hired at Texas, Mack Brown made it clear no group was more important to his efforts to rebuild the storied Texas football tradition than the high school coaches. In his first press conference, he talked about restoring relationships with the lettermen and with the high school coaches and of reconnecting with the tradition of success that men such as Darrell Royal built for the Longhorns.

He was true to his word.

Brown and his coaches have built a bond with their counterparts in the Texas high school ranks. Hundreds of high school coaches attend Longhorn games, and the Texas staff attends every clinic possible. At the Texas High School Coaches Association Convention each summer, Brown himself leads a delegation that practices, in part, what he has asked of the Texas fans. They come early, and they stay late.

It is Brown's style to meet every person he can, and he has an amazing gift for remembering names. At the coaches' meetings, he will locate a spot where he can get a chance to say hello to every coach possible.

In the summers, Brown asks his coaches to juggle their vacations to make sure one member of the offensive staff and one member of the defensive staff are in the football offices at all times. In case a high school coach or a player or a fan drops by to visit, someone is always available to them.

Once, late on a summer afternoon, a high school coach on vacation dropped

113

by the Moncrief-Neuhaus football offices. The doors were closed and locked, but a receptionist saw the coach and his family and spoke to them. When she learned the visitor was a high school coach, she opened the building and waited until they had a chance to see the stadium from the Mike Campbell-Bobby Moses trophy room. From the full-length windows, they could see the massive stadium and the green grass football field. In the room where rich, dark wood contrasts with stark white tile, the family saw the bowl trophies, national championship trophies, and the two Heismans won by Earl Campbell and Ricky Williams.

Mack Brown knows that his relationship with high school coaches is critical in recruiting, but for him, the bond goes much farther than that. It goes back to his roots, in the foothills of the mountains in Tennessee.

MB

My first memory of a high school coach is that of riding a school bus to a game with my granddad. I was five years old, and I even had my own letter jacket.

My granddad was the winningest high school coach in middle Tennessee history. His real name was Eddie Watson, but folks around Cookeville just called him "Jelly."

My dad had also coached a year and had been a school principal and superintendent.

The most important male influences in my life when I was growing up were my granddad, my dad, and my high school coach, Bucky Pitts. There is no way to put a value on what high school coaches do for kids, or on how hard their job is. They are, like other teachers, vastly underpaid, but very important to the future of our society.

In college, we recruit talent. Professional teams hire it. High school coaches take what they are given and pull them together as a team. Often, particularly with so many kids coming from single parent homes today, high school coaches are one of the most important factors in a kid's life when it comes to discipline. A high school coach is often like a second dad to a kid, and sometimes he's the only male figure in a kid's life.

In recruiting, it's important to build a bond with the high school coaches in the state. That's why one of the first calls I made when I took the Texas job was to Eddie Joseph, who is the executive director of the Texas High School Coaches Association. I knew it was important for Texas—the largest school in the state—to reach out to the high school coaches. Not only would that help us in recruiting, but it was just the right thing to do. I'd known Eddie before, but he's become a great friend since that day. After we lost to Oklahoma in 2000, Eddie told me to be sure I had at least six friends. I asked him why.

"Because you need six pall bearers at your funeral," he said.

In putting together a staff, I wanted people who would like and respect the high school coaches in our state. Our first goal was to visit every one

114

of the more than 1,200 high schools that plays football in the state.

Every summer, we attend coaching school, and it isn't just to be seen. We require our coaches to go to the panels. In the summer of 2001, they had a panel discussion of the nine winners of the state schoolboy championships. The group included John Parchman of Midland Lee; Mike Johnston, Katy; Chad Morris, Bay City; Sam Harrell, Ennis; Kiff Hardin, Gatesville; Tony Valastro, LaGrange; Jason Herring, Sonora; G. A. Moore, Jr., Celina; and Brad Thiessen, Stratford.

From that panel, I picked up at least five very valuable points. First, minimize distractions. Understand what is important to winning and eliminate the rest. Second, don't let your players drift. Be aware of your kids, both in their attention at practice and meetings and in their off-the-field activities. If one of your players is acting different from the norm, confront him immediately. Talk to him and his parents to head off whatever is bothering him. Third, take all mention of the previous season, regardless of how successful it was, and put it away. Put up rings, watches, and memories from past successes and build your own story. Fourth, be open to new ideas. And fifth, you must have fun.

What a gift they gave us! When guys who have won championships, at whatever level, are willing to speak to you, you need to listen.

The toughest thing about recruiting under today's NCAA scholarship limit is that we can't take all the players we would like to take. Schools can give a maximum of twenty-five scholarships a year, and there are times when we have to tell a kid—and his high school coach—that we can't take him because of the limit. The high school coach may not tell a prospect to come to your school, but they will sure tell him not to come if they don't feel good about your program.

It is hard for us to have to say no if a high school coach believes a kid can play for us, and he wants to see him happy. That is when you'd better have built a bond of respect with the high school coach so that he understands your job. Even though he may disagree with your decision, he will give you the same respect you have given him. With 1,200 high schools with top prospects and your ability to only take twenty-five, public relations becomes essential to your success. Out-of-state college coaches don't have to maintain an honest relationship and go back to each school each year, but at Texas we do.

I have made it clear that our office doors are always open to these three groups of people: a player, his parents, and his high school coach.

There's a picture in my office of my dad and my granddad, both of whom died just before I came to Texas. A lot of what I believe, I believe because of them. There's a part of me that coaches for them and my mom to be proud of me each week. My mom lives in Florida and watches all of our games, but I believe my dad, granddad, and grandma watch every game as well.

They were honest people, and I have always been obsessed with people telling the truth. That's why our staff always makes sure that a young man and his high school coach understand what we are saying, because I don't want them to ever think we've lied to them.

I make a point of introducing myself to every coach I have a chance to meet. I want to know their names and where they coach. I want them to ask questions, just like people used to ask granddad. Coaches have always reached out to me, and now I would like to give back some of that kindness.

After my dad got out of coaching, he ran the sporting goods store, and he always helped the high school coaches. If a coach needed some equipment and couldn't pay for it right then, he'd sell it to them on credit. A lot of times, he never collected. It was just how he was.

I enjoy being around high school coaches because they are the purest form of coach, and I feel as if I know them because that's how I grew up.

Whether you're at the junior high level or in the pros, if you coach, you are ultimately there for the players. The high school coach is, in my opinion, one of the most important members of a school's faculty. He has the chance to teach principles and values that extend beyond the classroom and the playing field.

He can touch a kid's heart when nothing else can reach him.

The Support System

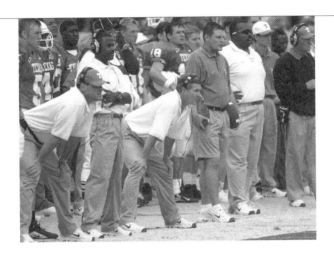

❝THE NUMBER-ONE PRIORITY IN GOING TO COLLEGE
IS EARNING A DEGREE, AND EVERYONE AT TEXAS
PUSHES YOU TOWARD THAT GOAL. THEY ARE ALWAYS
EMPHASIZING ACADEMICS AND ENCOURAGING YOU
TO WORK HARD IN THE CLASSROOM AS WELL AS
ON THE FIELD. OUR ACADEMIC STAFF AND FACILITIES
ARE THE BEST AROUND. AT TEXAS, EVERYTHING IS
IN PLACE FOR YOU TO FOCUS ON GETTING
YOUR COLLEGE DEGREE.❞

— *Major Applewhite,* 1999 Big 12 Offensive Player of the Year

◀ BEYOND THE COACHES – Jeff "Maddog" Madden *(white shirt, second from right)* is a major component of Mack Brown's program at Texas. Madden, the Assistant Athletics Director for Strength and Conditioning, teams with Brian Davis *(Assistant Athletics Director for Academics)* and Jean Bryant *(Lifeskills Director)* to help the players prepare for football and life afterward.

D own the hallway that leads to Joe Jamail Field at Darrell K Royal-Texas Memorial Stadium, just beside the plaques of the academic all-Americans, is the academic center where Brian Davis and Jean Bryant spend much of their time helping Longhorn players concentrate on the world beyond football.

The two are part of a long legacy devoted to the academic nurturing of football players at The University of Texas. When Mack Brown came to Texas, he took a system that was in place and upscaled it. But it had begun a long, long time ago—when Darrell Royal came to Texas.

Royal was the youngest head coach in America when he took the Texas job in December of 1956. The Longhorn program, once the scourge of football in the southwest, had fallen on hard times, dropping to a 1-9 record in the season just ended. People were beginning to wonder if college football at the highest level could exist in an academic institution driven to be one of America's greatest seats of higher learning.

As Royal looked at the situation, he realized recruiting good student athletes was not the problem. He had a solid coaching staff who understood recruiting, and they were on the cutting edge of the game in 1957.

"I looked around and said, 'We don't need another coach.' It seemed to me we had plenty of coaches; getting kids in school and teaching them football wasn't a problem. I could see right away that keeping them in school was the issue," Royal said.

So he went to Lockhart, Texas, just twenty-five miles southeast of Austin, where a respected school administrator named Lan Hewlett was the principal. He convinced Hewlett to become the first academic counselor for athletics in the country. Folks called him "the brain coach."

From that beginning, the athletics department budget for student athletes' academic support had grown to an annual figure of $2.5 million by the year 2000. Brian Davis, a former track athlete at Iowa State and a member of Brown's support system at North Carolina, is a veteran of almost twenty years in academic support. Jean Bryant assists the Longhorn football players not only in pursuing their degrees, but in preparing for life after football. A former teacher as well as a

118

long-time counselor, Bryant provides spring seminars for the Longhorns on everything from interviewing for a job and money management, to lessons in proper
etiquette in fine dining.

The two provide assistance on such matters as registration, degree planning,
and compliance with university and NCAA policies and procedures. They maintain
an excellent relationship with the university's administration, faculty, and deans.
Operating out of a 2,500-square-foot facility with thirty-six individual computer
stations, separate tutoring rooms, and a multi-purpose student hall, Davis and
Bryant supervise a support staff that includes several full-time assistants and a select
group of mentors and tutors. Class attendance is monitored, and the mentors and
tutors are provided to assist student athletes with their course work.

At North Carolina, over 70 percent of the players who lettered for Brown went
on to achieve their degrees. Through his first three years at Texas, Brown's staff
helped contribute to an overall graduation rate of 81 percent of all letter winners.

MB

I have been fortunate to work as a head coach at schools that didn't
take any short-cuts when it came to education. Somebody said that at
Texas we weren't going to "shorten the playing field or lower the
baskets" when it came to providing an education for our young
people. That's exactly what I believe a university should stand for.

As The University of Texas at Austin grew to be one of the nation's
great academic institutions, it was important to those in charge that it be
a place where all students in the state, if admitted, had a chance to
succeed. Louis Pearce, one of UT's greatest friends and supporters,
helped establish the Gateway Program, which allows top professors to
work with smaller classes at the freshman level. This gift has helped not
only athletes; it has allowed a lot of students to adjust to the difference
between a high school class and a college environment.

We have a system in place that allows for the maximum support of
our players in their classroom work. College should be about helping kids
grow up, so that they make a difference in the world after they graduate.
As we recruit good players, we know a number of them will have a goal to
play professional football, and we've been fortunate to have a lot of
players who have achieved that dream. But there is no way to overesti-
mate the value of a college degree. Brian and Jean give the players skills
that not only will help them graduate, but will help them function in a
business and social world beyond college.

When he was coaching, Coach Royal started a tradition of giving
players who lettered for him and earned a degree a "T" ring—a golden
ring with an orange stone topped with a white *T*. Earl Campbell, who was
making all-pro for the Houston Oilers, wanted that ring badly enough
that he came back to school to graduate and get it.

It is my job as head coach to provide the best staff possible to assist the players and then to support that staff. You can have the best academic support in the world, but if all the coaches, from the head coach to the assistants, to the strength and conditioning people and the trainers, don't support that, it doesn't work.

I've been in coaching for almost thirty years, and the one thing I know about kids is that they are kids. Sally says kids are pieces of adults, trying to learn who they are through trial and error. Some of them will stumble, as well-intentioned as they are. Kids need discipline, and we've been fortunate to have Jeff Madden on our staff to provide that counsel. If a kid misses a class, he goes to Maddog's "Dog House." After visiting with Maddog, it is likely he'll feel that attending class is way better than dealing with Jeff. Disciplining with conditioning and counseling is not a bad thing, but it takes someone with a gift to know how hard to drive a player.

Jeff has a gift in dealing out "tough love" that sends a message and also builds a special bond between Jeff and the players. He'll always hug the player after he disciplines him. The players will go to war for him. When the team was asked to give an award at the Holiday Bowl to the person who had been most important to them, they gave it to Jeff. If he could have shared it, part of it would have gone to Brian and Jean.

A degree represents a completion of a goal. It says that someone has finished something they started. That's important, but the things that Brian, Jean, and Jeff do help us educate young people about life, which is the reason universities were started a long time ago. I have a sign on the wall that says, "The value of a coach is measured not in what he knows, but in what his players have learned."

Our first year at Texas we adopted a theme which said, "Practice Winning Every Day." We didn't mean just football practice. It referred to going to class, showing up on time, keeping your word, taking care of your business in everything you do. As coaches, it is our responsibility to make sure players understand that being a winner goes beyond the field.

Chderse

Chemistry

"BUT IT IS CHEMISTRY—THE COHESIVENESS OF THE STAFF
OR THE ABILITY OF A TEAM TO PULL TOGETHER AS ONE—
THAT WILL DETERMINE HOW YOUR TEAM DOES
IN THE LONG RUN .**"**

—Mack Brown

◀ A VETERAN STAFF – With over two hundred years of experience, the Longhorn coaching staff brings maturity and experience to one of the nation's storied college football programs. Here assistants Darryl Drake, *(left)* Tim Brewster, and Tim Nunez greet quarterback Chris Simms after a touchdown pass.

Keith Jackson, the ABC Sports commentator who is perhaps the best-known figure in college football, tells the story of a trip he took to Maine. The old gentleman behind the counter was excited when Jackson walked into his Holiday Inn because he was the biggest celebrity who had visited the hotel in quite some time.

"Mr. Jackson," he had said when Keith walked in, "it is an honor to have you in our hotel."

They exchanged pleasantries as Jackson made the appropriate arrangements for a non-smoking room with a king-sized bed and inquired about a place to eat dinner. He would be on his way in the morning.

As they finished, the hotel manager asked, "Which credit card do you wish to use?"

"Oh," said Jackson in the familiar voice, "I'll just pay cash when I check out tomorrow."

The man behind the counter hesitated, then firmly said, "Mr. Jackson, I'll be needing a credit card."

"I don't understand," said Keith. "I'd rather just pay cash. You know who I am."

"Mr. Jackson, you're right. I know who you are. But I don't KNOW yah."

When Mack Brown came to Texas, he knew he had a lot of work to do. He had a football team that was bruised from a losing season, and he had fences to mend with the alumni and especially the Texas high school coaches. He knew the most important construction job he faced didn't have to do with finishing the football support facility or the stadium—it was in the creation of his staff.

To build that, he had to rely on people he could trust to do the job... people he KNEW.

His first hire was Cleve Bryant. As one of the first two African American head coaches in college football, Bryant's players had posted the best graduation rate in the country at his alma mater, Ohio University. He had been an all-star quarterback and is a member of Ohio University's Hall of Fame.

When Brown completed the staff, he assembled a group that had a collective 200 years of coaching experience. Every coach he hired had served as a

122

coordinator or—in the case of Bruce Chambers, who came directly from Dallas Carter High School, and Tim Brewster—as a head coach in high school.

Defensive coordinator Carl Reese was a veteran of over twenty-five years in the profession and served in a similar role at LSU. Wide receivers coach Darryl Drake, defensive ends coach and recruiting coordinator Hardy McCrary, secondary coach Everett Withers and offensive line coach Tim Nunez had been coordinators at Baylor, Rice, Louisville, and Marshall. Defensive tackle coach Mike Tolleson worked with Reese at LSU and had served as a defensive coordinator at three schools.

The final piece in Brown's puzzle was his strength and conditioning program, and to run that, he brought Jeff "Maddog" Madden from North Carolina. Madden assumed the title of Assistant Athletics Director for Strength and Conditioning. Other critical staff hires included his academic adviser, Brian Davis, and Jean Bryant, who managed the life skills and community relations side of the program. Dan Berezowitz, who helped design the facilities at both North Carolina and Texas, and later, Arthur Johnson, filled the important role of Special Assistant to the Head Coach.

There was a solid connection among the coaches. Most of them Brown had worked with before; others fit because he knew them, or they had worked directly with somebody on the staff.

He took no chances. It was like the scene in the movie, *The Magnificent Seven*, when a collection of gunfighters band together to save a little town. In this case, they had come to save a program that is more the size of a country than a small town.

MB

At a place like Texas, it is particularly hard to pick a staff because everybody wants to work here. I had talked to Cleve and Greg about the Texas job when the call first came, so I knew where they stood. Moving is never easy on a coach's family, and if you are comfortable with the new head coach and have a chance to stay, there are a lot of reasons to do that. So the first thing we had to do was sort out who was staying with Carl and who wanted to come to Texas.

Carl's keeping some of the staff members gave me a chance to hire some guys with ties to the state of Texas, so it worked out best for everyone. I've left three head coaching jobs, and in each case one of the assistants got the job after I left. I'm proud of that. That always worked well for our staff, and it also meant the university must have been pleased with our product.

Tim Brewster is a great young coach and an outstanding recruiter, and I felt he was somebody we needed. Every tight end that started for Tim at North Carolina was in the NFL. Tim said, "I don't care what I coach or what you pay me. I just want to go with you." He will make a great head coach some day, and part of the reason is that he understands what loyalty means.

I interviewed all of the members of John Mackovic's staff, and I liked them all.

They were really bruised by the way things had ended for that staff. A year earlier they had upset Nebraska for the Big 12's first title and had played in the Fiesta Bowl. The season of 1997 wasn't good for anybody at Texas. It is hard to keep a coach in a situation that had ended on such a negative note.

I knew we needed enthusiasm, and some of those guys were whipped and just needed a change. Most of all, we needed guys who could coach and recruit, and I was looking for three things: First, I wanted somebody who knew something about Texas high school coaching. Second, I wanted somebody who was good with kids. Third, I wanted people who would be excited about the challenge of bringing Texas back to the elite of college football. We needed guys who could coach, but who were tough enough to handle an environment that had been hard for a lot of coaches.

I didn't want anybody with an oversized ego, and I didn't want people who would snipe at each other. College coaching staffs spend as much time with each other during the seasons as they do with their families. It is critical that you be able to work together and get along.

The coaches we hired wanted to be at Texas. Greg Davis was a Texas native, and Carl Reese had admired Coach Royal's longtime assistant, Mike Campbell, for years. From the time he was a young coach in Missouri, he wanted to coach where Mike Campbell had coached.

There are some fine coaches at the high school, college, and professional level who are former Longhorn players, and I made a point to seek them out and explain what I was doing. I tried to hire a couple, but things just didn't work out. As much as I might have liked for them to work for us, I felt it was important for me to hire guys I had worked with or whom I knew. I told those former Longhorns I wanted to get to know them so that, in the future, maybe they could join us if they have an interest in winning. I would like to have UT lettermen on our staff because I think it speaks to our tradition.

When I started as a young head coach, I believed you had to work all the time, and we spent many hours in the office. I don't think that serves us now. I want our coaches to work hard, but I want them to get out of the office and take time for themselves and their families.

We stress recruiting. There is a sign in our staff room that says, "Write Your Recruits." Recruiting is about building relationships with kids and their families, and that's what we try to do. Once again—I can't stress it too often—you must be able to build that relationship based on communication, trust, and respect.

Our staff is our extended family, just like our team is our extended family.

We have been lucky at Texas because DeLoss Dodds and our university administration have allowed us to hire and keep, with good financial packages, the best staff in the country. We could not ask for more support, and we couldn't have the success we are having without that support.

We kept the same staff for three seasons, and when Everett Withers left to coach in the NFL, we hired Duane Akina, who had been the associate head coach and defensive coordinator at Arizona. Dick Tomey, who had been Duane's head coach when they were building the famous "Desert Storm" defenses at Arizona, is a close friend of mine, and when Everett left, he recommended Duane. He said Duane was the best assistant coach he has ever had on his staff. I wish Duane had not been on John Mackovic's staff at Arizona; it made it more sensitive for John because Duane chose to come to Texas. Even though it was a delicate situation, Dick was right. Duane is a great coach.

One of the most important things you can do as a head coach is to know the people in your profession. By the nature of our game, assistants will eventually move on. You want them to reach their goals if possible, but keeping the continuity of the staff is tremendously important. All you have to do is look at the success of the Penn States, the Florida States, and the Nebraskas to see that. They have good players, but they also have kept virtually the same staff for years.

I have always tried to look at other staffs and to be aware of guys I like and guys whose work I admire. When you have a great staff, there are going to be folks who want to hire your people. The opportunity to coach in the NFL is attractive to some coaches, and when a guy has a chance to be a college head coach or a coordinator at a high profile school, sometimes that's a position he can't turn down. If that's what he wants, he owes it to himself to go for it.

As head coach, you should be excited to see your guys progress in the business, even if you hate to see them leave. Mike Campbell is the only assistant Coach Royal ever offered a raise to get him to stay, and Coach Dietzel once told me, "If an assistant wants to leave, let him go. Most of the time, you will come out better with the new guy."

When that happens, you have to go looking for people you know will fit. Building that staff is about respect—for players, for parents, and for staff members—and with that comes responsibility for recruiting and the ability to coach a position.

Hire coaches who fit your philosophy. At Texas, we wanted coaches who had a lot of experience. That stability was important. We didn't want "yes" men. We wanted guys who would bring in some new ideas.

But it is chemistry—the cohesiveness of the staff or the ability of a team to pull together as one—that will determine how your team does in the long run.

The Lion King

❝I THINK I'VE FIGURED OUT THAT THERE AREN'T VERY MANY WAYS TO LEAVE A JOB AND HAVE PEOPLE HAPPY WITH YOU. THE ONLY WAY TO LEAVE A JOB AND HAVE PEOPLE HAPPY MAY BE TO DIE, AND IF YOU'VE BEEN WINNING, THEN THEY MAY NAME SOMETHING AFTER YOU.❞

—Mack Brown

THE TWO LIONS - Darrell Royal was one of the most successful coaches in college football history, and his friendship
with Mack Brown began with advice Royal gave him years
ago when Brown was at Tulane. His respect for Royal was a
major reason Brown came to Texas.

BL

I t was an all-star committee, four men summoned to New Orleans to assess the
athletics program at Tulane University. There were two athletics directors—
Gene Corrigan of Notre Dame and Don Canham of Michigan. There was
Chuck Neinas, head of the College Football Association and a respected
national collegiate administrator. The fourth member of the group was a former
athletics director who had gained his fame as a college football coach. His name
was Darrell Royal.

Mack Brown was in his first year as the head football coach of the Green
Wave. He had spent the season before as the offensive coordinator at Oklahoma.
Respect was a long-ago word when it came to Tulane football. The Green Wave
had played second fiddle to the state power, LSU, as long as most folks could
remember.

Never one to shirk from a challenge, Brown was putting notches on his
coaching gun. He had a remarkable year as head coach at Appalachian State in
1983, then helped coach the Sooners to an Orange Bowl bid and a narrow miss
at the national championship.

When Tulane beckoned, it was kind of like the old Steve McQueen line from
the movie *The Magnificent Seven*. Questioned why seven men would risk their
lives to defend a poor village, McQueen's character says, "It's kind of like a fellow
I knew once in El Paso...took off all his clothes and jumped in a pile of cactus.
People asked him why he did it...he said it seemed like a good idea at the time."

Brown was just thirty-two years old when he accepted the head coaching job
at Tulane, and he suddenly found himself named athletics director as well, head of
a department that had just eliminated a basketball program filled with scandal.

Into the turmoil rode the consultants. Corrigan was one of the most respected
figures in college athletics, and Canham had proven to be a marketing genius
in the world of the Wolverines. Neinas's knowledge of college sports would eventually lead him to become one of the premier advisers to many programs. Royal
had been out of direct association with athletics for six years, but he was the one
person on the committee Brown was anxious to meet because he was one of
Brown's heroes.

When Mack Brown was growing up in Tennessee, Darrell Royal was winning more games than any coach in college football. He had also served as Texas's athletics director for seventeen years. For most of that time he doubled as the head football coach, just as Brown was attempting to do.

When Royal was suggested as a consultant, Brown could not have been happier. But he got way more than he bargained for. Throughout his life, Royal had always been honest, and he wasn't about to back off now. When Brown met Royal, he found honesty, and he also found a friend.

"They asked us to come down there and write a report, and we were to get a fee," Royal recalled. "But I never wrote a report, and I didn't get a fee. There were just too many problems for me to be enthusiastic, and I wasn't about to candy coat something that wasn't the truth.

"I remember Mack as being young, aggressive, shiny, and I knew he had a future, but not if he stayed there."

For the next twelve years, Royal didn't have much direct contact with Brown, but he followed his career, and he knew of his success at North Carolina. When the two met again in December of 1997, it was to discuss the future of Texas football and the future of Mack and Sally Brown.

MB

I was named head coach at Tulane in December of 1984. We'd won the Big 8 championship at Oklahoma, and we were playing Washington in the Orange Bowl. If we had won the game by more than ten points, we might have won the national championship.

I had taken the Tulane job while we were still working on the bowl game. We didn't play very well and we lost the game, so I have always felt guilty because I could have done a better job of preparing if I hadn't been trying to do two jobs. It was a tough case of overload. I felt for Mark Richt in the 2000 season when he took the Georgia job. He was still the coordinator at Florida State and they were playing for the national championship against Oklahoma.

When you're hiring a staff, recruiting for one school, and trying to get a game plan ready for another, you are pulled in too many directions. Your players are thinking about who the new coach is going to be, so it is a difficult time.

Once the game was over, I was excited to officially be the head coach at Tulane. But things were about to change in a hurry.

After I had been there for two or three months, our basketball team was involved in a point-shaving scandal, so Tulane dropped basketball the first day of spring football practice. The athletics director resigned and within a week they made me the athletics director and head coach. I was thirty-three years old. We had fifty-nine players on scholarship, and forty-one of those were on academic probation. I learned that our players had individual charges to the university in excess of $41,000 for different reasons. We were playing six teams that had competed in bowl games the year before. Needless to say, I was once again overloaded.

The day we dropped basketball, I didn't find out until 11 o'clock that morning. On the first day of spring practice, the media went immediately to our football players and said, "Hey, does this mean they're going to drop Division I sports? Are they dropping football, too?"

All the kids were coming to me, panicked, on what should have been a great day, saying, "Are we out of here?"

The school immediately appointed a fourteen-member blue ribbon committee—of which I was a part—to determine whether we would stay in Division I-A sports. There were students, faculty members, and alums on the committee.

It was a hard time. I had been involved in some of the meetings, but I was trying to coach the football team, then go to a meetings to see whether we were going to have football. It was getting to be a conflict of interest for the old coach. We sent Wright Waters, our associate athletics director, to the meetings because I was too antagonistic and it was better for everyone if I didn't attend. It was during the season, and it was hard to talk about dropping football during the week and then try to beat Florida State and LSU on the weekends.

The university vice-president, Chuck Knapp, who later became president of the University of Georgia, decided Wright should come in my place. He picked the right guy. He's a great friend and an excellent administrator. In my opinion, Tulane made a mistake when they didn't keep him as the athletics director after I left. He and Greg Davis, who got the head coaching job, might still be at Tulane if they had, because they were both very good at what they did.

Friday night before our Southern Miss game—one week before our last game of the season with LSU—the committee was meeting to see whether we were going to keep football. Wright was coming to Hattiesburg to see me Friday night to tell me what had happened. He didn't show up, and I couldn't find him. The vote was a tie, so he didn't want to tell me before the game.

They voted again on Monday, the week of the final game, and they actually broke the tie by one vote and decided to keep football. Over the years, that one vote has meant a lot to Tulane. Their football program today is healthy and on the right track.

When the year was over, we were in financial trouble, we were 1-10, and we didn't know where we were going with our program because basketball was gone. Fund-raising was an issue, and we were having trouble drawing crowds. Wright proposed the idea of bringing in a consulting team to look at our situation, and Chuck Knapp took it to the president, Amon Kelly. They wanted a coach and some athletics directors, and they wanted Chuck Neinas because of his ties with the College Football Association, as well as his association with the Big 8 conference and the NCAA. The university wanted the committee to come in and look at what we were doing.

It was exciting for me because I knew Chuck through CFA, and I knew of Gene Corrigan and Don Canham as two of the great athletics directors in the country. But the most exciting thing to me was that Coach Royal was on the team because, as a football coach, when you can bring in a guy who's won three national championships to evaluate what you're doing and tell you what you're doing wrong, it's really a good thing.

Those guys came in for three days. They interviewed everybody in the department, they interviewed administrators, and they interviewed faculty members.

I remember walking out on the field with Coach Royal, and he said, "Where is your practice area?"

I said, "Coach, this is it." We had a little grass field and a fifty-yard artificial turf field. I'll never forget our team running out on the field for spring practice and Coach said—and he wasn't being rude—"Where's the varsity?"

I said, "Coach, this is the varsity."

I remember asking, "Coach, how did you ever turn your team around after a losing season?" And he said, emphatically, "I never had a losing season."

I thought, "Well, this isn't helping much...."

On Sunday, after their visit, I met with the four men. Don, Gene, and Chuck said, "You've got a chance here. You're working hard and you've got a great staff. We need to get $2 million dollars more in your budget so you can at least try to break even, to give you guys a chance." The administration asked us to include revenue from bowl games and TV games in our budget. Since we weren't winning, we weren't likely to go to a bowl or be on TV, so we were in a budget hole before we ever started. But they said, "You've got a good chance here, so just keep working."

I looked at Coach Royal, and he said, "I'd get the hell out of here as fast as I could, because you've got no chance. And I would go to a university that has *The* in front of it, because that's the only way you're going to make it."

The other guys said, "Darrell, you can't say that."

And he said, "The boy paid me to come here and be honest, so I'm being honest. He needs to get out of here as fast as he can."

He also said, "Don't ever take a job where they don't care enough to fire you, and they don't have enough money to buy you off if they do fire you." Only he could say that.

After that, I'd write him a note every now and then, and I'd see him at the National College Football Foundation dinner in New York, but we really didn't have much contact.

We had some really good kids at Tulane, and by our third year, we were fortunate enough to go 6-5 and earn only the fifth bowl bid in school history. As hard as it was to leave, I knew the time was right. The Tulane fans who followed us to the Independence Bowl were angry at me, but I think I've figured out that there aren't very many ways to leave a job and have people happy with you. The only way to leave a job and have people happy may be to die, and if you've been winning, then they may name something after you.

I am really pleased to see that Tulane now has some good people in place and is getting things together. Athletics should be important there. Jim Wilson has built a beautiful athletics complex, and it really is a great place. I am so happy they voted to keep sports. I am a Tulane fan, and every time they win, I feel a sense of pride for our time there.

I thought of Coach Royal when I took the North Carolina job. Every time I wrote *the* University of North Carolina, I smiled a little in his honor.

The next time I had a chance to visit with him at length, I was meeting with the Texas search committee in Atlanta. When we had some time to be alone, he told me, "You need to take this job."

I said, "Why?"

He said, "Because we need help, and if you do at Texas what you did at North Carolina, you'll be appreciated more."

And it does have *The* in front of its name.

To See Ourselves

❝UNDERSTANDING WHERE YOU CAME FROM
GETS YOU ON A PATH TO WHERE YOU
WANT TO GO. IT IS A ROADMAP TO
CONQUERING FEAR, WHICH CAN BE DEFINED
AS 'FALSE EXPECTATIONS APPEARING REAL.'**❞**

—Bill Little

STORIES OF THE MIND

◀ THE ART OF SELF-EVALUATION – **When Brown came to Texas,** then-Governor Bush gave him good advice about Texas football fans and people in general.

BL

"O h," wrote the 18th century poet Robert Burns, "would some Power the gift give us, to see ourselves as others see us! It would from many a blunder free us, and foolish notion."

In America's book market, a startling number of self-help books regularly appear on the *New York Times* bestseller list. On the couches, in the corners, or at the tables in Starbucks all across the country, thousands look inward for answers.

"What did I do wrong?" asks the troubled soul whose business or marriage has failed.

All are seeking the answer to the simple question: "What can I do to improve?"

That is the question Mack Brown asks himself at the end of every day, every week, and every season.

Webster says *evaluate* means "to appraise value."

Understanding where you came from gets you on a path to where you want to go. It is a roadmap to conquering fear, which can be defined as "false expectations appearing real."

Football coaches use videos of games and practice as a teaching tool, not to place blame, but to show how it could have been done differently and to reinforce the positive things that were accomplished.

Terry Jastrow, a movie producer who was a pioneer in televising live sports events, tells the story of a highly successful West Texas oilman.

In the sun-bleached weeds of the flat land just outside Midland, an oilfield worker couldn't see an oil well head cap, and he ran over it, breaking it and creating a big leak.

Distraught, the foreman exclaimed to his boss, "I'm gonna fire the S.O.B."

"No," said the oilman. "We aren't going to fire him. He's the only S.O.B in the company who now knows where the well head is!"

MB

I think self-evaluation is the hardest thing any of us have to do. It contradicts self-image in some ways, and we all—particularly in athletics—promote a strong self-image and feeling good about yourself and being positive.

Many of us are raising our children now with better self-esteem than self-evaluation. We try to teach our players how to evaluate their performances, not their capabilities. It doesn't help them to say, "I'm not as good as he is." They can, however, benefit from saying, "I'm not playing as well."

We've said that God has given each of us gifts—things we do better than we do others—and we need to use those as our strengths.

About ten years ago I was struggling with a coaching problem and I called Sally. She was able to help me work through the decision. It is important to realize the resources that you have, whether or not you're in the coaching profession. Sally never coached, but she understands people, and things that worked for her in business weren't all that different from things that work for coaches. Sometimes it's a matter of helping a person identify the tools they've been given, then putting them in a position to use those tools.

When you ask people to open themselves to self-evaluation, you have to build on trust, and you have to be able to communicate. Until you have those two things, there's no chance for honest self-evaluation. Everyone's got insecurities and if there is not already trust built up when you talk to people about evaluating themselves, they go into a shell and they won't listen.

A great example of that is a team meeting we had this summer. We talked about a lot of things—the games that were scheduled for television, how much had gone well. But what the players heard was a discussion about hair codes and going to class. All they heard were the only two negative things brought up at the meeting. They didn't hear the positive things. It is important to understand that self-evaluation isn't only about the negative things.

If we have an issue with a player that involves his parents, we bring him into my office and we call the parents together, or we make him tell us about the problem, and I write it down so I know exactly what he is thinking. Then I read it back to him to be sure I'm clear about the issue. That's why the information and evaluation sheets that the players fill out are so important.

That's a real valuable thing that I didn't do when I first became a head coach. Instead of just saying, "Is there anything you want to talk to me about?" I make players write down answers to direct questions. It forces them to have a conversation.

Once, one of our regular players ranked one of our assistant coaches at the bottom of a one-to-ten scale. The player had been hurt and he hadn't played much. The coach was after him to work harder and play better. The player ranked the coach as a three and a poor communicator after that tough year. The year before, when he was healthy and starting, the same player ranked him at the top as a great communicator.

So the player said, "I just don't trust my position coach."

I said, "Well, have you ever trusted him?"

He said, "No, I've never trusted him."

I said, "Really? In this meeting last year, did you rate him three or four...do you remember?"

He said, "Yeah, it was down low."

I pulled that evaluation out and said, "You had him rated a ten and said he was a great communicator and a father figure. Do you think the problem has anything to do with you instead of the coach?"

We never say a player has weaknesses; we call them "areas of concern." We say, "Here are the areas where you have strengths, and here are the areas where you have some concerns. If you expect to play more, you have to take care of these concerns and make them better."

When you're considering a player's strengths and his areas of concern, you'll really miss out if you think that just because it is a strength, it doesn't have to be tended to. That's why you hear "play to your strength" so much. If that's what I do best, that's what I'm gonna do more of.

Everything we ask of our players, we ask of ourselves. During the year, I am constantly looking at what our staff is doing and what I am doing to determine how I can help us do it better. At the end of the season, I take a long, hard look at what we have done. That works in coaching, in business, in a family...anything you do.

When we came to Texas, we ran the football effectively with Ricky Williams. The next season, Hodges Mitchell had a great year. The third year, we were not as effective as we had been. In my opinion, we became too predictable. When I looked back on the year, I sat down with Greg Davis and our offensive staff and we figured out how to fix that. As coaches, sometimes it is our nature to be stubborn, to stick with something we like, even if it isn't working. That goes for a lot of folks in a lot of businesses, too. Our staff has done an outstanding job and a lot of teams would be happy with the record we have. But we want to get better, so we are constantly re-evaluating our offensive and defensive schemes.

It is important to get a plan you believe in and stick with it. Then, at the appropriate time, take a look and see what is working and what isn't. For me, it is important to see what role I am playing in the situation and how I can do it better. I ask every one of our staff members to take that same look at themselves.

It serves no purpose to beat yourself up for failure. It only works if you take that negative and turn it into a positive. And that only happens if you take a good look at how you helped create it.

A Matter Of Time

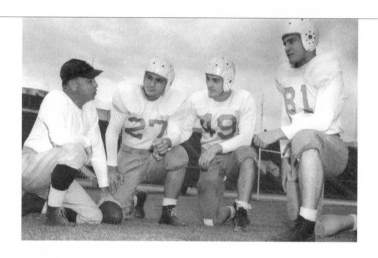

❝MOTIVATIONAL SPEECHES ARE GREAT,
AND THEY CAN SOMETIMES HELP PROPEL
TEAMS TOWARD DEFINING MOMENTS,
BUT IT IS ON THE PRACTICE FIELD
THAT GAMES ARE WON AND LOST.**❞**

—Bill Little

◀ EARLY ORGANIZATION MAN – Mack Brown prides himself on
being organized, and a great example for him is a book
on football by D. X. Bible, the legendary Longhorn coach.
From practice times to game plans, Bible's sixty-year-old
ideas apply today.

BL

The faded blue book rests on the corner of the polished oak desk. Its table-mates—a book of quotes from Darrell Royal and a 1965 *Sports Illustrated* with a cover story about Tommy Nobis—shift from time to time, but are always in evidence.

The neat gold lettering is dimmed with time, but the principles on the yellowed pages remain sound, and the advice works more than fifty years after its publication.

There is simplicity in its message and in its title:

Championship Football.

By D. X. Bible.

For Mack Brown, and for a generation of Texas football followers, the auto-graphed book is a blueprint for success from a man who achieved much success.

Dana X. Bible came to Texas in 1937 with a charge to save the once-powerful Longhorn football program. With a long championship record at Texas A&M and Nebraska, he was recruited to become the Texas coach and athletics director and was paid more money than the school president, which was unheard of at the time.

Before Bible left, he had restored the Texas tradition and had won more foot-ball games than any coach except Pop Warner and Walter Camp, both of whom coached years more than Bible.

It was not lost on Brown, a student of the history of the game, that Bible, like Brown, was a native of Tennessee, nor were the similarities between the hiring of Bible and Brown lost on those Texans with a knowledge of history. After all, the Volunteer State had produced such Texas heroes as Davy Crockett, Sam Houston, and many of the defenders of the Alamo.

Bible and Brown both came to Texas at the top of their game. Bible's teams at Texas A&M had posted a 72-19-9 record before he moved to Nebraska. All he had done there was win six league championships and compile a 50-15-7 record in eight years.

Brown's record at North Carolina over his last six years was 54-18, and only spirited but unsuccessful battles with national powerhouse Florida State kept him from a run of Atlantic Coast Conference titles and maybe a national title.

137

When Brown came to Texas, it didn't take long for him to remind some of Bible's former players of their former coach.

"They both cared about their players and they both loved the game," says Noble Doss, who became a Texas legend on Bible's famed teams of the early 1940s. "But what I see most of all is the organization they have. I look at Mack's practices, and I am reminded of things we did sixty years ago. Of course, there is a difference in that we played both offense and defense, and we had to practice both."

"But there are a lot of things that haven't changed at all, such as making sure every player knows what to do against every scheme and making sure that practices aren't too long and that they are extremely efficient. We didn't fool around at practice, and Mack's teams don't either. We'd run the same play over and over. We didn't have too many plays, but with the ones we did have, we were prepared for everything that our opponent might do."

Motivational speeches are great, and they can sometimes help propel teams toward defining moments, but it is on the practice field that games are won and lost. And for Mack Brown, as it was for Noble Doss and Coach Bible so many years ago, being repetitive leads to being successful.

On the Texas practice field, there is a sign that says, "Practice winning every day."

Figuring out how to do that is critical to achieving it.

MB

We've all heard the cliches.

"You play like you practice." "Practice makes perfect." Even "practice makes permanent." There is truth in every one of them.

That's why I feel that one of the most important responsibilities of a head coach is planning your practice time.

The best thing I've done from an organizational standpoint is that I've kept notes for seventeen years. I update them every year, so I don't go back to the first year I coached. I go back to last year's notes, where I update them after every practice in two-a-days.

I'll find notes like, "This one was hot...four kids got cramps. We stayed out too long. We should have cut practice."

Among the organizational demands on a head coach are: How often do you practice? How long do you stay out there? How much do you hit? How many plays can each guy play and still be successful?

You have to hit enough, because, as Joe Jamail so aptly put it, "You can't learn to swim without a pool."

You can't play football without pads and without hitting. So figuring out how much you can hit without getting hurt, and how long you can stay out in the sun before getting tired and dead-legged—which can lead to an injury—is one of the hardest things a head coach has to do.

We found that out in our preparations for the Southwestern Bell

Cotton Bowl game, which we lost to Arkansas. In hindsight, I felt like we worked the kids too hard before the game.

We organize our practices so that all of our players have a chance to get a good number of reps. Receivers, running backs, and quarterbacks will all get practice time with each other. It's important to have a working relationship with more than just the same guys all the time. You never know when you may have to win the game with somebody other than the guy you ran out there on the first series.

We try to be efficient with our drills, running identical drills from the first and second units at the same time. That's another thing: We don't call our units "first and second teams." We've found that if you call a guy a "second teamer," he believes he's supposed to play like one. We have an "Orange" team on offense and a "White" team on defense. The next groups are called the "Storm" and the "Attack".

We also work one-against-one, and we insist that players never allow each other to hit the ground. That's where injuries occur, when there are guys falling on each other. Over and over again in practice, you'll hear, "Stay up! Stay up!"

The key is to practice as close to "game speed" as you can without getting anyone hurt. I learned that from Dick Coop, who is one of the top sports psychologists around. I said to him, "Tell me what we've got to get done here. How can we practice and not get people hurt?"

He said, "It looks to me as if you have to simulate the game as fast as you can and get as close as you can to game speed in practice, but not get them hurt."

Another valuable thing to understand about each player—I learned this from Dean Smith at North Carolina—is how playing time affects his performance. Coach Smith retired as the winningest coach in college basketball history, and he and his assistant at the time, Bill Guthridge, were always good about sharing information with me.

How many plays could a reserve play without his performance dropping off, as compared with a starter? Coach Smith figured it out using minutes played, but what I tried to pick up from him was based on number of plays. Some players are twelve-play guys. Some are fifteen-play guys. And if a tired veteran player is not as effective as a full-speed rookie after twenty-five plays, then the coaches have to make that adjustment. We need to try to understand each player that we have, and understand how long we can go with him in the game. If we are doing our job right, we don't have to take chances. Every player we recruit at Texas should be able to play if his attitude is right.

A coach has to balance how much to play his reserves. You need to play as many players as you can because it keeps team morale up and it helps you with your depth. Plus, tired players have more of a chance to get hurt and let up on a play.

That is particularly true with a player who has been injured. In the

2000 season, Shaun Rogers had a chance to be as good a defensive tackle as we've ever had at Texas. He and Casey Hampton were by far the two best tackles in the country, but Shaun got hurt in the Houston game, and he never regained full speed the rest of the season.

Our defensive staff had to figure out how many plays we could count on from Shaun, based on the fact that a team will run an average of sixty to eighty plays a game. If we could count on Shaun for twenty plays, we had to get some young players ready to play. Marcus Tubbs was a great example of that; he played as a freshman. All we asked is that everybody play as hard as they could when they were in there. We count on our team to communicate with us when they feel that they can't go full speed.

Trying to be a hero, staying in when you have nothing left, gets you beat.

The young actor Matthew McConaughey is a Texas graduate who has become not only a huge Longhorn fan, but a great friend. He once talked to the team about how similar making a movie is to the teamwork we ask from our guys. His point was if the sound guy doesn't do his job one day, then it's a bad shoot. The same is true if you put in a guy who's worn out. But if he can give you one good play, it might be enough.

I love action movies, and there was a great message in Matthew's war movie *U-571*. At the end, Matthew and his crew have just one torpedo left, and it is their only chance against a German battleship. If they miss their one shot, the German ship will sink the sub that Matthew is commanding.

Matthew's team made that one shot count, and it saved their lives.

In football, giving your best shot whenever you are on the field can save a game. And it is the coach's responsibility to put his players in position to do that.

The Eyes Of Texas

"IF YOU MISS OUT ON A KID, AND HE GOES SOMEWHERE ELSE AND PLAYS AGAINST YOU, YOU'LL SEE THAT KID MAYBE FOUR TIMES THE REST OF HIS LIFE. IF YOU SIGN HIM, YOU'VE GOT HIM 365 DAYS A YEAR, AND HE'S YOURS."

—Lou Holtz

◄ HONESTY ABOVE ALL – Mack Brown's experience at Vanderbilt with brother Watson helped him understand the importance of being honest with recruits. Brown, pictured on the left as a freshman, transferred to Florida State for his final collegiate years.

BL

A s the stainless steel elevator doors close for the ride up in the Moncrief-Neuhaus Athletics Complex, the piped-in music features the Longhorn Band's spirited rendition of the Texas fight song, "Texas Taps." On the way down, it plays "The Eyes of Texas."

Everything Mack Brown does is about his players, the Texas tradition, and recruiting.

With every note of the songs, every Longhorn emblem, or every drop of orange paint, with every picture produced by staff photographers, Jim and Susan Sigmon, every trophy collected to represent the Texas tradition, Brown and his staff make a pitch to the best teenaged football players in America to be a part of a program whose number one goal is to win a national football championship.

From websites to media guides, from notes to phone calls, nothing is done in the Texas football offices without thinking about how it can help recruiting. For in college football today, recruiting will ultimately determine the success or failure of a program. It has always been so, but in other years, numbers made the odds a lot better.

When D.X. Bible was reconstructing the Texas football program in the late 1930s, the freshman class he recruited—the seniors on the famed 1941 team—included 128 players. And that was when players played both ways.

For part of Darrell Royal's career, schools could issue unlimited scholarships. It was not unusual for a recruiting class to include as many as six or eight quarter-backs. They may not have played that position in college, but because most schools put their best athlete at quarterback, they likely would contribute at another position. James Saxton, for example, moved from quarterback to running back and became an all-American. Bill Bradley, maybe the most heralded recruit in Royal's tenure, finished his Texas career at defensive back and went on to star in the NFL at that position.

One of the reasons for the success of the Wishbone offense under Royal was the Longhorns' ability to collect a stable of quality running backs, as well as depth in the offensive line.

Fred Akers, who succeeded Royal as the Texas head coach in 1977, once said

142

of his program, "At Texas, we don't rebuild. We reload."

The dynasties in college football lived in a high profile world, and for a long while, it was as Royal once said, "The big 'uns will eat the little 'uns."

That was the case until the NCAA decided to mandate a diet plan.

Scholarship limits were imposed in all sports. In football, the numbers began at sixty per year, dropped to fifty, then forty-five, then thirty, and finally, in the last decade of the 20th century, bottomed out at twenty-five scholarships per year, allowing eighty-five total players on full rides.

In the seventeen years Mack Brown has been a head coach, those are pretty much the numbers he has faced.

At some schools, such as Big 12 partner Nebraska, walk-on programs supplement the numbers with quality players. The Cornhuskers have had their share of walk-ons who became significant contributors to their success.

But at Texas, entrance requirements are high. Receipt of a scholarship in his or her chosen field, whether it's music or athletics or something else, puts an applicant in a different pool, and an athlete on scholarship who meets the NCAA standards is eligible for admission.

In order to "walk on," a student not on scholarship must meet the same standards as any incoming UT freshman, which include a finish in the top 10 percent of the student's graduating class or an exceedingly high test score on a college entrance exam.

So, with only a maximum of twenty-five possible recruits, the magnetic board in the recruiting "war room" in the football offices becomes a critical point in hopes for success.

The puzzle is far from easy to solve, but is relatively simple in theory.

Coaches look at players on film, decide whether they want them, offer them a scholarship, and if they accept, the deal's done.

But the journey to that moment, when a young man decides to commit his future to a university, is the reason Mack Brown wins, and the reason he's still in college coaching.

MB

There are over 1,200 high schools playing football in Texas, so it is pretty easy to see there are a lot of good players. When you can take only a maximum of twenty-five, the most important thing you can do is evaluate talent. And the first thing you have to do is decide whether a player will fit the profile of players you want in your program.

You have to decide how you are going to make the numbers balance out. The twenty-five a year isn't the only thing you have to consider. If you take twenty-five a year, that's one hundred on your squad. Somewhere along the line, based on the eighty-five player cap, you'd have fifteen kids you would have to cut, and no coach wants to do that. So some years, you won't be able to give twenty-five scholarships. I'd say most colleges take between eighteen and twenty-two players.

This is something I have struggled with every year. How do you take the numbers and build a team? How do you pick the right guys?

In recruiting, we try to replace the juniors on our team, even though we know they still have a senior year coming. That way, a recruit won't have to come in and start as a freshman. There'll be a senior in his spot. He can play as a sophomore and have two years to get into the system, to become a difference-maker who doesn't hurt your team or have his confidence destroyed.

You have to balance your numbers and still sign the best players. If you don't need any receivers, but two great ones want to come, you have to take 'em. You'd better always take the best players.

The margin of success today is really thin. You have to be prepared for some tough scenarios. We faced one in 2001 at defensive tackle. A couple of recruits didn't get into school, we lost Cole Pittman tragically, and another player transferred. Suddenly we looked up and what should have been a strength on our team had changed. You have to have good players who are capable of stepping in and filling those roles, and they have to come out of that player pool.

We look for leadership in recruits. Were they captains? Did they take leadership roles on the team? We also consider whether they played on a winning team. They need to have strong family values and good core grades so they will fit in with the kind of players we want on our team.

Evaluating recruits and handling attrition are critical factors if you want to win year in and year out, and that's what we want. I don't want people to think, "Is this our year?" I want every year to be our year.

Recruiting has changed dramatically over the last several years. More and more kids are commiting early. Joe Paterno started that at Penn State, and it is really a lot more comfortable for the kids. When we all had to wait until February for signing day, it was hard on the players and the coaches. The NCAA has limited the contacts between coaches and recruits so much that kids are getting way more calls from recruiting services and reporters than they are coaches.

The summer before a recruit's senior year in high school is now the time that a lot of decisions are made. It's good because a kid and his parents can take time in the summer to visit a campus, rather than taking time out of school. It is a lot better for the high school coaches because once a kid decides where he wants to go, he can concentrate on his senior year and his high school team.

In Texas, we get a great chance to see kids during the NCAA-allowed visitation period during spring practice. We can actually see them work out. Kids also are coming to camps, and we get a chance to spend time with them personally.

That's one of the strengths of a camp—you get to actually be around the player. The way the NCAA has restricted recruiting visits, a coach really gets to visit a kid only once or twice. That makes it hard for you to get to know one another.

When we were recruiting Chris Simms, I never got a chance to visit him in his home. We were in New York when Ricky Williams won the Heisman, and Chris was being honored as one of the outstanding area high school players at a Heisman breakfast. Before we went to the New York Stock Exchange so Ricky could ring the opening bell to start the market's day, I ran into Chris at the Downtown Athletic Club. It was just a chance thing, and all we did was say hello, but somebody reported that as an official visit, so I was not allowed to visit him and his folks in his home. That's how tight the rules are.

In our evaluation process, we count a lot on our own players. When a recruit comes for his official visit, we have one of our players show him around. If our team members don't think the guy will fit into our program, we'll pull off of him, regardless of how good he is. I sometimes struggle with that, because I want to help kids who are troubled, but I'm not willing to do it at the expense of our football team. Our players are our best judges of character, and they are also our best recruiters. Your players can sell your program better than you can. If they aren't happy or don't like you, you have little chance to recruit good players because their attitudes will discourage kids from coming here.

I once asked the great Michigan coach Bo Schembechler about recruiting, and he had a pretty good system. He would bring a kid in, and if the assistant coaches and the players liked him, he'd talk to the kid. If Coach Schembechler wasn't comfortable with the kid, he would reject him. Coach Royal used to call that his "eyeball test".

Lou Holtz told me, "If you miss out on a kid, and he goes somewhere else and plays against you, you'll see that kid maybe four times the rest of his life. If you sign him, you've got him 365 days a year, and he's yours."

When a young man visits our campus, we try to give him a complete view of Texas. He'll visit with professors. We have an outstanding group of coeds who are supervised by Brenda Preston in Cleve Bryant's office. They are called the Texas Angels, and they "adopt" the recruits. When they visit, the recruits have a chance to learn about student life from the Angels and from our players. We want them to be as comfortable as possible with their decision. The Texas Angels are a classy group of young ladies who represent our program and their families well.

The single most important thing to me is that we are straight with the recruits.

I've said this before, but it's worth repeating: My parents and grandparents were honest people, and I have always been obsessed with people telling the truth. That's why our staff always makes sure a young man understands what we are saying, and that he gets a fair evaluation of his chances to be a Longhorn. I don't ever want him to think we've lied to him.

I take a commitment as a deal. If we offer a scholarship and it is accepted, we aren't going to take it back. That means if a kid gets hurt

145

during his senior year of high school and can't play anymore, we will make sure he has a chance to get his education as we promised.

But if a kid commits to us, I'm taking him at his word. I expect him not to go visit any other schools.

I tell him it's like getting engaged to be married. If you meet the right girl, ask her to marry you, and she says yes, then you don't go date somebody else.

The same is true in recruiting. We usually bring in no more than thirty-five players for official visits, and will make offers to no more than twenty-eight of those. We know we will lose some because they won't fit, they won't make their grades, or they choose to go somewhere else.

The reason we sign such a high percentage of our recruits is that we recruit kids that belong here. If a kid is an absolute jerk, and I give him the class speech and I know he's not going to go to class, and I give him the drug speech and he's smoking pot...he's not coming. So why bring him in?

We have been fortunate to hold on to most of the kids we want, and we have lost very few who committed early.

While we can't visit the kids much in person, we are in constant communication with them. We write our recruits regularly and keep up with their lives. NCAA rules restrict the number of phone calls we can make to them, but a recruit can make unlimited phone calls to a college coach. To facilitate this, we installed an 800 number which they can use to call us.

By signing day, the kids are like family, which is what you seek when you start organizing your recruiting effort in the first place.

The Audience Is Listening

❝IT IS THE PROVINCE OF KNOWLEDGE TO SPEAK, AND IT IS THE PRIVILEGE OF WISDOM TO LISTEN.❞

—Oliver Wendell Holmes

◀ HAIR IT IS – When his Longhorn players asked about different hairstyles, Mack Brown had only to look back at his own photo while at Florida State for a reminder that hairstyles change over the years. Determining what is important and what influences winning and losing is critical to a coach.

BL

O liver Wendell Holmes was a 19th-century author and physician who knew nothing of Texas football, but he would have understood a lot about Mack Brown.

"It is the province of knowledge to speak," wrote Holmes. "And it is the privilege of wisdom to listen."

Brown's great gift is to be a good listener.

"He is amazing," says Cleve Bryant, who has worked with Brown for nearly ten years. "He can go into a recruit's house, and before he leaves he will know the kid's grandparents' names, all about his family, who his girlfriend is, and even the name of his dog."

And he will remember them.

Dick Coop recalls a time in North Carolina after they first met.

"We were in this little restaurant, and we had a waitress who had just moved down from Vermont," said Coop. "She was wondering if she had made the right move, coming so far from home. By the time Mack finished his lunch, he had her convinced she had absolutely done the right thing, and she was walking on air. He completely changed her attitude."

When Brown came to Texas, he made a whirlwind tour across the state, speaking to Longhorn Foundation meetings in ten cities. Altogether, he had over fifty speaking engagements that first spring and turned down hundreds more. By the season of 2001, Bryant—who handles those requests for Brown—was turning down as many as seven hundred requests per year.

"He could speak every day, twice a day," says Bryant. "If he accepted all the offers, he wouldn't have time to coach football."

The most important communication for Brown, however, comes with his players and those he believes will fit well in his program at The University of Texas.

The NCAA, in its efforts to protect prospective student athletes, has strict rules about when and how recruits can be contacted. Phone calls and personal contacts are severely restricted. Even the kinds of mail that can be sent to a recruit are defined.

But the human touch—Brown's touch—can be carried on a simple personal note card. Kasey Johnson, Brown's administrative assistant, estimates that he

148

hand-writes as many as nine hundred cards to his selected pool of prospective student athletes over the course of a year. Assistant coaches are expected to write them as well. The colorful front of the card may vary—a picture of the team charging onto the field, a symbol of tradition, or a simple touch of orange on a football. The NCAA restricts what may be printed on the card, but it doesn't legislate or restrict the message.

In addition to the letters he sends to recruits, he writes personal notes to supporters and individualized responses to people who write during the year.

The time it takes for all that writing, however, doesn't match that spent in one-on-one sessions with his players. At the end of every season, Brown sits down with each player and reviews everything from the player's relationship with his position coach to his experience with all phases of the support staff.

Every area of Brown's personal office serves a purpose in communication. There is a flag that flew over the State Capitol the day he was hired, provided by Alpha Phi Omega, the student service organization which runs the Texas flag at the football game. There are replicas of the Heisman trophies won by Earl Campbell and Ricky Williams. A full bank of windows provides an artist's dream view of the field and massive structure of Darrell K Royal-Texas Memorial Stadium. On display are a cowhide rug, a hand-stitched saddle, and a showcase of Mack Brown's watches and rings from a dozen bowl games, ACC Coach of the Year Awards, and thirty years of successful coaching.

A bookcase contains not only books about football, but books about life in general. And a display case holds special memories, from pictures of family to those with Presidents Bill Clinton and George W. Bush.

A fish tank is a conversation piece, and the occupants become Brown's solo companions during late-evening note writing after everyone else has gone home.

"One of his best qualities," says Greg Davis, "is his desire to have people who are connected with the program be involved in the decision making. Part of that is the 'buying in' theory—if people feel they have a part in building the program, they are more invested in its success."

Davis, too, marvels at Brown's ability to listen.

"He has the ability to take in a thought, weigh it, and bank it for future consideration," Davis says. "It may come back to you sometime later, when you think he's forgotten about it, and you're caught totally off guard. When we were at North Carolina, we weren't allowed to wear jogging suits to work at any time. I argued that some of the jogging suits today are nicer than some of the regular clothes people wear. Last year, out of the blue, he decided we could wear jogging suits during spring training, as long as we weren't sloppy. That was three years later, but he hadn't forgotten the request."

Players have experienced the same thing. The best example was a request for a relaxation of the hair-style rule. Ever since Ricky Williams wore dreadlocks and Wane McGarity had his hair braided, other players requested the same. With the summer of 2001 featuring basketball star Allen Iverson with his hair braided in cornrows, the style of the moment rode contrary to Brown's policy. In a player's meeting, Brown's team asked him to reconsider the policy.

149

There are many motivational signs in Brown's corner office at the Moncrief-Neuhaus Athletics Complex, but one that is missing is one of the most famous desktop signs.

"As much input as he seeks," says Davis, "he reserves the tough decisions for himself."

Or, in the words of the late President Harry Truman: "The buck stops here."

Mack Brown doesn't need a sign to accept that responsibility.

I've said this before, but I believe that honesty and trust are two of the most important attributes of a person. They go together. To have trust, you have to be honest. And to be honest, you have to be willing to be open.

The NCAA rules restrict contact with recruits so much that it is important for me to communicate with them every way I legally can. I write them at least weekly. I wish them well in their upcoming game, remind them of the importance of maintaining good grades and a great attitude, and tell them what's going on with us. I want them to feel as much a part of our program as they can. And—I sincerely mean this—I want them to feel good about Texas, even if they decide to go somewhere else. We only want players who want to be at Texas.

I want to know how our players feel about their progress in every area of their college life, and in those conversations, I want to be certain they understand what we have said. Too often, people only hear the negative. You can tell them six positive things, and the seventh one can be, "You need to pick up your blocking." They'll hear the criticism rather than the praise, or in some cases, they'll miss the challenges to improve.

That's why, after a conversation with a player, I ask him to repeat the conversation as he heard it. I want him to hear what I said, not what he thought he heard me say. Saying it back removes all doubt of the message. To help players with that, we give each player a survey to fill out and sign. It deals with every facet of our program.

If I have an issue with our staff, with our players, or something I just feel I need some advice on, I try to find out how others see it. I may call Coach Royal, DeLoss, Red McCombs, who owns the Minnesota Vikings, Tom Hicks, who owns two professional sports franchises, Joe Jamail, or other close friends whose opinion I greatly respect.

Our staff is not a democracy. I get paid a lot of money to make the tough decisions, and I'm not going to put that off on somebody else. I like the responsibility of making the tough decisions. If you don't, you will not make it as a head coach.

As head coach, there is a thin line between being a friend to your players and being an authority figure to them. I think it helps kids grow when you involve them in making decisions.

The summer of 2001 was interesting in that regard. I have always told our team that every public appearance they make, whether it is on camera or in a photograph, is a job interview. Therefore, issues such as style of hair, tattoos, and body piercing should matter to them. I don't know many attorneys with nose or tongue rings, so if you want to be an attorney, you should think about the future.

But part of growing up is determining how you want to look. Crew cuts and sideburns have come and gone. When I was in school, I wore my hair pretty long and had sideburns. Cleve Bryant had a big Afro, as did many of the other African American athletes in the country then.

Michael Jordan shaved his head, and so did many of America's young athletes. Michael's one of the nicest people I have ever met, and he has worn an earring for years.

The NCAA wants kids to stay out of trouble, but in the summer coaches are not allowed to have much supervision over their team. You can't have a team meeting. You're allowed to have an academic meeting, and it was at such a meeting when the kids brought up the subject of hair. They'll discuss the things they need to discuss, whether it is on the agenda or not.

When the issue of hair was brought up, we all agreed that hair is not a factor in winning or losing. I tried to be honest with them. Hairstyle is a factor in personal impressions that may remain for years and may affect your ability to get a job.

Drugs, for example, have a direct relationship to winning and losing. You can't play if you use drugs. Drinking has a direct effect on winning and losing because it lessens your edge for the game. Beside that, if you're under age, it's against the law.

Coach Switzer told me you shouldn't make everything important, so emphasize the issues you feel most seriously about. It was important to me to explain to them in my best fatherly way where things really fit. And that goes back to choices and options.

In the meeting, three kids stood up and said, "Coach, you ought to let them do what they want with their hair. You've told them it may cost them a job ten years from now. If you feel that way, don't help 'em get a job. If they want to wear their hair that way, it doesn't affect the team or winning and losing, it only affects them—you've told 'em it affects them—and that's part of growing up."

I told the team I could bring in our top ten supporters—people they might one day want to ask for a job—and ask those people if they wanted to hire them.

The point of my telling this is to show that it is important to listen to your players and to be sure you are making rules for the right reasons. I do realize things are constantly changing, and it is important to pay attention to style and fashion. In raising kids—in every aspect of life, for that matter—you have to pick your battles.

We've talked a lot about Ricky Williams. I believe that if I had fought him on the issue of hair, there's a good chance he would not have come back for his senior year, and what a shame that would have been for us and for him. Ricky's hair had absolutely nothing to do with the way he ran and the heart with which he played.

When Greg Davis, Carl Reese, and I coached in the East-West Shrine game, we had an outstanding receiver from Oregon State who had hair down to the top of his belt. Watching him on television, it was easy for people to judge him, but when we met him, we found that he is a really nice young man and a fine football player.

Because of the team's input, we relaxed our hair rule. But we will not relax discipline, and the team will know exactly what we expect of them. I still believe that you must feel good about the image you present. If you look sloppy, odds are you'll play sloppy. I will always want our teams to keep their hair, whatever style they choose, clean and neat.

It is a coach's responsibility to let the players know they are constantly being evaluated by everyone. You don't want them to make a life-changing decision now because they didn't understand that their actions have consequences.

It goes back to the kind of kids you recruit. At age fifty, I have seen a lot of hairstyles come and go, and I have no doubt it will happen again. Some kids are back in Afros thirty years after Cleve abandoned his. Even styles like my long hair and sideburns are back. James Street had long sideburns when he won twenty straight games and led Texas to a national championship in 1969. His hairstyle has changed in the years since, and there is not a finer, more respected former Longhorn today than James Street. But short or long, his hair didn't affect how he competed.

The most important part of this story is that coaches and players have to talk with each other. Because the head coach is the boss, he's going to make decisions that his players or his assistant coaches don't always agree with. They will feel it is their team only if they are part of the decision making process. They have to believe they will be heard and that you'll give them a fair hearing and a fair answer.

That's why we are here.

Choices

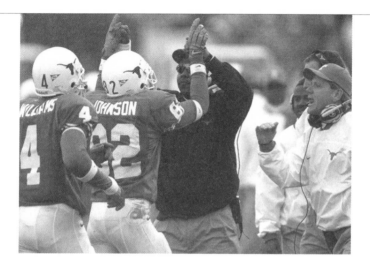

❝AS COACHES AND AS PARENTS, WE CAN ONLY
TEACH OUR KIDS THAT LIFE IS A SERIES OF OPTIONS,
JUST LIKE FOOTBALL. IF YOU MAKE GOOD DECISIONS,
YOU ARE LIKELY TO SUCCEED. **❞**

—Mack Brown

◀ FATHER FIGURE – Assistant coach Darryl Drake greets two of his young stars, Roy Williams *(4)* and B. J. Johnson *(82)*. It is the responsibility of the coaches to help players make the right choices about their lives on and off the football field.

BL

or a young football player at The University of Texas, there is tremendous irony in Austin's famous Sixth Street.
    For 49,865 of the 50,000 students who attend the campus located twenty blocks to the north, the heart of the city's entertainment district is a release, a draw, and one of the reasons they choose Texas.

The live music and the alcohol flow at equal levels from the clubs lining the remnant of the street that was known as Old Pecan Street when they laid out the city nearly 150 years ago. It was a main thoroughfare then, with carriages and trolley cars carrying senators, students, and those who just wanted to be a part of a young Texas. After all, it was the state legislature which decreed that a "university of the first class" should be established on a forty-acre tract way up north.

Equally important then and now is a warehouse district a few blocks west of mighty Congress Avenue. Here, merchants and livery folks worked and stored the supplies that would feed and clothe those 16,000 or so who called the young capital city home.

By the 1880s, work was being finished on the State Capitol building five blocks to the north. When The University of Texas opened its doors in 1883, Old Pecan Street was, next to The Avenue, the most important street in Austin.

The trolley car tracks were removed in the middle of the 20th century, and when the old Capitol Theatre closed in the '60s, it left only a drug store and a few jewelry merchants to try to survive. When the interstate highway cut through the eastern half of the street, it severed an artery that linked the Hispanic residents near Chicon Street with the dwindling end of the once flourishing street.

The Fentress Corporation, a small newspaper chain that featured the *Austin American-Statesman* and the *Waco News Tribune*, opened a state of the art newspaper plant in the late '50s. This modern structure located at Fourth and Guadalupe stood only a few steps from Tom Miller's old warehouse and livery building.

In the '70s, all of that changed.

A round, bearded disc jockey named Rusty Bell began playing songs by Willie Nelson, David Allen Coe, and Kris Kristofferson and called the sound progressive country. Across the Colorado River a few blocks from the warehouse district, Eddie Wilson reopened an old National Guard armory and called it Armadillo World Headquarters.

In the beer garden outside Wilson's venue, beer and marijuana blended with the music of Seals and Croft, and a new culture was born. To house it, those who wanted to make Austin the "Live Music Capital of the World," turned to the alluring vacant buildings on Sixth Street. Clubs and restaurants jumped right in where the old Ritz Theatre had sat closed for years, and suddenly, Lewis's Drug Store and Jewelry had neighbors again.

By 1980, Longhorn basketball coach Abe Lemons was entertaining fans at lunchtime during the taping of his television show at Madison Square Garden, an early sports bar and restaurant that took residence where a dry goods store used to be.

As Kevin Costner learned in the movie *Field of Dreams,* "If you build it, they will come," and from the campus and all parts of Austin, they did.

Mr. Fentress sold his newspaper to the Cox chain out of Atlanta. They vacated the warehouse district, and with a change in location and a change in attitude, moved just across the river. With the journalism of the '90s, athletes all over the country suddenly found themselves living in a fishbowl. If a student under the age of twenty-one got caught drinking, the media was all over it. Do something good and you make the sports page; do something bad and you make the front page.

No one knows about areas like Sixth Street better than Mack Brown. In his years at Tulane, he had to contend with the most famous entertainment venue in America—Bourbon Street in New Orleans. He understood the peer pressure his players felt from fellow classmates who were not bound by the same strict training regimen or the media scrutiny as his football team.

A university is far more than just bricks and mortar, and a football team is more than just blocking, tackling, and scoring touchdowns. Both are about people, and Mack Brown's challenge in the vibrant environment that Austin provides is to steer his players from the classroom, to the football field, through a growing-up time that includes travels through tears and temptations, as well as textbooks and triumph.

MB

Every one of us who is a parent, or who is in a position to deal with young people, has heard them say, "You don't understand me...." And every time I hear a player say that, I want to answer him by repeating what Coach Lou Holtz once told his players: "I have been eighteen. You have not been fifty, so trust me when I say 'I do understand.'"

The difference between growing up in the 21st century and growing up in Tennessee in the '60s is that there are a lot more chances to get into trouble today—I mean bad trouble—than there were when I was a kid. Choices are tougher and more critical to teens in the 2000s.

A mistake used to mean a whippin' or a stern conversation with your parents. A mistake today can cost you your life. Fast cars and fast living

155

have changed a lot of things. Today, everything kids do is about choices.

One day last summer, our academic counselor was talking to one of our players who is really a good student and a great young man. But he had missed a class and was behind in another. The player was upset that we had called his parents.

"I'm twenty years old," he said. "When am I going to be treated as an adult?"

I looked at him and then at the counselor.

"We called your parents because if you keep going like you're going, they are going to find out there's a problem, and then they'll be calling us. We're trying to keep that from happening. And you will be treated as an adult when you act like one and consistently make good choices."

Choices. That may be an important word for all of us, but it is particularly important when we talk about our players.

First, it is our responsibility as coaches at The University of Texas to recruit players we believe will make the right choices. They have to have the right values because every town has places like Sixth Street, and college students are hammered with chances to make the wrong decisions.

When I was a young coach at Tulane, I probably didn't realize the impact an environment like Bourbon Street could have, so I don't know that I handled it very well. Later I realized that every school and every city has its own version of Bourbon Street. College students are going to party, and we ask our team members to commit to staying away from that scene.

The first year we were here, we sent Brian Davis, our academic counselor, to Sixth Street with a media guide. Brian showed the book to every club manager and bartender. He opened the guide to the player section, which had a player's picture and his biographical sketch, which included the player's birthdate.

The legal drinking age in Texas is twenty-one, and there are serious penalties for underage drinking. The penalty is also severe for an establishment serving alcohol to a minor.

"Here are our players, and here are their birthdays," Brian told the club owners. "If you serve them and they are under age, you are placing your license in jeopardy."

That took care of the "choice" for the club owners, but it did not remove the responsibility of doing the right thing from our players.

After every Thursday practice, we remind our players of what it means to be a part of this team. If there is value in winning and in playing well, then their choice will be to stay in on Thursday night.

We help them with that decision by having them lift weights at 6:30 A.M. on Friday mornings, and all players must check in with their position coaches by 9 A.M. Friday.

The toughest team issue I've had to deal with at Texas involved some wrong choices made by four of our players preceding the 2000 Cotton Bowl game against Arkansas. We had to suspend the players two days before the game. They are great kids, and the last thing they wanted to do was intentionally hurt the team, themselves, or their families. But they made a mistake, a decision that changed the direction of our chances in the game and jeopardized their futures.

Two nights before the game, I had to tell those kids they couldn't play. A lot of us cried that night. Teams become a family, and when your family hurts, you all suffer. I'll never forget seeing big Shaun Rogers, all 340 pounds of him, sobbing in the back of the room.

The good news is, they survived. As badly as it hurt, they moved on with their lives, learned from what happened, and let it serve as a lesson to all of us.

In the time since, I've come to have a healthy respect for the word *choice*.

As coaches and as parents, we can only teach our kids that life is a series of options, just like football. If you make good decisions, you are likely to succeed. A quarterback's right choice or a defensive back's split second decision can make the difference between success and failure.

It is all about training people to understand the deal, and when there is nobody else around, to make the right choice.

Shut Up And Deal

❝IF LOSING EVER STOPS BOTHERING YOU, IT IS TIME TO DO SOMETHING ELSE.❞

—Mack Brown

◀ DETERMINED TO WIN - Offensive tackle Mike Williams works out in the weight room. After a loss, Texas's approach is to deal with it and move on. Williams's weight work is a good example of how a player turns a negative into a positive.

BL

I
t's a saying that came from long ago, perhaps from the poker tables of the Old West.
   Winners tell jokes; losers say, "Shut up and deal."
   In the fall of 1971, Texas was riding one of the most successful periods in its history. From the third game of 1968 through the last regular season game of 1970, the Longhorns had won thirty straight football games. A loss to Notre Dame in the 1971 Cotton Bowl game had ended the string, but after starting the next season with three victories, Texas had posted an incredible record of 33-1 over its past thirty-four football games.
   Each Wednesday, following victory after victory, Darrell Royal would load his 16mm game film—one of those oversized reels that clipped onto a gray Bell and Howell projector—and head for the Paramount Theatre on Congress Avenue in downtown Austin.
   It was a pilgrimage requested by members of the Longhorn Club, a support group headed by Wally Scott, an Austin attorney and former Longhorn player who loved his school.
   Austin was different then. Parking on Congress Avenue did not require an hour of your time looking for a space, and many of those who came to the showing could simply walk from their downtown offices.
   At night, the Paramount was the premier movie house in Austin, but Wednesdays at noon, it was all about boxed lunches and Longhorn football.
   While an assistant would ready the film, Royal would give a brief overview of the past week's game and a report about the upcoming opponent. He was frank, folksy, and, well…just very Darrell Royal.
   It was there that many of the "Royalisms," those simple phrases that became part of Austin's culture of the '60s and '70s, were born.
   In the fourth game of the 1971 season, with his star quarterback, Eddie Phillips, hampered with a pulled hamstring, Royal's Longhorns lost to Oklahoma, 48-27. The next week, with both Phillips and his backup, Donnie Wigginton, out, the team—which remarkably would bounce back and win the Southwest Conference—lost to Arkansas, 31-7.

That was the scene in the ornate theater when Royal got up to speak the next Wednesday.

"You know," he began philosophically, "I'm told Oliver Wendell Holmes, on his deathbed, said that every person should experience defeat at some time in his life. He said losing builds character. I have thought a lot about that over the last two weeks, and I am sure there is something in what he said."

Then, in a serious voice, he continued.

"But after two straight losses, I have decided...piss on Oliver Wendell Holmes."

Little could Royal know that thirty years later, his Texas team would be led by a guy who hated to lose every bit as much as he did.

Royal, who never had a losing season as a head coach, could only imagine what Mack Brown had endured during rebuilding efforts at Tulane and North Carolina. At Tulane, he had taken on the challenge of a program which hadn't won in years. The Green Wave had won only nine games in the previous three years, so when Brown's first team bottomed out at 1-10, it was painful, but not unexpected. Two seasons later, he was taking the Green Wave to only its fifth bowl game in more than forty years.

North Carolina, however, was different. In the early '80s, Dick Crum had made a strong effort toward returning the Tar Heels to the football glory of a far distant past. With the likes of Lawrence Taylor, he produced several outstanding clubs, but the program had leveled to pretty much break-even when Brown arrived in 1988.

In fact, interest had so waned when Brown first arrived that Ron Green, Sr., wrote in the Charlotte Observer, "If Mack is 7-4 and gives the fans something to do until basketball season, everyone will be happy."

Nothing Brown had experienced could have prepared him for the next two seasons. At a school where the basketball team sets a high standard for winning, Brown's first two teams went 1-10.

In the midst of that, as he was heading to a Carolina Foundation meeting to talk about his future, Brown pulled into a service station for gasoline.

The attendant filled the car and was cleaning the windshield when he noticed Brown's Big 8 Championship ring, earned in the 1984 season at Oklahoma.

"That's a nice ring," said the attendant as he sloshed water on his dirty jeans.

"Thanks," said Brown. "We need to get things going here so we can get some of these."

"I'll tell you what," said the attendant. "As long as that Mack Brown is your coach, you ain't winning nothin'."

To this day, Brown has driven by the station many times and has never stopped again. In the middle of his third year, his team turned the corner with a come-from-behind victory over Bill Dooley's Wake Forest team. Then came a 13-13 tie with eventual national champion Georgia Tech.

His car may have needed gasoline, but determination and hard work fueled Brown, whose career came out of the darkness. Starting with that third season, his teams would post winning records in his final eight years at Chapel Hill, climaxing with two ten-win seasons that produced top-ten teams.

I f it hadn't been for Bobby Ross, the coach at Georgia Tech who went on to win a national championship there and later took a San Diego Charger team to the Super Bowl, I might have given up. He had struggled through the longest losing streak in ACC history, and as we talked together on the field before we beat them for our only win in 1989, I asked him, "How can you keep doing this? How do you stand the losing?"

He told me, "You have to remain positive. The faculty, the students, the fans, the media, and even the parents will be negative. Everybody, including your players, will look to you to see how you are handling it. If you give up, so will they."

I think of that now, and I realize how true that is. It also fits with something Coach Royal told our team that I think is really important.

He said, "Teams don't quit. Players quit. And if enough players quit, then the team loses."

I don't remember when I first started hating to lose; maybe it was when my Dad jerked me out of that Little League game for taking a called third strike. I know it has always eaten on me. I am terrible to live with after a loss. But I have figured out a way to deal with it. Rather than just sitting around and pouting, I have found the best way to deal with it is to get back to work.

When we lost to Arkansas in the 2000 Southwestern Bell Cotton Bowl, I wasn't happy at all. Our team didn't show up, and that comes back to us coaches. We met at 10 A.M. back in Austin the day after the game to get to work and find out what had happened.

The same was true after we lost to Oklahoma in 2000. Going into the game, we thought we were going to win. None of our players or our coaches had ever lost to Oklahoma. We had fallen behind, 17-0, the year before and had come back and won. This time, we played poorly and we got killed. I was embarrassed for our team, our coaches, and myself. We had a team meeting the next day and we did a lot of talking about what went wrong. We turned things around after that, and we won the next six games.

The only other time anything like that had happened to me was when we were at Tulane, and Florida State beat us, 73-14, on homecoming. After the game, when people asked me if I felt that Coach Bobby Bowden had run up the score, I told them that it was my responsibility to put a team on the field that wouldn't give up seventy-three points. It's not my place to coach the other team.

The next week, we came back and won 30-19 over a good Mississippi State team coached by Emory Bellard, a former assistant for Coach Royal at Texas, and once the head coach at Texas A&M.

Our challenge after the OU loss at Texas was to get ready in a week to go play Colorado at Boulder. We hadn't beaten them there in five straight trips, and they'd just beaten Texas A&M in College Station. We made it clear to everybody in the program that we needed to get on that plane to

Colorado with a different attitude.

I learned from Coach Bear Bryant and Coach Royal to publicly take responsibility for a loss. As the head coach, it is ultimately my responsibility. We will deal with the loss as a team, but we'll do it behind closed doors. I try to deflect the criticism from the players and the assistants so they can get back on track.

At Texas, there may be a small group of people who want to complain, but there is a much bigger bunch who will stand by you. We have good people like Rooster Andrews, a former Longhorn legend who has more friends than anybody I know, coming out to practice just to show they still care and they still believe. Roy Spence and his people at GSD&M created an inspirational banner that we hung in the locker room.

Sally says something would be wrong with me if I didn't hurt when we lost, because it shows how much it matters. I try not to dwell on the reasons for the loss, except to make sure we fix them so we don't repeat them. It serves no purpose to replay mistakes over and over again, unless you plan on correcting them. After a loss on Saturday, I have trouble sleeping until about Tuesday. Terry Donahue, who was so successful at UCLA and is now with the San Francisco 49ers, warned Sally when we married about how coaches take losses. He said after a loss he felt sick for days, until he got serious about the next opponent. Losses stay with coaches a lot longer than wins. You must learn to enjoy the wins as much you hate the losses.

When I was younger—when I started at Tulane and North Carolina—I was naive enough to believe we could win, no matter what. Looking back, I can understand that wasn't true, but at the time, I didn't see that. I couldn't see the program, I just saw a game. That's important to understand. There are times when you may risk a game because your goal is to build a solid program.

In those first years at North Carolina, I wanted to win so badly that a couple of times I wound up costing my team. I remember a game against Maryland my first year. They scored late in the game to tie us, 38-38. When we got the ball back at our own 20, I was throwing every down, trying to get in position to win. They intercepted and kicked a field goal to beat us, 41-38. That probably wasn't fair to that team, but it did send a message for the future that we would always play to win.

The next year, against Wake Forest, we had won only two games in two years. We scored late in the game to cut their lead to 17-16. We went for two, and we didn't get it. Looking back, a tie would have felt really good to a bunch of kids who needed some self-confidence. Sometimes not losing is just as important as winning. But I thought I did the right thing at the time because we still sent a message.

At Texas, we want to get back to a place where we are in the top ten all of the time and put ourselves in position to win all the games. That's how the Florida States and the Nebraskas did it in the '90s. If you win all the games, you most likely will be the national champion. We need to focus on winning each game more than talking about the end results.

I look back over my career, and I realize how many times I almost allowed losses to destroy me. My second year at North Carolina, we lost to Navy, 12-7, and it was the first time in three years that they had beaten a Division I team. After the game, I went out to my car and just sat there and cried because I knew we had better players and had lost a game we shouldn't have lost. That is a horrible feeling for a coach. After I regained my composure, I had to do my coach's show for television and start preparing for the next week. Sometimes being a head coach is very lonely.

Losing those first two years at North Carolina affected me, my marriage, and my family.

What I have come to learn, even though I still hate to lose, is that there is a much bigger picture than just winning and losing. I think Coach Royal's point is the most important: When a coach looks at his team he realizes that, most of the time, 90 percent of the kids are trying as hard as they can. They haven't quit.

It is my responsibility as a coach to find out which ones aren't pulling their load and try to keep them from slowing down the others. If you get down on all of them, you'll not only lose the game, you'll lose your team.

That's why now after a loss, regardless of how tough it was, we go back to work. I try to make it clear to our kids that I am not mad at them, I am mad at what we did or didn't do, and that we will get it done better, either by them or by somebody else who wants to do it right.

If losing ever stops bothering you, it is time to do something else. After a loss, I'm hard to live with because I am crushed. But if you don't learn to deal with that and fix it, you will destroy yourself and everything around you.

And when you do that, you ruin your chance to win.

Sticks And Stones

"AS FAR AS THE PRINT MEDIA IS CONCERNED, I LEARNED A LONG TIME AGO YOU NEVER PICK A FIGHT WITH A GUY WHO BUYS INK BY THE BARREL, SO MY POLICY WITH THE LEGITIMATE MEDIA IS PRETTY SIMPLE: BE AS HONEST AND AS OPEN AS YOU CAN BE WITHOUT CRITICIZING YOUR KIDS AND COACHES."

—Mack Brown

◀ HIGH SCHOOL HERO - Nobody understands better than Mack Brown what it is like to be a publicized high school star. Learning how to deal with daily media attention is an important part of learning to be a Texas Longhorn.

I̲ittle Bit Cat was a small black feline whose curiosity seemed to predetermine that she would spend at least several of her nine lives in harm's way, but never more so than one winter evening when the family's laundry was being finished. As the clothes dryer was turned on, there was heard a distinct thumping, as if a tennis shoe were included among the sheets and towels.

Quick thinking was all that saved Little Bit that night, and from that time forward, after she was pulled, frantic, from a wad of wet towels, her picture was pasted on the outside of the appliance as a reminder: Folks needed to check to see if there was a living being inside.

Coaches, players, politicians—you name it—are victims of similar oversights. In the callous world of talk radio, hypercritical media, internet chat boards, and fan newsletters, the public sometimes forgets that underneath the helmet, beyond the television screen or radio dial, and behind the newspaper account, there is somebody who is not all that different from themselves.

It may have begun with the Watergate scandal in politics, or the emergence of caustic reporters such as Howard Cosell, but somewhere in the '70s, coverage of sports went from conversational to adversarial.

Jones Ramsey, the sports information director at The University of Texas from 1961 through 1982, was once asked by a young sports writer to define the difference between Darrell Royal and Fred Akers, who was in the midst of his successful ten-year run from 1977 through 1986.

"Well," said Ramsey, "for one thing, Darrell didn't have to put up with you."

During Royal's tenure, it was simply an issue of journalists covering sports. A few years later, coverage would become more pervasive, as radio stations changed formats to begin airing "sports talk" shows. At first, they went by names such as "Sports Day," or even just "Sports Talk," and they were hosted by the station's sports director, or maybe even a local sportswriter. In time, as AM radio sought programming, all-day sports shows emerged, and in some cases, the hosts were selected from the most vocal of the callers. Radio talk shows became a place where angry people vented. The same became true with internet message boards.

The new media brought both challenges and opportunities for college coaches.

It became impossible to stop the untruths and half-truths that were fostered, but the same technology that brought them also provided a vehicle to tell the real story.

One of the first things Mack Brown did when he came to Texas was start his own website. By the fall of 2001, MackBrown-TexasFootball.com had four million hits in the first three weeks of preseason practice. The innovative, action-filled site was rated the best in the nation by several national services and was a runaway winner among the Big 12 sites, as judged by the *Dallas Morning News*.

What the media relations industry discovered was that far more people were interested in legitimate news about their universities, and that the people who cared and were knowledgeable were not on the internet at 2 o'clock in the morning bashing the coaches and players.

Mack Brown understood that criticism of the coach went with the territory; he got paid a lot of money to take it. But when it came to the bashing of his players, he took issue. Behind the face guard, inside the numbered jersey, was a nineteen- or twenty-year-old who was only human, yet was brave enough to seek victory and risk defeat on a Saturday in the fall in front of 85,000 people.

For them, he would go to the mat.

I once asked Coach Royal why I should take the Texas job...what was the best thing about it.

"Because 20 million people care about Texas football," he said.

"What's the toughest thing about it?" I asked.

"Twenty million people care about Texas football," he replied.

Since we came to Texas, we could not have asked for better or more positive support. People ask me about the "pressure" of the job. I tell them, "It's not pressure at Texas, it's interest."

When we have more than 50,000 season tickets sold and a waiting list of over fifty for our sixty-four stadium suites, I don't believe our fans have a problem with our program. When they don't come, they're letting you know there's an issue.

I want our fans to care, and as much as they hurt when we get beat, the coaches and players hurt worse. We came to Texas because we wanted to win a national championship, and we won't be satisfied until we do. It is very important for fans to feel they are a part of what we are trying to do.

As far as the media is concerned, I understand they have a job to do. As long as they get the facts and seek an understanding as to why something happened or is happening, I respect their opinion. They don't have to agree with us, they just have to be fair in trying to understand the thinking that went into it. I do understand they can't have as much information to evaluate the situation as we do. They are at a real disadvantage because they have to fill their paper. They have to write something.

I will never criticize a player or an assistant coach to the media. There's a big sign inside our locker room and inside our coaches meeting room: "What we say in here, what we do in here—when you leave here— stays in here."

When we recruit a player, we make that clear to him and his family. We're teachers. It would serve no purpose to publicly flog a player or a coach. When we lost to Oklahoma in 2000, we stunk. But as the head coach, that was my responsibility. It wouldn't have been right to blame it on somebody else. On Sunday, or more correctly, on the way home after the game, we began to figure out how to fix what had gone wrong.

The season of 2000 probably was the most interesting we've had from a media coverage standpoint. The media thought I was being too sensitive when we were ranked in the top five in preseason, and some publications ranked us number one. I knew we had some serious questions, and I had seen every practice, so I said I felt we should be in the top fifteen. If things fell right, by the end of the year we could be in the top ten.

We also had a question at quarterback. On January 1, Major Applewhite had suffered an injury in the Cotton Bowl game that required surgery, and as hard as he tried to get ready, I knew his rehabilitation was not complete. Major is such a competitor that he would never admit that because he wanted so badly to believe he was ready. Chris Simms, on the other hand, had very little experience because we had not been able to get him in many games the year before. So our choice was to start an experienced player who was limited because of an injury and bring the youngster off the bench if we had to, or to start the rookie and, if necessary, bring in the experienced player.

We talked constantly with both quarterbacks, and they fully understood what we were doing. But to some of the media and some of the fans, it was as if they thought we got together on Saturday and drew a name out of a hat. Looking back, the media coverage of the quarterback situation hurt our team. It became bigger than the team, and football is the ultimate team sport.

Our job is to win football games. Parents love their kids. I have no doubt that one mother likes her son better than the other mom's son at whatever position you're talking about. Every parent wants to see his or her son play. Just go to a Little League game if you doubt that. Our job is to put the people on the field who will give us the best chance for victory, and we don't play favorites. I like every single player we have on our team. I wouldn't have brought them to Texas if I didn't believe in each kid's potential. I want to see each player excel, but most of all we want to see our team win. I owe that to our fans, to our university, but most of all, I owe it to our players.

I appreciate how well most of our fans have reacted. When we came, we asked them to be positive, and they have been. We asked them not to sit in the stands and talk about how dumb the coaches are, because a recruit's mom and dad might be sitting in front of them. The same is true on the internet. Every single word written about our program makes its way into the hands of recruits. So if somebody has an issue, we ask them to write us, and I answer every single letter I get, as long as it is signed.

I remember Barry Switzer telling me about answering a letter from a "fan" who was highly critical. Barry wrote back, saying, "Some idiot sent me this letter and signed your name, and I just thought you ought to know about it."

I haven't reached that point, but there've been times in my career I was tempted to do that. I am keeping all the crazy letters, and I'll probably put them in a book one day. So be careful what you write; you may see it again.

People ask my opinion about the internet and the message boards. For all the reasons we've discussed, I wish people would be careful what they write. I have also found that, in a way, recruiting services and the internet have become undercover agents for the NCAA as far as cheating in recruiting. With all of the contact that is out there, with all of the phone calls to recruits from services and rumors from fans, if there is anything that even smells of being illegal, somebody is going to print it. And that is positive. Our best chance to win is if everyone goes by the rules.

During the season, I do not read the papers, look at the internet, or listen to radio shows. I encourage our players and staff to do the same. If Sally or somebody on the sports information staff feels I should see or know something, they'll bring it to me. I find it works better that way.

Fans who call radio shows and post messages on the internet are anonymous. There is nothing to keep an opponent's fan from calling a station and ripping your football program under the guise of being the other team's fan. So when people come to me and say, "The fans are upset," my response is, "Whose fans?" Most bulletin boards and radio call-in shows represent a recycling of the same people. A lot of them are just unhappy. As Sally says, they didn't like what they had for breakfast and they hate their job, so don't take it personally...they are mad at everything.

Modern-day radio talk show hosts are paid to start controversy so they get more callers and more opinions on their shows. It is also significant to note the relatively few callers who really do participate in those shows. That's why you can't take them personally.

As far as the print media is concerned, I learned a long time ago you never pick a fight with a guy who buys ink by the barrel, so my policy with the legitimate media is pretty simple: Be as honest and as open as you can be without criticizing your kids and coaches.

And be accessible. During the season, we have a media telephone conference call on Sunday, a Big 12 media call on Monday morning, a press conference at noon on Monday, and I'm available after every practice. We also set aside an hour window once a week before practice to return phone calls to media and radio shows.

The media demands on our players are extensive—five major

newspapers and at least seven radio and television stations cover us on a daily basis. While we try to accommodate the media, it is critical for us to be protective of our players' time. They are available at a Monday noon luncheon. Offensive players are available after practice on Tuesdays, and defensive players are available on Wednesdays. Freshmen are not allowed to be interviewed until they have played in a game. The assistant coaches and I do not do interviews that are not set up through Assistant Athletics Director Bill Little, and the players have the same policy with Media Relations Director John Bianco. We aren't trying to limit the access to our players from the legitimate media, but there are too many bad agents and gamblers who try to get to the kids. Anybody on the phone can say they are "with the media."

Folks like Mr. Bible and Coach Royal put this program in the national spotlight years ago, and right now, our job is to represent them, The University, and our football team as well as we can.

It is the media that tells our story, and I want it to be a good one.

27

Attitude

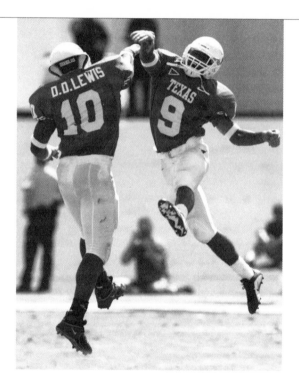

❝THE REASON GREAT TEAMS WIN ALL THE TIME IS THAT THEY BELIEVE THEY CAN WIN ALL THE TIME. ❞

—Mack Brown

BL

T he night chill had set in outside the weathered brick building nestled not far from the massive football stadium looming in the darkness across the wide expanse of parking lot.

The Texas basketball team had finished its work on old Autry Court inside Rice Gymnasium, and the players hustled from the steamy showers to the bus waiting outside on the street.

It was a three-hour ride back to Austin, and after a stop at Wendy's for burgers, it would be up to Denise to pilot the big bus back down Interstate 10 to the Columbus cutoff, then on home to Jester Center Dorm.

Early classes the next morning dictated the need for speed, and no one was better at that than Denise, the heavy-set African American woman with the Technicolor hair.

Rice was an interesting opponent for Texas in the old Southwest Conference. It was widely recognized as one of the country's top academic institutions, and it was always sparring with its huge neighbor in Austin as to which school—the giant state university or the small private institution—ranked as the better place to get an education.

Rice students reveled in exercises of the mind, and they lived for the feud. A sharply placed barb, a quip or a zing, would be the talk of the campus the next morning. Pranks and practical jokes were as much a part of life at Rice as a stroll down University Avenue, and games of the mind were far more successful than the Rice Owl teams usually were in the arena of athletic competition.

So it didn't surprise anybody that, as the Texas team prepared to leave the gym, a sleek new Mazda sneaked into the parking space in front of the bus.

As the coaches and the players filed out of the gym, gleeful students practically danced from the fun. With the little red car safely inserted in front, and another car blocking the rear of the bus, it would be a while before anybody left for Austin. It was sweet revenge for the narrow loss the Owl basketball team had just suffered inside the gym.

There was irony in the fact that the Longhorn coach's message before the game had dealt with playing with an attitude, and suddenly they were faced with seemingly no recourse to deal with a demonic plan from some wily future wizards.

After the coaches fruitlessly tried to reason with the students, they climbed off the bus to wait out the siege. That was when Denise stepped off the bus.

She was all business as she glared at the students and then looked at the shiny new car.

"My name is Heavy D," she announced, the fire in her dark eyes visible even in the dim light from the street lamps. "And I am going to move my bus. Now, I can get another bus. Can you get another car?"

From the pack, a long-haired young man in worn jeans and a silly hat stepped forward, got in the Mazda, and drove away.

So did Heavy D and her bus.

"Now that," assistant basketball coach Eddie Oran would recall later, "was attitude."

MB

I've said this before, but my earliest introduction to attitude in sports came from my dad, when I took a called third strike in a Little League game. He told me to never take a close one; if I didn't have enough guts to swing, then I shouldn't even go up there.

We want our players to walk with a swagger. There is a huge difference between being boastful and in being solidly confident about who you are and what you can do. The reason great teams win all the time is that they believe they can win all the time.

I have tremendous admiration for Lance Armstrong. When we first moved to Austin, Lance and Kristin were our neighbors. He has overcome a lot of things to become the best cyclist in the world, and for three weeks on the Tour de France, the most important factor in his racing—aside from the training he's done, of course—is the attitude with which he approaches the race and his fellow competitors.

The same is true for Tiger Woods in golf. He's won a lot of tournaments simply by being Tiger Woods. That was one of the things I learned when I worked that year in Oklahoma as an assistant to Barry Switzer. Coach Switzer had the best relationship with kids of all different backgrounds that I've ever seen. Nothing was a crisis to him. He just worked through things. More than anybody I've ever worked for, he gave the kids confidence on a day-to-day basis, and he had them walking with that swagger.

He told his guys that there were games they were supposed to win, and others that would be a fight. He would tell guys they were supposed to win, say, these seven games, and these other four…you'd better get ready to go. But he always made them feel like they were going to win the game. They believed there was never a chance that they weren't going to win.

But after a loss, he handled it well. He'd say, "Give them credit, and let's move on."

When we were playing Kansas, Danny Bradley, our starting quarter-back, had a sprained ankle and couldn't play. Mike Clopton was our second team quarterback, and he'd been ruled academically ineligible because of some technicality involving his transfer from a junior college. So Troy Aikman had to come out of being a redshirt, and he hadn't taken a snap all year.

We started Troy in that game, and we were down 10-7 at halftime to Kansas. I chewed out the offense and said, "You're not helping, and we're gonna get beat...we're gonna get beat...we're gonna get beat." And I convinced our kids that we were gonna get beat. We lost the game to an inferior Kansas team, and after the game, Barry said, "We've got to be real careful, don't we, not to convince our kids that we can lose."

A few weeks later, we were playing Kansas State. We were behind 7-6 at halftime, and as we were walking in, Barry grabbed my arm and said, "We're in great shape, aren't we? Because the longer the game goes, the team with the best players wins."

I said, "I gotcha."

He would walk in with an attitude of "We haven't done a thing right, and we're still ahead 7-6. Boy, are they in some trouble." He would make light of it.

In the Nebraska game at Nebraska, we were sitting there at halftime, tied at 7-7, and they had beaten the heck out of us. They had a great team, not a good team, and we honestly weren't as good. We squirted the fullback in the wishbone for about a sixty-yard touchdown, and they'd just been moving up and down the field. They had Mike Rozier, Greg Remington, and Turner Gill. It was a great bunch of football players.

We walked into the locker room at halftime, and I'll never forget Barry walking in and saying, "Boy, are they good! They are a helluva lot better than I thought they were. They are beating the crap out of us!" Everybody kind of looked up, and we were all trying to figure out what he was doing.Then he stopped and said, "But it's still OU and Nebraska, and they don't think they can beat us, but we know we can beat them, and we're gonna kick their ass the second half."

And we beat them 16-7.

With a team that was not nearly as talented as theirs, we went to the Orange Bowl and almost won the national championship.

Barry had a magic with the kids when it came to attitude. He had the ability to put his team at ease, even when somebody else might have thought they were in trouble.

One of the greatest things about Ricky Williams that year he won the Heisman was his attitude. Ricky was as great a competitor as anybody I've ever been around.

When we were preparing for our game with A&M, he was going for the NCAA all-time rushing record. He needed only sixty-four yards, but I knew the Aggies would do everything they could to stop him, because if they stopped Ricky, that was their best chance to stop us. You always try to take away a team's strength.

I was talking to Ricky in practice a couple of days before the game, and I told him not to worry about the record.

"Oh," said Ricky, "I'm not worried about the record. I always do well against the Aggies. I'm going to get that. In fact, what I want is Napoleon McCallum's record for all-purpose yards."

Then he asked, "If I'm close to that, will you let me return a punt or a kickoff so I can get that record, too?"

I told him to just worry about running the football. You can't tell a guy not to set his sights so high. He did indeed get the rushing record and McCallum's record without returning any kicks. Late in the game, when he had broken both records, Ricky walked by and said, "Coach, you can forget about that kickoff return. I don't need it. I've already broken both records."

I once asked Joe Jamail to speak to the team about pride. Joe is one of the greatest friends of The University of Texas, and has given millions to other colleges as well.

"I'll tell you one thing," he said, "I've won more cases for more money than just about any lawyer in the world. If you come up against me in the courtroom, if you have pride, you have a chance. If you don't have pride, I'll whip your ass every time." Joe understands about attitude.

You see the great teams in sports, and all you have to know about them is the emblem they wear on their hat or the name across their jersey. There is a mystique to attitude, and a swagger shows honest confidence, not inflated ego.

"It"

**❝IF YOU'VE GOT IT, YOU'LL MAKE IT.
IF YOU DON'T HAVE IT, YOU WON'T.❞**

—Darrell Royal

◀ ALL ABOUT "IT" – Willie Nelson, Darrell Royal, and Ben Crenshaw
join Mack for a picture during the "Ben, Willie, and Darrell
Charity Golf Tournament," which has raised almost $4 million
for underprivileged youngsters. There are no better examples of
Royal's "It" theory than Nelson, the legendary songwriter and
performer, and Crenshaw, two time Masters Champion.

I t was midway through the Longhorns' practice on Frank Denius Fields. The 5
o'clock traffic was droning to a standstill on the busy highway just beyond the
chain link fence that separated green grass from solid asphalt. As twilight
approached on an early spring day, a young high school coach had his bags
packed, ready to challenge the road home in the school van with "Go Eagles"
emblazoned on the side.

With his muscles bulging from a Nike shirt in his school's colors, the young
high school coach certainly looked the part. His jacket with the school logo was
slung over his shoulder.

He was a marked contrast to the man in the golf cart—the man wearing
sneakers, a golf hat, and a wind breaker. The watchful eye, the ability to talk and
see every move of the players at the same time, made it clear this was not the
rider's first time to step on a practice field.

Fifty years before, Darrell Royal was a young coach visiting practices and
seeking answers. He had spent thirty of those years becoming a coaching legend
and then, at age fifty-two, he retired. There are few true living legends in any field
of endeavor, so that spring afternoon in Austin, the young coach decided he'd just
go ask the man his secret.

Mack Brown was in the middle of a conversation with Coach Royal about
offense and pass routes and blocking assignments. Brown looked up to see the
young coach standing beside the golf cart.

"Coach Royal," said the young man, "I just wanted to meet you and ask you
for some advice."

Brown looked at his cart partner, expecting a question about the finer points of
the Wishbone offense that Royal helped create, or maybe even about practice times.

"I want to be a successful college coach," began the young man, "and you've
been around a long time, so I'd like to ask you what I should do to make that happen."

Royal looked at Brown and then at the young man. "How long you got?" he said.

"Well, I have to be getting on the road pretty soon," the young man replied.

Royal paused for a second, then locked his eyes on the eyes of the questioner.

"If you've got it, you'll make it. If you don't have it, you won't," Royal said.

The jacket with the logo shifted as the young coach glanced at Brown, who simply returned a shrug that said, "I heard him, too, and I can't help you here, coach. He's the master."

The young coach waited in the silence as Royal turned back to the orange-shirted players on the field in front of him. Then he thanked Royal, turned, and walked away.

When he was out of earshot, Royal, still fixed on the play being run, smiled a knowing smile and said, "Nice guy. 'Hope he has the drive for it.'"

MB

A couple of years ago, Bill Duvall and Baker Montgomery, two of our good friends who are successful Dallas businessmen, invited our head basketball coach, Rick Barnes, DeLoss Dodds, and me to play in the Byron Nelson Golf Tournament Pro-Am. With my golf game, I thought I might get embarrassed; I didn't want to hit someone as I was teeing off on the first tee. We were paired with Sergio Garcia and we had a great time. Sergio was just starting on the tour. He knew nothing about American football. He invited me to the annual running of the bulls in Pamplona, Spain. That would be something to see, if you wanted to learn about determination...on the part of both the runners and the bulls. I told him he should come to a football game in Austin and see the running of the 'Horns. It was interesting to see the ease with which he played. He was relaxed, and we laughed a lot. I think he shot even par despite us.

What I remember most about that day in Dallas was, as we were packing up to leave in the late afternoon, walking by the practice tee and looking up to see Tiger Woods hitting balls. He had been hitting balls at 7:00 A.M., he had played eighteen holes, and at 3:30 P.M., he was hitting balls again, from different positions in the practice sand trap. With people pulling him in every direction, he maintained great focus, and the people cheered every practice shot.

That had a great impact on me. Here was the number one player in the world, who played golf every weekend and had just finished playing a practice round. And here he was, working on his game.

When Tiger came to our Stanford game in California, I had a chance to talk to him about that. It was clear he had a gift of talent, but, at his young age, he also had a gift of wisdom: No matter how good you get, you can always learn something.

I'll never forget a piece of advice Coach Royal gave me when I first came to Austin. He was talking about his early success at Texas. In the early '60s, Texas put together one of the greatest runs in college football. From 1961 through 1964, they won forty games, lost three, and tied one. Then, they had three consecutive 6-4 seasons.

I asked Coach what happened.

"I got too comfortable," he said. "You don't ever want to stand in the shade too long."

Having grown up in farm country, I understood what he meant. If you stand under the shade tree too long, rather than working in the hot sun, you won't accomplish what you need to accomplish, and your competition will run past you.

Successful people always do more than is required. Gil Brandt said Tony Dorsett, when he was with the Cowboys, would run all the way to the end zone on every practice run when he broke in the open. He wanted to get used to going the distance. Tony did everything the other backs did and then did more.

That works not only in sports, but it works in any business you go into. There are several keys to running a good program. Obviously, there are givens: You have to have good players. I have tried it with good players and with bad players, and you win a lot more games with good players.

It is tempting to say, "You have to work harder than the other guy," but you need to be careful with that. If you judge "working hard" based on the hours you put in, you may not be accomplishing what you want.

There are a lot of ways to waste time.

As we entered the 2001 season, we made some changes in our pre-season workouts. The first three years we were here, we took buses out to the Whitaker Intramural Fields, about twenty minutes north of the campus. During two-a-days, that meant forty minutes on the buses, twice a day. That's nearly an hour and a half. At the Denius Fields, two blocks east of the stadium, it's a ten-minute turnaround. So this year, we decided to practice on campus

We also considered the heat, and wondered if we were wearing out the guys by practicing in the heat of the day. So we changed that to include more night practices and fewer workouts in the hot sun. We could still get them in shape, but it was safer and more productive.

So how does this fit with business?

It is a matter of constantly looking to improve your operation, and a matter of working smarter than the other guy. Working smarter doesn't mean simply working longer. When I first started coaching, I didn't believe in taking vacations. Donnie Duncan told me that people are going to take vacations, whether or not you give them one. If you give them time off, everyone is happier and more productive. If you don't give them time off, they'll take time off on the job.

Tiger Woods wasn't on the practice tee just to be out there longer than anybody else, it was to tweak something that would make a difference in his game, and to practice it until it was perfect. He also has taken up fly-fishing to take some time away from golf.

Times have changed in our business; today it is more important than ever to be efficient with practice time. During a school year, the NCAA limits practice time to twenty hours a week, and we have to give players one day a week when they are not required to do anything pertaining to football. When I was playing, there were no limits. It was nothing to practice four or five hours every day.

Now, we try to limit our longest workouts to no more than two hours. We go over Saturday's game film on Sunday afternoon, and the players take Monday off. The coaches and I establish a game plan on Monday, and we take care of media obligations. Our heaviest work is done on Tuesday and Wednesday, followed by a short practice on Thursday. We do not practice on Fridays. On road games, we usually have a walk-through at the stadium where we will play, and sometimes that includes a very light workout in sweats.

For a head coach, just as it should be for the manager of a company, it is important to seek input from your staff and players. We have a player's leadership committee that regularly gives us advice on what the players are thinking, and often they are able to see things we don't. Everybody from the trainer to the strength coach to the equipment manager can have a valuable piece of information that may help us win.

Coach Royal said, "Luck is when preparation meets opportunity." That's why we've heard all our lives that you make your own luck.

I notice that every now and then when I'm watching golf on television. When Tiger sinks a long putt or pulls off a miraculous shot, I remember that twilight practice in Dallas.

And I think about that young high school coach who wanted success to be so simple.

II

ONE HEARTBEAT

The First Goal

**"YOU WON BECAUSE YOU NEVER QUIT.
REGARDLESS OF WHAT HAPPENED, YOU KEPT
COMING BACK. YOU HAD EACH OTHER,
AND YOU BELIEVED YOU COULD WIN.
THERE IS A LESSON IN LIFE THERE. KEEP FIGHTING,
STICK TOGETHER, AND BELIEVE."**

—Mack Brown

◀ IT STARTS HERE – Center Lyle Sendlein (62) calls out a play prior to snapping the ball to quarterback Vince Young in the Longhorns' showdown with Ohio State. The strength of the offensive line was one of the major assets of the 2005 team.

"Anybody who wants to beat Ohio State, meet at the practice field tonight at eight," read the note on the board in the Texas Longhorn locker room.

It was early summer, 2005. As twilight descended upon the western sky beyond The University of Texas campus, the lights on the Frank Denius Practice Fields alongside Interstate 35 etched a sharp contrast between the green grass and the shorts-clad figures working on it.

Texas and Ohio State, two of the nation's universities with equally renowned football programs, had never met on the football field. But on September 10, 2005, they would.

Outside of bowl games and a few Oklahoma games before the Longhorns and the Sooners were united in the Big 12 Conference in 1996, this was the biggest non-conference game for Texas in recent history. It wasn't the season opener—that would be at home against the University of Louisiana Lafayette on September 3—but it certainly had the focus of every football fan in Texas and Ohio. For that matter, it had also captured the imagination of the whole country.

ABC television quickly seized the moment and moved the game to prime time, meaning a nationwide telecast at 8:00 P.M. eastern daylight time. Defending national champion Southern Cal was a preseason pick to repeat, and Texas was a solid second. Ohio State was in the mix, ranging generally from number four to number seven in the top ten.

Vince Young, who had been voted the Most Outstanding Offensive Player in the Longhorns' Rose Bowl win over Michigan six months earlier, was the ring-leader of a group of determined seniors and underclassmen who had made a commitment to themselves and to one another.

In the summer, according to NCAA rules, coaches cannot participate with players in workouts. That left the hot afternoon conditioning work to Strength and Conditioning guru Jeff Madden and his staff. The rest of the time belonged to the players.

That was when Young and the others planned their practices, and basically the whole team showed up at Denius. They also came up with a plan to work against members of the Division I-AA Texas State Bobcat team, located thirty minutes south of Austin in San Marcos. Texas State itself was preparing for what would be a stellar season.

The 38-37 last-second victory over Michigan had earned the Longhorns a respect that had validated their program as a legitimate player in the quest for a national championship. Young's performance in that game, a veteran offensive line including tight-end David Thomas, plus the return of seniors such as Michael Huff, Cedric Griffin, Aaron Harris, and Rod Wright on defense, had all of the preseason magazines buzzing.

The idea of a return to Pasadena, where the 2005 national championship game would be played, was a driving factor as these "boys of summer" used the extra work to get better and better.

It was in that window of time that Young's receivers—a season removed from being an inexperienced crew whose main forte had been downfield blocking—grew up. Limas Sweed, Billy Pittman, Nate Jones, Jordan Shipley (who had missed the 2004 season with a knee injury), and former pro baseball player Quan Cosby were Young's primary targets, along with the dependable Thomas.

Shipley was lost again to a pulled hamstring during fall practice, but the offense received a boost from the running-back position. Selvin Young's return after missing a season with injury was aided by the emergence of freshmen Jamaal Charles and Henry Melton, along with the multi-talented Ramonce Taylor, who played both at running back and wide receiver.

Ahmard Hall, the senior who had earned a scholarship after walking on following a stint in the Marine Corps, became the starting fullback and an inspirational and wise leader.

The coaching staff had also undergone a change, with the departure of three members from the 2004 staff. Greg Robinson and Dick Tomey had become head coaches at Syracuse and San Jose State, respectively, and running-backs coach Mike Haywood had been named the offensive coordinator at Notre Dame.

To replace them, Brown had blended success, experience, and passion. Gene Chizik, who had helped Auburn to an unbeaten season in 2004 as its defensive coordinator, took Robinson's position as co-defensive coordinator along with the returning Duane Akina. Brown replaced Tomey with Oscar Giles, a former Longhorn who lettered in 1990 and had built a good resumé in college coaching since that time.

With Haywood's departure and that of Doak Walker Award-winner Cedric Benson at running back, Brown went with a well-traveled fatherly figure in Ken Rucker, who was a perfect fit with a stable of recovering and young running backs.

Every Mack Brown-coached team at Texas begins the season with five basic goals. They include winning the "state championship", a mythical title they can accomplish in their games against teams from the State of Texas, winning the Big 12 South Division, winning the Big 12 Championship, and winning whatever bowl game in which Texas participates. The first of the five goals is always to win the season opener.

But when fall practice was accomplished and Louisiana Lafayette was dispatched in the season opener, it was time for the game which everyone had been waiting for.

And the game, with all of its hype, did not disappoint.

Long after the game was over, the famous home stadium of the Buckeyes of The Ohio State University stood sentinel to an important moment in recent college football.

It was empty now, with only a few security guards and a couple of clean-up crews working in the distance. The "thud" that broke the eerie silence came from the falling of a support beam as workers took down the set of the TV production above the tunnel at the southwest corner of the stadium.

The portable lights peered over the rim of the massive facility, as if they were giant birds perched and gazing, focused on the green grass nestled in the canyon of gray concrete.

As Mack Brown walked back onto the field, there below the lights and the concrete for one last time to tape the opening to *Longhorn Sports Center,* the north end of the stadium looked ghostly in the empty stillness.

It was his last look at the Horseshoe.

Only a few hours before, Ohio Stadium, known to the locals and the followers of college football simply as "The Shoe," had welcomed two teams and more than 105,000 fans for a classic college football game.

The crowd, plus the national television audience who watched, was one of the largest ever to watch a Texas football game. It was the number two-ranked Longhorns against the number four-ranked Ohio State Buckeyes—the "Show-down In The 'Shoe'," in prime time, in the biggest September match-up in recent college gridiron history.

Over one thousand media credentials were issued. Both ABC's studio crew and ESPN's *Game Day* were there. There were Heisman Trophy winners, celebrities, and true American heroes. The distinguished-looking fellow who boarded the elevator with his gracious wife really was John Glenn, and Jack Nicklaus was there, too, sitting in the plush suites below the massive press box.

And that is where our story begins:

"Take Dead Aim."

Nicklaus, of all people, would have known the expression and known what it meant. In 2005, the Texas football team had taken the philosophy of the late master teacher of golf, Harvey Penick, as its theme.

It was a simple plan, with a simple meaning. Choose the target, block out everything else, and Take Dead Aim.

"Blocking out" means that when things have gone badly, you push them aside mentally. It means when one thing isn't working, you try something else. It means that you concentrate your efforts, and simply refuse to be distracted from your primary object. But most of all, to activate the premise, you have to believe in yourself.

It is hard to put into perspective how history will remember this first meeting between Ohio State and Texas and the Longhorns' dramatic 25-22 come-from-behind win. By the numbers, it ranks as perhaps the most significant non-conference victory (discounting the Oklahoma game) since the 1934 Longhorns went to South Bend, Indiana, and handed Notre Dame their first home opening loss, 7-6.

For the legion of Longhorn fans who cheered Texas's meeting with Michigan in the 2005 Rose Bowl game, it offered a validation of where Brown and his staff have brought the UT program. Brown had talked of "visiting the neighborhood" of college football's elite. His team's goal, he had said, was "to buy a house there."

Ten- and eleven-win seasons over the past four years had purchased the property. The Rose Bowl had allowed the Longhorns to have an open house. That Saturday night in Columbus, they invited the whole wide world in for a party.

A day before the game, Brown had been waiting for a radio interview near the southwest corner of the stadium. He looked up and saw members of the Ohio State band arriving for practice at the north goal post, deep into the horseshoe. Brown walked the length of the field to talk to the kids.

"I'll see you guys tomorrow," he had joked. "But I'll probably be a little too busy to say hello. I want to tell you how much I admire your band and appreciate what this place means to college football." The drummers put down their sticks, and the trumpet players, who had just given a cheer that ended with "Texas sucks," sheepishly gathered around the coach and willingly accepted his compliments.

A day and a few hours later, he was in the middle of the tension, watching as the Longhorns reversed all of the precepts of the game. Eighty-one-year-old Darrell Royal, who watched from the press box as his late friend Woody Hayes was honored at halftime, would tell you that any "big game" will be decided by "turnovers and the kicking game." Although there were positives in the Longhorn kicking game, Texas lost both, and still won.

It is important to remember that sport is not a matter of life and death when pondering its significance. Our country has troops standing in harm's way, fighting to keep us safe and free. After Hurricanes Katrina and Rita, there were brave volunteers and refugees who struggled every day to survive the ravages of nature.

But sport does teach us much.

In the locker room after the game, Brown gathered his team around him. They knew that at times they had not played well, but they understood that they had played hard.

"You won," he had said, "because you never quit. Regardless of what happened, you kept coming back. You had each other, and you believed you could win. There is a lesson in life there. Keep fighting, stick together, and believe."

Standing on the bench near the north wall of the locker room, Vince Young asked to say something to his teammates.

"I just want to thank the defense," he had said. "Because when we messed up, you guys kept playing and gave us a chance to win."

People had spent up to one thousand dollars a ticket; one military pilot had taken a two-week leave from combat to come all the way from Iraq to see the game. In the dangerous al Anbar province in Western Iraq, Marines from Texas and Ohio gathered in a chapel at 3:30 in the morning to watch the game.

No, this game wasn't about a trophy or a championship, and there was much more season left for both of these outstanding teams. But what Ohio State and Texas gave us for almost four hours on Saturday night, September 10, 2005, was a respite from the troubles that seem to constantly surround us.

Brown said he would coach his team hard that following week, because you can do that after a victory, particularly one that had obviously correctable flaws. He brushed aside talk of a national championship and pointed out that it is important to look at the journey, not the destination. Each week, he told his team, will present new and different challenges. To win all the games, you must win the next one.

Ken Rucker, the new Longhorn running-backs coach who is a veteran of the coaching profession, said that what you hope for in a game like that is that it is a place "to grow from." A chance, if you will, to get better.

And the truth is, that's why football fans across the country loved the game. Because it gave us a message that if a bunch of kids on a football field can fight through adversity and come out winners, maybe we can, too.

Longhorn golf coach John Fields, who watched the game from the Texas bench, said Harvey Penick would have loved it. It really was like a round of golf.

"You start birdie-birdie-par. Then you are in trouble with a couple of double-bogeys. And you finish eagle, birdie, birdie," he said.

The heroes were many; almost every Longhorn made a play that made a difference. Limas Sweed clutched Young's touchdown pass in a catch that erased tough memories of past "almosts." Billy Pittman realized the work of the summer could be translated into immense success for him in the fall as the leading receiver. Drew Kelson dropped a sure interception early, but stripped the ball to seal the game. David Pino both believed and took dead aim on field goals and extra points that made the difference in the game.

The lines, offensive and defensive, dominated play; Michael Griffin and Aaron Harris were spectacular in leading a defense that absolutely refused to lose. When Selvin Young went out with injury, freshman Jamaal Charles stepped up. And in perhaps the most unorthodox play of the entire game, Ramonce Taylor couldn't hear his teammate's instruction to stay in the end zone on a kickoff return and somehow went from a dead stop to a thirty-five-yard return that almost broke for a touchdown.

Brown took one last look at the Horseshoe, and as the team headed to the airport for a charter flight that would get them home at five in the morning, he reminded them of what he had told them before the game.

"I want you to enjoy this, because you are going to be a part of history. Years from now, you can tell your grandkids that you played in this game, in this place."

And maybe they'll have the opportunity to tell them about believing and about the importance of choosing a target. And of taking dead aim.

They had taken the first step—a major one—in their quest.

They were on a path of goals and dreams. What we learn is that goals are stated and attainable. You set a goal to lose weight, to clean your garage by the end of the month. You choose your goals, and you can go after them.

Dreams are bigger, and they usually require you to muster help and support from others to realize them.

As Brown said later to an ABC crew doing the Missouri game two weeks later, "Somebody once said that life is like a cleaning crew...the young janitor may work quicker and harder, but the old janitor sweeps out the corners, and cleans the

whole the floor."
So there you have it: the goal is to sweep the floor.
The dream is to sweep it clean.

MB

We started working on Ohio State, along with Oklahoma, in the spring, because we knew those games were huge, and they had similar offensive philosophies. So every day we would work on the team we were preparing for that week, and then we would stick in something for Ohio State and Oklahoma without talking about it to the kids. They were working on them without knowing it. We were taking dead aim on the job that we needed to do. At the same time we were preparing for plays that were going to come up, but were not preparing for those teams.

The kids had had the best summer workouts of all our years at Texas. Summer workouts are voluntary and the kids worked better than ever for Jeff. They were working out three nights a week, throwing the ball after they had run in the heat during the day. So they had tremendous chemistry and work ethic throughout the summer. There were some early signs that this year would be different and that this group was about team and not about individuals. We had some really good seniors on this team, and those guys realized that they had a chance to accomplish something special.

We also made some changes in our fall practices, simply because of the Texas heat. Looking back over past seasons, I think we had made some mistakes in handling the intense heat. It is the nature of a coach to always worry about his kids being out of shape, and in the past we took the wrong approach because we worked them so hard early. We were listening to the wrong messages. When you want to win all the games, you consider a lot of factors. Sometimes we wonder if we're working them hard enough and as a result we probably wore them out some.

When they looked tired in the fourth quarter of a ball game, it was probably because they were exhausted, not because they hadn't worked hard. The Texas football player is fashioned in high school so that after he gets here, he is going to work. At this level, a coach has to be more careful about overworking than he does about under-working his players. So we decided to change our approach.

During the heat of two-a-days, we'd stay outside for the first hour and do all of the individual work—the throwing, the catching, and the kicking game—in the sun and in the wind. Then we'd go to the indoor facility, which is air conditioned, for the last hour of practice. Because of their summer work, they were already in great shape, and we got more work done by using this system. We had better practice sessions and did a better job of keeping fluids in them, keeping their electrolytes up, and not depleting them so much. The heat beats players down over time. It may not affect them until the third or fourth game, but if a coach wears out his team in two-a-days, it is going to take awhile before they can get the energy back.

As we approached the Ohio State trip, we tried to build from the success we had had on the road. Since the season of 1999, we had lost only two road games in our opponents' home stadiums. In a number of those games, we had to come from behind, or we had to hold off an opponent late in the game.

As we have tried to figure out the secret to our success, I think it really comes down to three things. First, have confidence and plan on winning. Second, don't panic. Too many teams, when things don't go well, turn away from what got them there. It's important to realize that the other team will likely have a surge, so be prepared to withstand it; maintain control. And finally, just keep playing. The game will come back to you if you just keep playing.

We approached the Ohio State trip by talking about the fact that it was the experience of a lifetime. We didn't hide from the magnitude of it. No one at the University of Texas had ever been there. No one at the University of Texas had ever played in that stadium. What a wonderful experience. This would be something that they could talk about that no other player in the 112 years of Texas Longhorn football had done. So it was a big event to be a part of, but it was early in the year. If we lost, we'd be fine. We could get back on track for the rest of the season.

We didn't hide from the ramifications of it, either. We reminded them that it was a non-conference game, and it was a national game. If we won, even though it was early in the season, it would immediately put us in the mix of all the stuff that would happen at the end.

We had been told by everybody that it would be loud, and even though we'd been in a lot of hostile stadiums, I don't think we had any way of realizing how loud it would be. We told the team that it would be loud, it would be tough, but most of all, it would be fun. We said, "They are really good and we have great respect for them." We showed them a picture of the Buckeyes' stadium. We talked about the history of Woody Hayes and all of the Ohio State all-Americans. We told them that there were a lot of similarities in the two universities; they're in the state capital, they're in a city similar to Austin. We said, "Guys, this is just the University of Texas up north. This is fun. You just played Michigan and beat them, and now you're playing Ohio State. Win this one and you'll be Big Ten champs."

After we had finished practicing the day before the game, we noticed that some of the Ohio State band members were coming in for their practice. We have a great band at Texas, and I have always thought the Ohio State band's "dotting of the i" is one of the great traditions in college football. I believe it is important to respect other people's traditions.

I thought it would be neat to walk down there and tell those kids that. They were pretty antagonistic as we were walking up, but before we left we were all taking pictures together. All we wanted to say was, "We really appreciate you guys and what you stand for." What a neat thing in college football for those two teams to get to meet on national TV. With all the interest and publicity surrounding this game, it's important to remember that the game is really about the kids.

The setting was wonderful at the game. The crowd is everything they say it is, and I thought the Ohio State fans treated our team, our coaching staff, and the tradition that we brought there with a lot of class.

People have asked me if I thought, when we won that game, that we had assured ourselves of a national championship. That was a little premature, but when Limas Sweed caught the ball in the end zone at the end of the game and we went ahead to win, as I was walking off the field I thought, "This team has a chance to go all the way." The game didn't decide the national championship, but I thought it might be for the right to play for it. We still had to run through our conference. But later, when Ohio State beat Notre Dame in the Fiesta Bowl and got after them pretty good, I watched and thought that two really good football teams had played in Columbus that night, and we just happened to make the last play.

The Second Goal

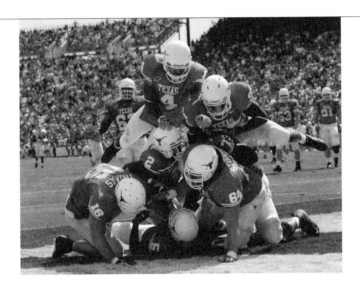

" ...AS THE BUSES CARRIED THE LONGHORN
FOOTBALL TEAM BACK OUT OF THE TEXAS
STATE FAIRGROUNDS AND ONTO THE HIGHWAY
HEADING TO DFW AIRPORT, THE SETTING SUN
WAS DEAD-SOLID BURNT ORANGE. AND WHEN IT SET,
THE SKY WAS THE DARNDEST ROSE-COLORED SUNSET
YOU EVER SAW. **"**

—Bill Little

◀ PILING ON THE POINTS – At the bottom of this pile in the Texas-Oklahoma game is receiver Billy Pittman (5) who is joined in the end zone by his teammates after scoring a touchdown on a 64-yard pass against the Sooners. Texas went on to win the game in a landslide, 45-12.

Isn't it strange how princes and kings
And clowns that caper in sawdust rings,
And common people like you and me
Are builders for eternity?

Each is given a list of rules,
A shapeless mass, and a bag of tools.
And each must make, ere life has flown,
A stumbling block or a stepping-stone.
—*R. Lee Sharpe, "A Bag of Tools"*

The Texas-Oklahoma meeting in 2005 was the one-hundredth game of a series that had begun even before Oklahoma became a state. It had been well-known as a series of streaks, and since 2000, the Sooners had owned the streak.

Several years ago, after a resounding victory in a Super Bowl, the guy who was voted MVP of the game was being interviewed in the winning locker room on national television. When the commentator asked him about his performance, his reply was classic.

"Look," he said. "I do what I do, and that fella over there," he said, pointing to a teammate, "he does what he does."

If you want to understand the "secret" of success in games like Texas and Oklahoma, there it is. This is not rocket science or brain surgery. It's really simple. Go out and "do what you do."

That had been the mantra of the Texas team that had strung together eleven straight victories, the nation's second-longest winning streak. Coaches worked hard analyzing opponents and developing game plans, and players went out and played.

That is why the speculation surrounding the upcoming meeting between Texas and Oklahoma in Dallas became amusing. Some members of the media scrambled, trying to get one team or the other to say something outrageous about its opponent. They all seemed to agree that Texas had the experience and the physical talent to win, but they pondered the "mentality" the team would bring into the Cotton Bowl.

The "streak" usually came up in interviews and in fan conversations. "Pressure" was a major word of the week. The most interesting phenomenon of the game, the winning string of one team or the other, had extended to five straight Oklahoma victories.

And what we know about streaks is that they end.

Following its victory over Ohio State, Texas beat Rice at home and then opened Big 12 Conference play with a win at Missouri. Oklahoma, on the other hand, had struggled uncharacteristically, losing to TCU and UCLA.

The annual ritual of the State Fair of Texas and the meeting of Texas and Oklahoma provided the perfect test.

In the previous five years, Oklahoma had entered the game ranked higher than Texas. Three of the last four games had gone into the fourth quarter with no more than six points separating the teams.

Excluding the Oklahoma game, Texas had lost one regular-season Big 12 football game over the last five years.

That's a record of 35-1. In the months of October and November, including games against all opponents, Texas was 32-1, excluding the losses to the Sooners. Oklahoma had gone on to play for the national championship three of the five years. In two of those, a Texas victory would have put the Longhorns in the Sooners' place.

What you had was a match of two of the great college football programs in the 2000s. In the days when this series earned its national reputation, it was unique in that it was a match-up of two powerhouses from different conferences. They met one time a year at a neutral site for bragging rights, and then went their respective ways. Oklahoma could win the Big 8 and go to the Orange Bowl; Texas could win the Southwest Conference and return to the host spot in the Cotton Bowl.

All that changed ten years ago, when the Big 12 came into existence. Not only are the teams in the same league, they are in the same South Division. For the fans, this game may be about bragging rights and streaks. For the teams, it had been about more than that, and that was particularly so for Texas in 2005.

We've talked about this before. Streaks, momentum changes, the power of the pendulum that swings back and forth across the Red River at this annual October classic—all of those subplots of a common football game come down to one thing: the best team usually wins.

Going into Saturday's game in Dallas, Texas knew it, Oklahoma knew it, and before it was over, the whole world knew it.

By the time the final snap was done on the floor of the ancient stadium and the Longhorns had won, 45-12, it truly was all over but the shouting.

The day had begun with the Longhorns boarding buses at their hotel in Richardson, having heard Brown's final comments about the game. Newspapers and electronic-media outlets had set the tone with a week's worth of coverage reminding Texas of its recent frustrations, and the fact that this was an historic one-hundredth meeting between the two schools in the two states separated most of the way by the Red River.

And much of the conversation focused on "the streak."

Ah, the streak. Five straight games. Everyone wanted to help. Former players and caring parties all stepped up and offered to talk to the team. Surely somebody could say something that would be profound.

But what we know about streaks, if you are on the wrong side of them, is that you don't need talk, and you don't need reminding. Streaks end when the losing side gets fed up with hearing about it. And they end when you have a better team than the other guys.

The Longhorns knew all of that as they boarded buses to head to the Cotton Bowl down Central Expressway that Saturday. The reminders came all too frequently along the way. Actually, to put it into perspective, it was pretty much a ride to the office at the beginning, but when the buses turned off the expressway and headed toward the fairgrounds, business picked up.

The Texas-Oklahoma game in the Cotton Bowl has always been a collage of sights. To their credit, hopeful Longhorn fans were much in evidence, flanked by red-clad Sooners who held one hand high with five fingers, and the other with the Hook 'em 'Horns sign pointed downward. If the football team needed a reminder, it was conveniently provided by the opponent.

Because of the State Fair and the field preparations, the two teams never go to the stadium on Friday for a "walk through," so when the team arrived at the stadium on Saturday, Vince Young led a small contingent of players in street clothes to the field to loosen up. Television cameramen, already stationed at their posts two hours before the game, caught Young and his teammates grooving to their iPods. The guys who had been labeled "uptight" before this game in years past were "chillin'."

Two hours later, Texas lost the only thing it would fail to win that day, and that was the coin toss. So they took the opening kickoff and drove the length of the field. Young hit a leaping Ramonce Taylor for the first touchdown of the game.

When Young hit Billy Pittman in full stride with a perfect pass just before the half, the hunt was, for all practical purposes, over. The defense was stifling, the kicking game effective, and the offense varied and vicious.

Only the final score was in doubt, and the defense punctuated that with Brian Robison's hit and Rod Wright's long touchdown run with the fumble.

Brown said afterward that this game was never about him, but that he was happy and proud for the Texas fans and the Longhorn team. By Sunday, radio talk shows in Oklahoma were accusing their coaches of being "too conservative." They were calling for the offensive coordinator's job, proclaiming that such a performance was unacceptable, and were even questioning the ability of the Sooner strength coach.

The immense irony, of course, was that those were the same issues that chat boards and radio talk shows had maligned the Longhorns for during the aftermath of the past five games.

Brown, who is now 3-5 against Oklahoma, stayed above all of that in the postgame media conferences. Like the Ohio State victory earlier in the year, there was little time to enjoy this one. One more time, the theme of the season came into play: Texas had to put the victory behind them and "Take Dead Aim" at the upcoming target.

In contrast to the non-conference game the 'Horns played after beating the Buckeyes in the Horseshoe, Saturday's Big 12 opponent Colorado was hot and formidable. Texas Tech followed that, then road trips to Oklahoma State and Baylor.

For the last five years, the Oklahoma game had forced Texas to play catch-up for the rest of the season. Now the slate was clean. The challenge Brown and his staff had conquered so well—putting a loss to the Sooners behind them—now switched to putting the victory behind them.

One of the stated goals of this Longhorn team had been to win the Big 12 South, and to get its first league championship since the inaugural one in 1996.

As the buses drove away from the stadium, fans dressed in burnt orange celebrated. Most of the people dressed in red had departed, save for one soul who tottered back and forth as he stared blankly at the buses and held up six fingers. Obviously, he had missed something.

This much we know is true: late in the afternoon, as the buses carried the Longhorn football team back out of the Texas State Fairgrounds and onto the highway heading to DFW Airport, the rain and the clouds, which had frequented the evenings in recent Octobers past, were nowhere to be seen. The setting sun was dead-solid burnt orange. And when it set, the sky was the darndest rose-colored sunset you ever saw. The Longhorns had played five games, including two that will be remembered for a long time in UT history: the win over Ohio State and the victory in the one-hundredth game of the OU series. All of that was important.

But when you choose to play at the level Texas was seeking, your most important game is your next.

MB

Because we hadn't beaten OU in five years, the pressure on our kids made that game big. Oklahoma had struggled early in the season, but they had gotten better leading up to that game. Besides, this is a true rivalry and in rivalry games, you can throw out the rankings and records.

The Texas-Oklahoma game was one of the reasons I came to Texas. When I coached at Oklahoma in 1984, it had made an impact on me. I thought it was one of the great traditions in college football, and I wanted to be a part of it again.

This year, the game was as much about overcoming a hurdle as it was about just beating Oklahoma. It was something that had kept us from getting to where we wanted to go. I talked to Coach Royal about how streaks stopped and he said, "When you're good enough, and your team gets tired of getting beat by that same team."

I think that's what happened. We were better than Oklahoma, and our team was tired of losing that game. And the dominating way that we won also sent a message that this wasn't just a team that wanted to beat Oklahoma, this was a team that wanted to be really, really good and continue to grow.

The telecast of the game featured that shot of Vince and some of the players enjoying their music while they were loosening up at the stadium before the game.

A lot was made out of my iPod and music, as if we'd all reached some special level because of the music we listened to. That had all begun when I walked through the locker room one day and they were playing music that I didn't think was appropriate. That is when our conversations started, and two very valuable things came out of our discussions. First, it was important that the players understood that even though they believe everybody listens to music that talks about beating up women and police officers and is very vulgar and talks about sex and drugs, that doesn't mean it's okay. And as the fifty-four-year-old head coach at The University of Texas, I cannot condone them listening to that around me, because it's not who I am, and they know that's not who I am.

At the same time, I had to reach out and say, "Let's find something that will fit your needs that's conducive to what we want to achieve here." We cared enough to say, "Let's talk...there's a common ground here that helps you and that helps our team," instead of saying, "To heck with you; we're not doing it. Put it up and I don't want to hear about it again." So they came up with an instrumental that they could play in pregame that still accomplished what they wanted, but it didn't have the vulgar language.

That probably was one of the huge communication and trust builders for our team. It carried over to the practice field, because we started letting them have the music in pre-practice. They ended up finding stuff that would work, and by the Rose Bowl, some guys had actually written some songs specifically for the team.

It never really was about the music. It was more about communication. Young people will cry out, "Listen to me," in a lot of ways, and it's a coach's responsibility to hear them. From our standpoint, we tried to get them to understand that just because that was the music they listened to in the dorm or on their iPods, that didn't mean their girlfriends or their mothers should hear it, and it might not be best for them, either, in the long run. I believe this...they won't want their children listening to it.

After the way we played in the Oklahoma game, I thought we had a great chance to play for it all and go to the Rose Bowl. The OU game had been such an emotional stumbling block, not just a physical one. I felt that, until we took care of our business there, it was easy to talk about it, but the guys had to do it. We had a long way to go, but to that point, the team had done everything we had asked of it.

We had broken the season down into separate parts. The first part
ended with the Ohio State game, the second with Oklahoma. Now we
were facing a conference run that included Colorado, which appeared to
be the best team in the North Division, Texas Tech, which would be
ranked in the top ten, and trips to Oklahoma State and Baylor before our
final home game with Kansas.

After Kansas, we had a weekend off before we played Texas A&M,
and we hoped to end with a trip to Reliant Stadium for the Big 12
Championship game.

A lot of people kept trying to make the Oklahoma game a competition between Bob Stoops and me, but it never was about us. I have great
respect for what Bob has done at Oklahoma, and I have great memories
and good friends from my time as an assistant there.

When I got to Texas, we won the first two games in the series and
then lost five. We had our chances in most of those five, but we didn't get
it done. This team wanted to make a statement, and they did. Now it was
time to go back to our theme. It was time to put that victory behind us
and "Take Dead Aim" on Colorado.

The Third Goal

**"THE MARK OF A GREAT TEAM IS TO HAVE
THE CONFIDENCE AND THE ABILITY
TO COME FROM BEHIND."**

—Mack Brown

◀ HOLD ON THERE, FELLA — Longhorn defensive end Brian Robison (39) separates the ball and the jersey from Texas Tech quarterback Cody Hodges in a top ten match up in Austin. The Longhorns wrecked the Red Raiders' aerial game and came away with a 52-17 victory in a battle of unbeatens.

BL

In the mountains of Montana, in historic Glacier National Park, there is a highway called the "Going-to-the-Sun" road. It is, without question, one of the most scenic passages in America.

Tours through the park and up the narrow road are conducted in unique buses, built in the 1930s by the White Motor Company and refurbished for use in the 21st century. When the driver rolls back the canvas top of the red bus, the tourists in the half-dozen or so rows of the big sedan have a panoramic view of some of nature's most spectacular displays.

Ahead are the majestic, snowcapped peaks of the Rocky Mountains; to the side are infinite canyons, with a valley seemingly miles away, veiled in a blue-gray mist.

On a crystal-clear, late-spring morning, you will begin a tour that will take you most of the day. The sights are amazing, and the journey is worth the ride. The secret of success is the driver. A good one can point out the bears in the forest and the white mountain goats hidden in the snow, or note the awesome glaciers of another millennium and pause at the reflection in the stone-still lake—all the while keeping his or her eyes on the road.

A wrong turn, and the whole deal is history.

As Texas turned past the Oklahoma game, that is exactly the kind of path the Longhorns were traveling. With six regular-season games remaining, Texas was on the high mountain road. In fact, following the victory over unbeaten Texas Tech, a nationally recognized ranking—the BCS—had Texas as number one for the first time since 1984. And while percentage points and rankings in the BCS changed weekly, the standings for the week of October 24 were significant. It was validation of a program that had worked very hard to get to where it was.

The Texas football staff had broken the 2005 schedule into several "mini-seasons." The first had ended with Ohio State, the second with Oklahoma. Now there was a five-game stretch, all against Big 12 Conference schools, which would carry them all the way up to the week off before the Texas A&M game.

Since the beginning of the season, Southern California had been ranked number one and Texas number two in every national poll. The weekend of October 15, Texas returned to Austin after its big win in Dallas and prepared for a Colorado team that had overcome a lot of obstacles to be the power in the North Division of the league over the last several years. There were concerns as to how Texas would respond after the emotional victory over Oklahoma, but when the lights of the UT Tower turned orange at the end of the day on October 15, signifying victory, it marked an ironic difference from exactly one year before.

The Sunday morning newspapers and the television sports-news reports featured raves of quarterback Vince Young's impressive performance in the Longhorns' 42-17 victory over Colorado. One year prior, a segment of fans and a lot of reporters were projecting his impending move to wide receiver.

Young's "lights out" performance against Colorado, when he hit twenty-five of twenty-nine passes for 336 yards and two touchdowns, and ran for fifty-eight yards and three more scores, began a string of successes that would take his already growing legend to immense heights.

When the Colorado game ended, Texas fans and the Longhorn team in the locker room found themselves glued to television sets as their new national rival, Southern Cal, struggled with Notre Dame. In fact, when the Irish took a late lead and SC faced a fourth and nine deep in their own territory, it looked for a moment as though the Longhorns might move to number one. But when the Trojans rallied and scored as the game ended for a 34-31 victory, the two titans of 2005 remained number one and number two, on a collision course for Pasadena.

The win over Colorado—which had begun the "third season" of the year—coupled with Florida State's loss to Virginia moved Mack Brown past Bobby Bowden to number one in the NCAA's winningest coaches over the last ten years.

The next week was show time on the UT campus, as ABC's national crew and ESPN's *Game Day* and *Cold Pizza* shows arrived for the game of the number two-ranked Longhorns against the number-ten Red Raiders of Texas Tech. It was a battle of the unbeaten, but it didn't take the Longhorns long to dispatch the Raiders, and when Texas rolled over Texas Tech, it appeared that the way to the Big 12 championship game would be smooth sailing—that is, until a trip to Stillwater to play Oklahoma State the next week.

With Colorado and Tech disposed of, the Longhorns were heavily favored over Oklahoma State, Baylor, Kansas, and Texas A&M. But the Cowboys had other ideas. Historically, the Longhorns had not played well in Stillwater, and sure enough, it was happening again.

Oklahoma State, a team that had struggled without a Big 12 victory, had jumped to a nineteen-point first-half lead at 28-9. For the Longhorns to overcome it, they would have to erase a deficit equal to the second biggest they had ever overcome. David Pino's field goal as time expired in the half cut the margin down to 16, but Texas realistically needed three scores to lead.

A year before in Austin, a much more powerful Oklahoma State team had jumped to a 35-7 lead, only to have Texas erase that and win 56-35. In a halftime TV interview, Brown had seemed calm and upbeat. He believed in his kids, who somehow blended talent with pride and emotion just at the right times.

But none of that would matter if Texas couldn't move the ball against an inspired Cowboy defense that had frustrated the Longhorns in the first half.

Vince Young knew this as he brought his team to the line of scrimmage on the third play of the second half before a frenzied crowd at Boone Pickens Stadium. He dropped back, headed right, pump-faked a Cowboy defender off his feet, and took off down the sideline.

On the sidelines, Mack Brown looked at the down-and-distance marker. When he saw Young break past the line of scrimmage, he remarked in the headset to Davis, "He's going to get the first down." Davis, who had a full view of the play from the press box, replied, "Oh, he's gonna get a lot more than that."

He covered the eighty yards in just thirty-six steps, an amazing average of six feet, eight inches per stride. That's like stepping over a prone Limas Sweed, with room to spare with every stride. The run set the tempo for the second half, which would result in a Longhorn landslide of thirty-eight unanswered points and a 47-28 victory.

Throughout the week, Brown had warned that the Longhorns traditionally had experienced slow starts in games with Oklahoma State. Texas had trailed, 16-14, at halftime in Stillwater in 2003 before rallying to a 55-16 victory.

The record for the Cowboys against ranked teams included stunners in 2001 and 2002 over archrival Oklahoma. This season, first-year coach Mike Gundy rebuilt his team after key losses to graduation and to a strong stance he took on some discipline issues. Then injuries took a heavy toll. Turnovers plagued the offense.

But Saturday, for one half of football, everything fell into place. Two blocked kicks, a surprise play, a freak bounce of a pass that turned into a touchdown, and a couple of Longhorn turnovers had Texas on the Cowboys' heels. In the dressing room, Brown and his staff simply went to work. Where in 2004, Brown had prophetically written a score of "42-35" on the board when UT trailed 35-14 at intermission, this time there was no such drama. The coaches made adjustments, and players recognized mistakes and developed a plan. When they came out of the locker room, Oklahoma State entered from a walkway outside the OSU basketball arena, Gallagher-Iba Hall, which is located at the east end of the stadium. Texas came out of the same area. The Cowboys were surprised by what they saw.

Here was the number-one team in the BCS, trailing by nineteen points, with only thirty minutes of football left to play. They had been outplayed by OSU, and some teams would have been uptight with the pressure of the moment.

The Texas players, instead, were singing.

"Keep them focused," Greg Davis had said to his star quarterback as he left the locker room to return to the press box.

"We're fine, baby," Vince had said.

Going into the week, Brown had reminded his team that their season theme of "Take Dead Aim" now had an interesting twist to it. "Right now, you've got a bull's-eye on your chest, and everybody is going to be 'taking dead aim' at you," he said.

Oklahoma State fired the first arrow. Baylor, Kansas, and Texas A&M would follow during the regular season, each understanding that a victory over Texas would make their season.

"Right now, we're everybody's national championship game," Brown said.

The Oklahoma State game was a wake-up call for Texas, and with easy victories over Baylor and Kansas, the 'Horns went on to clinch their goal of winning the Big 12 South.

The Longhorns had learned a hard lesson: they had reached a pivotal point in the season—the danger of traversing the road and the mountain really isn't just about getting there, it is about staying there. We all know if you are going up stairs, it is important to look where you are stepping rather than at the top.

That is why the story of the Red Bus and the mountain is so important. The driver knew where she was headed, and even took the time to enjoy the ride. But she also made sure she kept the bus on the road. At the peak, the highway was narrow, the safety shoulders were non-existent, and it was a straight drop of over one thousand feet to the bottom.

It could have been scary, but it wasn't, and that is the key to all of this. The purpose was to have fun, to enjoy the ride, and to stay on course.

MB

The longer you coach, the more you realize that your teams are going to be in trouble in two or three games each year. The mark of a great team is to have the confidence and the ability to come from behind. All season long, I believed we had a great chance to get to the Rose Bowl, and I thought we would play Southern Cal. When USC faced that fourth and nine against Notre Dame, I wasn't so sure. But when they pulled it out, I knew they'd be there. It was now up to us to get there.

It was pointless to tell our team not to think about Southern Cal, because everybody in the country kept talking about the match-up. So we came up with a way to include them in our thoughts without ignoring our opponents. We told the team that they needed to play to a standard. Halfway across the country, Southern Cal was putting up impressive numbers and adding to a winning streak that led the nation. So we told the team that we needed to play to a standard, the standard that SC was setting.

We still stressed "Take Dead Aim" on our opponents, but we allowed ourselves to think about the end in the midst of the season.

The Oklahoma State game was probably the game that scared me the most. It had been a hard place for us to play. We'd had close games there every year, and there had been a couple in Austin that we really struggled to win. This time, OSU had not played very well. They were talented, but had turned the ball over a lot, and that always scares me. They can be dangerous if they don't do that. It was a night game, and night games on the road are always troublesome because they make for a long day. It was also right after we'd played a lot of exciting games, and people weren't talking about this game very much.

At that point, they were still buzzing about the way we handled

Colorado and Tech, and the Notre Dame-Southern Cal game had made people think that the Trojans were vulnerable.

Our fans were already into the Rose Bowl. We had people making hotel reservations for Pasadena as soon as the Ohio State game was over, and after the Oklahoma game they were buying plane tickets for L.A. The year before, we'd come from behind and beaten Oklahoma State so easily that I did not think they had our full attention that week in practice, and I was right.

Even down 28-9, there was an amazing calm about our team. It was like, "Can you believe this? It's happened again, and we've allowed it." It was unique and unusual, and even though it seemed a devastating blow at the time, it was funny. And when the ball bounced up in the air at the same place on the field on the same hash mark as the year before and they caught it and ran it in for a touchdown after two of our guys should have intercepted it...that's when we said, "Okay, we gotcha." We knew we had better go to work and play here, because this was exactly the same scenario as last year.

That was a huge building block, because at halftime our coaches and our players did not panic, and we went back to work. It was really weird that everybody in the stadium seemed to think we were going to win the game.

I heard somebody say that when you know you're good, you're right, and if you're unsure, you're right, too. And the Longhorns knew they were good. But they didn't take the reasons they were good for granted, and those were their work ethic, their character, and their confidence. They knew they could continue to do what got them there. You're going to be behind, and you're going to be behind in the fourth quarter, and your ability to come back and win those games makes the difference between the really good teams and the great teams.

The Final Steps

❝ON THE DAY WHEN IT'S NOT YOUR BEST DAY, YOU STILL HAVE TO GO TO WORK. AND ON THAT DAY, IT OFTEN ISN'T ABOUT SKILL OR TALENT OR SIZE OR STRENGTH...WHEN YOU WANT SOMETHING BADLY ENOUGH, YOU SOMETIMES JUST HAVE TO PLAY WITH YOUR HEART.❞

—Bill Little

◀ SEMPER FI – Fullback Ahmard Hall (46) scores a first half touchdown to give the Longhorns the lead in their annual battle with Texas A&M in College Station. Hall, a former Marine, became a true American hero because of his service in the Middle East and his success story as a walk-on who became a starter and a team captain.

BL

For a handful of change and a degree of determination, you could buy a kite at Mr. Middlebrook's five-and-dime store on Main Street. It was a simple package: a sturdy piece of paper with string sealed around the edges, with just enough twine protruding from each corner to serve as hooks.

The infrastructure, if you want to call it that, consisted of two thin pieces of balsa wood, with notches on the ends to fit into the hooks. The paper was wrapped around the sticks, and you didn't have to be a structural engineer to bind the wood into a "t" and secure the paper.

As the winds of winter gave way to the breezes of spring, the grass on the playground at the elementary school was fighting to turn from brown to green, and when the rains didn't come, the grass lost the battle.

The most popular kite of the day was red, white, and blue, in keeping with the theme of patriotism common in the '50s. But as a kid, I remember asking my Dad a simple but important question. With blind faith and significant hope, I somehow knew the breezes of nature would get the kite off the ground.

What I wanted to know was, "How high will it fly?"

As the Texas Longhorns secured their fourth Big 12 South Division trophy in Mack Brown's eight years at Texas, that question, which had been strictly speculative for an entire season, now became very real. Midway through the month of November, after an impressive Veterans' Day recognition at the Kansas game, Texas had earned the first of what would become an extensive collection of award hardware. But no one, not the team nor the coaches nor the fans nor the media, could gauge exactly how good the team really was. They had won close and won big, and had brushed away all challenges.

While the Longhorns got a well-earned weekend off on November 19, Southern Cal was in a battle for survival.

Three time zones away, Joe Paterno's Penn State Nittany Lions stayed up until the wee hours, hoping for an upset that could thrust them into the championship game, as Fresno State took the defending national champions to the limit. But once again, Southern Cal survived, coming from behind for a 50-42 victory that wasn't decided until well after 2 A.M. on the East Coast.

Now, the magic number for the two teams to reach Pasadena was down to just three wins. Southern Cal had its annual cross-town match with UCLA on December 3, and Texas had to get by archrival Texas A&M at College Station and then the Big 12 Championship game in Reliant Stadium. At that point, the opponent from the North Division was undetermined. The Longhorns had thought it would be Colorado, but Iowa State and Missouri both were in contention late in the season.

But the Longhorns had to focus their full attention on Texas A&M.

For two weeks, all the media had talked about was how Texas was going to humiliate Texas A&M. What we know about the game of college football is that good players don't get into it without having pride. For two weeks, all the Aggies heard was how cruddy they were. And when it seems the whole world is against you, you have to prove it wrong, if only to save your pride.

Even more, Texas A&M, which was 5-5, knew it could salvage far more than just a trip to a mid-level bowl game with a victory. It could establish itself as one of the most memorable teams in school history…the team that knocked its archrival out of the national championship race.

It was the opportunity of an age: if they won, their names would be remembered with those of the greatest of Aggies.

Texas, on the other hand, was heading into a trap. Despite its record, Texas A&M had excellent football players, top recruits who had come with dreams, just like the Longhorns.

It is really hard to win all the games. Both Darrell Royal and Fred Akers had told Mack Brown so during the past two weeks. Brown understood it. He had seen his own hopes dashed by Florida State and Oklahoma over the last ten years. He had heard about how the 1961 Texas team lost to TCU, 6-0, when the Frogs crossed the fifty-yard line just once, on a flea-flicker pass. He knew that Royal's 1959 Cotton Bowl-bound team trailed Texas A&M, 10-0 at halftime, before rallying to win.

He had heard how the 1963 national champions survived in the mud in College Station, 15-13. He knew Royal had made his famous halftime move in 1965 when, trailing 17-0 at Kyle Field, he wrote the final winning score of 21-17 on a chalkboard as intermission ended. And he knew the last Texas team to go unbeaten through the regular season, the 1983 Longhorns, had trailed the Aggies 13-0 before coming from behind to win, 45-13.

The oldest of the Longhorn followers even remembered 1941, when number-one Texas saw their national championship hopes dashed by a tie with Baylor and a loss to TCU.

There is an old rodeo saying: "There never was a hoss that couldn't be rode… there never was a cowboy that couldn't be throwed."

All of that they knew, and all of that was true.

But when Texas jumped to a 14-0 lead in the first quarter, it appeared to be just another day at the office.

"They'll hang half a hundred on them," folks had predicted, and Texas was on its way.

But college football games are not played with computers, and sometimes the human factor, call it biorhythms or whatever, just won't cooperate with the predictors. That is when things get dicey; that is when upsets are born.

It was not the best of days for the Longhorns, but it revealed what this team was all about. Suddenly, after what appeared to be a routine beginning, the game was turning out differently than anyone expected. With only four minutes left in the first half, Texas trailed, 15-14, and faced third and seven at the Aggie fourteen, and that was only because Limas Sweed had scrambled to recover a Vince Young fumble that could have ended the drive.

At that point, offensive coordinator Greg Davis did what any red-blooded American would do. He sent in the Marines. And there, wide open in the right flat, was Sergeant Ahmard Hall, who took Young's pass and ran untouched for fourteen yards into the end zone for the go-ahead score.

Hall had been one of the best stories in 2005 college football. He was a Marine who had served in Afghanistan and Kosovo, a walk-on who earned both a scholarship and a starting position as the Longhorns' fullback. The scoring play and Ahmard are particularly important here, because his is the first name you hear from a stable of unsung heroes who stepped up to help bail out their team on a day when teamwork would prove to be crucial.

Rashad Babino, who was not the tallest of the Longhorn linebackers, knocked away a pass and then took a fake field goal on fourth down for a first down on a drive that would overcome A&M's second lead in the game. With the Longhorns clinging to a 34-29 lead late in the third quarter, there was Young hooking up with that Marine again, and this time Hall fought for twenty-five yards to set up David Pino's field goal, which took the cushion to eight points at 37-29.

In a game where field position was so important, it would be redshirt freshman Ryan Palmer who would scratch and claw and recover a fumbled punt that helped turn the field around in the fourth quarter.

Young would be the first to give credit to his teammates. On a day that was not his best, he did what a quarterback is supposed to do: he led his team to victory. Texas didn't reach the "half a hundred," but when you score forty points against your rival on the road and win by eleven, it's not a bad day.

In the locker room after the game, Libby Wright, the president of the Tournament of Roses in Pasadena, told the Longhorns she was proud of them, and she hoped they would win their next game. Then they could come back to the site of the "miracle of the valley" when the Longhorns beat Michigan on January 1 to start their amazing run.The State Farm people gave Texas the trophy for the "Showdown" between the two schools, and one more time, the Texas Longhorns sang "Texas Fight," as they do after every victory.

For eleven football games, this team had answered every challenge. It was the first unbeaten regular season for UT in twenty-two years, and only the sixth in the last eighty years. It is, after all, hard to win all the games.

There are moments in games and in life when you have to go to Plan B. On the day when it's not your best day, you still have to go to work. And on that day, it often isn't about skill or talent or size or strength, although those are certainly

207

qualities which sustain you. When you want something badly enough, you some-times just have to play with your heart.

With only Texas and Southern Cal unbeaten, and ranked as the number-two and number-one teams in the country, the Longhorns met and overcame the trap that had been set for them. Now there was one last hurdle remaining—the Big 12 Championship.

At the beginning of the Big 12 a decade before, it had seemed so easy. Texas was a twenty-one-point underdog to Nebraska, and the Longhorns surprised the nation with a dramatic victory in St. Louis in the first-ever Big 12 Championship game.

Twice in the Mack Brown era, Texas had represented the South Division in the game. Both times, they lost the rematch with a team they had beaten during the regular season. First, it was Nebraska in San Antonio in 1999, and then there was the devastating loss to Colorado in 2001, with the national championship game and the Rose Bowl within their sights.

Four years later, Colorado had again won the North Division, almost by default. The Buffaloes had lost to Nebraska, seemingly giving the right to represent the North to Iowa State, but the Cyclones were beaten by Kansas in their final game. To that point, Gary Barnett and his team had been survivors. Despite off-the-field turmoil, the team had pulled together and played some solid football. Colorado had played in the championship game four of the last five years.

Media speculation noted the similarities between 2005 and 2001, when Texas easily handled the Buffaloes during the regular season, only to fall in the championship game.

By now, the conversation of goals and dreams and taking dead aim was all pointed at the championship game. The archery target was adjusted, with the words "Big 12 Championship" forming a ring around the bull's-eye, which now had a rose in the middle of it.

Matthew McConaughey, the actor and former Longhorn who has been such a supporter of his alma mater, stopped by practice on the Thursday before the Longhorns left for Houston. "Get your goal," he had said, "and then go after your dream."

It was the first time that the correlation between season-long goals and an ultimate dream had been presented to the team.

In Houston, the Longhorns were housed at the Renaissance Greenway Plaza Hotel, a property that has stood the test of time. Longhorn teams in the late 1970s had stayed there, when it was under different ownership.

The top floor of the hotel once housed one of Houston's coolest nightspots, a bar with music and dancing that offered a panoramic view of the city's skyline. But in 1983, Hurricane Alicia had taken away the glass windows and most of the top floor of the hotel. When remodeling was complete, the hotel used the space for a banquet room instead.

Early on the morning of December 3, 2005, as the Texas Longhorns ate their pregame meal prior to the noon kickoff of the Big 12 Championship game, a strange phenomenon occurred. As the sun rose in the east and fog hugged the bayous of the city, in an opening in the cloudbank, Reliant Stadium seemed to rise as a castle on a hill.

The target was right there in front of them. And that day, they answered the question about how good they really could be, crushing Colorado, 70-3. In California, Southern Cal completed its season with a rout of UCLA. The yearlong quest of both schools was finished, and the path to the national championship game was now complete.

MB

First, we knew we would be in for a fight in College Station. Texas had had enough near-misses there that some of our fans were on edge because of the Aggie game. There were a lot of uncertain issues as we began to prepare for them. Reggie McNeal, their senior quarterback, had gotten hurt, and it wasn't known if he would play. We had already earned the South Division championship, but even though we would be playing for the conference championship, none of it would have been complete without a win at Kyle Field.

The Texas-Texas A&M game has always been the game that all Texans talk about on Thanksgiving weekend. So as unique as the Oklahoma game is as a border rivalry, the in-state rivalry has been, and will always be, with Texas A&M. Therefore, with all of the great things that were on the line in the future, this game meant more than anything to the Texas fans.

I thought the final two games, the Texas-Texas A&M game and the Big 12 Championship, gave us some insight as to how good this team really was. When we go to A&M and win 40-29 and we're disappointed and our fan base is disappointed, that tells you something. It's been hard for Texas to win at Kyle Field over the last twenty or so years. But I thought the concern was a good message: we had better get back on track; we had better quit talking about SC and the Rose Bowl; we had better talk about Colorado and the championship game. Our team now had full focus.

The Texas A&M game is always very special to me, because I've developed a lot of good friends who are Aggies. Before the game, I had a chance to visit with Gene Stallings, one of the great coaches in our sport, with John David Crow, and with former President Bush, whose presidential library is on the A&M campus. We found some common bonds with Texas A&M when they had the bonfire tragedy, and I think we all saw then that this particular rivalry is one of respect.

I was also pleased that Ahmard Hall wound up scoring our go-ahead touchdown. A young man who went to the Marines out of high school, he took a hard path through Afghanistan and Kosovo to get here, and he got here on his own and walked on. We didn't know who he was. He was a linebacker, and we moved him to fullback. We really didn't plan on him playing much, other than on special teams. But he not only became a significant team member and a leader, he also became a unanimous choice for captain.

At a time when war is real, he taught us that we had better enjoy a game, because it is not war; he lived the war. We learned more from Ahmard and his experiences than we taught him. We'd actually called the play that he scored on before, but the ball didn't go to him. This was a year when we didn't use the fullback in that role a lot. But it was fitting that when we needed a tough guy to turn the momentum in a ball game, we went to him. When you've been to war in the Middle East, I don't think a third and four at Kyle Field is tough. So I promise you, he didn't feel pressure.

We were glad to be playing the Big 12 Championship game in Houston. The last times we'd lost the championship games, we were in front of our fans in San Antonio and Texas Stadium in Arlington. So this was really important for our fans, because we had not played like we wanted to in those two games.

They were games, especially the Colorado game, which had earmarked our program. We were the winningest program in college football over the last eight years, but the kids and the coaches still didn't get the credit because of a game, the 2001 Colorado game.

We had played Rice in Reliant in 2003, so some of our kids had had a chance to play there, and we had a lot of players from Houston who were going home.

As the game approached, I was concerned because I felt like Colorado had a chance to be really good. They were sound and well-coached, and even though we did some exceptional things in Austin against Colorado, I didn't want to underestimate them. They had a chance to beat Miami, and if they hadn't blown a couple of games because of turnovers, they would have been 9-2. They had lost a tough game that embarrassed them against Nebraska, and usually you play your best right after you get embarrassed.

But Colorado had so many distractions surrounding their program that they didn't play well. It got out of hand, and we were as dominant a football team as I have ever seen. It was over so quickly, and the outcome was decided so early, that I really struggled as it came to an end. Gary Barnett and his wife have been good friends of Sally's and mine. I felt for him and his job at a time when it should have been a euphoric moment for me. We had finally won the conference championship and had completed an unbeaten regular season. I was really proud of our coaches and our kids, but I felt compassion for the other coach. As I said, this is not a war.

We sat at breakfast that morning and we looked out the window and saw Reliant Stadium sitting there in the fog. We were able to turn to the guys and say, "That's the target you've been aiming for since the spring. There it is; it's in your sights. Let's go get it." We had taken dead aim and, as Matthew had said, gotten our goal. Back in Austin, Roy Spence of the advertising agency GSD&M wanted to help us all celebrate the moment, so he did a tremendous job of creating a "Live The Dream" campaign, which will be something that we'll all remember for the rest of our lives.

The Dream

❝THE FOURTH-AND-TWO PLAY WHERE WE HELD THEM WILL GO DOWN IN UT HISTORY. OUR GUYS DECIDED AT THAT MOMENT THAT THEY WERE GOING TO WIN THE NATIONAL CHAMPIONSHIP. ❞

—Mack Brown

◄ RUN FOR THE ROSES – Quarterback Vince Young (10) breaks behind the blocking of Jonathan Scott (73) and Justin Blalock (63) in the 2005 BCS National Championship game victory over Southern Cal in the 2006 Rose Bowl. Young was named the offensive MVP in the game as he rushed for 200 yards and passed for 267 yards in the 41-38 victory.

A s the American Airlines jet roared off the runway in Dallas toward New York's LaGuardia International Airport, things seemed eerily the same, and yet they were so different.

DeLoss and Mary Ann Dodds sat beside each other, directly across the aisle from Mack and Sally Brown. The destination, as it had been exactly twelve months before, was the Hall of Fame dinner of the National College Football Foundation. The weather in New York would be chilly, with light rain. A car would be waiting to take the Texas party to their hotel.

Had it been only a year?

One year before, Brown and Dodds had left the ground hoping that Texas would edge past California and get a BCS bid.

Several times during the flight, air phone calls were made to try to find out what had happened. Finally, when the big jet touched down in New York, Dodds turned his cell phone on and got the message.

"We're in," he had said to Brown. "You're playing Michigan in the Rose Bowl."

In retrospect, it was one of the most important moments in Brown's thirty-two-year coaching career. After years of excellence, Mack Brown and his 2004 Longhorn team had a chance to step straight into the limelight in the most famous venue in college sports, the Rose Bowl.

In the span of the next twenty-five or so days, Texas linked its grand tradition with that of the tradition-rich Rose Bowl. In its first-ever trip there, in its first-ever game against Michigan, history would be made. Dusty Mangum would kick that game-winning field goal, and Vince Young would run and pass himself straight into the national college-football limelight.

In the end, Texas would have the 38 and Michigan the 37, and the ghosts that linger in the canyons of the Arroyo Seco would smile and say, "Well done."

There was immense irony about it all, because the 2004 Longhorn football team was fraught with miracles. You always knew they would somehow have one left, and sure enough, they did. But the greatest coincidence of all was how the Longhorns, a group hooked together with a special bond of love, wound up in the Rose Bowl, which had as its theme "Celebrate Family."

213

Brown and Dodds didn't need to wait for phone calls on the ride this year. The Longhorns' team plane returning from Houston had circled the burnt-orange Tower on its way into Bergstrom International Airport. This year, "Big 12" referred not only to a conference; it stood for the twelve wins this unbeaten team had put together as well.

That was slammed home with an exclamation point in the 70-3 victory over Colorado in the league championship game. Now, as they waited for their bags in the same area where they had made excited phone calls a year ago, they knew their destination.

On the podium accepting the trophy for the win over Michigan and for being the game's Most Valuable Player, Vince Young had said it first: "We'll be back."

That, of course, meant more than just another trip to a BCS bowl in California. Young and his teammates had their sights set on the national championship game, which in its rotation between the Orange, Fiesta, Sugar, and Rose bowls, fell to the Rose in 2005.

Since early in this season, the college football world—excluding, of course, opponents and those who had designs on crashing the party—had hoped for this match-up. For three months, Southern California had been number one and Texas number two in most ratings. Week after week, the two teams, both sporting ever-growing winning streaks, answered every challenge.

The much-maligned BCS, which had been Texas's frustration for the first four seasons of the 21st century, finally looked as if it had a chance to work. As Texas and Southern Cal prevailed, others fell from the ranks of the unbeaten.

"It would be," wrote a Chicago columnist, "what every college sports fan has dreamed of...a game for the ages."

And sure enough, as Brown headed to a national television appearance, here it was. Brown was the first to spread the praise for all of this, and it was, indeed, about a tremendously talented group of Longhorn football players and a coaching and support staff who worked every day of their professional lives for this chance. He would also be the first to say that nobody in burnt orange wanted to stop just yet.

It had been about goals and dreams—how goals are visible, attainable things. The Big 12 Championship was the next step in the Longhorns' annual series of goals. At the start of the season, that is all they could count on. It was the last thing they could completely control. They could still reach their final goal by playing in and winning a bowl game, but a chance to play for the national championship would be determined not by what they did, but by what other people thought about them. Thus, that became the dream.

Dreams are us human folks' way of imagining. There are good dreams and bad dreams, big dreams and small dreams. Athletes are taught to dream big, and Texas did. In spring practice, on warm summer nights, in two-a-days... they dared to dream.

Texas had never played the two biggest names in the Big Ten—Michigan and Ohio State—and by the luck of the draw, they did it in a span of three games in 2005. Since Mack Brown came to Texas, he had built his program with the goal of bringing the Longhorns back to the national spotlight. Those two wins accomplished that.

Then there was the matter of Oklahoma. The truth was, the Sooners and the Longhorns had both become dominant college football teams, but Texas seemed to get overlooked or discounted because of losses to Oklahoma—losses that often proved the only real blemish on a spectacular five-year record.

When Texas hammered Oklahoma in Dallas in October, folks who had already begun making tentative arrangements for a trip to Pasadena now made non-refundable reservations.

Now, the nation got what it wanted. It was a wintry day as the stretch limo made its way across the East River into downtown Manhattan. The results of a yesterday snow were still in evidence alongside the streets. For many of the nation's top football coaches, the National Football Hall of Fame dinner marks the completion of another year of college football. But Brown and Dodds' trip to New York was marked with ironies.

First, it was December 4, eight years to the day from the time Brown had been hired as Texas's head football coach. And it was exactly one month until the game that everybody had been waiting for—by all definitions, The Game of the young 21st Century.

As Brown made his appearance on the set of CBS's announcement show, back home in Austin his team was gathering to celebrate the news. The Monday morning papers sent up red flags for the Texas coach. He felt that, in their enthusiasm, some of the players hadn't shown enough respect to Southern Cal, and he wasn't about to let the media turn the game into a battle of words.

On Wednesday, as Brown headed off to awards shows to honor his players, members of the Texas athletics staff had gathered in Pasadena for a meeting with the Rose Bowl officials. Most of the details were pretty easy, because the Longhorns were staying at the same hotel and practicing at the same site as they had a year before.

As the staff wrapped up their preparation, they made one final, secret stop— the Airport Hilton Hotel in Burbank. It was not a visit that was talked about, nor did the name of the hotel appear on any of the Longhorns' literature. But it would figure significantly in the grand scheme of things before the story played itself out.

A bowl trip for Texas Longhorn players is different from those taken by a lot of universities. Since his days at North Carolina, Mack Brown has taken advantage of an NCAA rule which allows a school to pay for players' standard airfare to and from their homes to the bowl site. As soon as the Longhorns qualify for a bowl, players are advised to seek out the best airfare and travel arrangements they can find. This allows players to spend more time with their families and it underscores the coaches' faith in them to act responsibly.

The coaches, staff, and student-support staff travel by charter from Austin, and the team convenes after their Christmas break on the evening of the day before they are to begin practice and bowl activities. In the case of the 2006 Rose Bowl, that meant the Longhorns arrived on the night of December 27.

After he returned to Austin from New York and the Longhorns had begun bowl practice back home, Brown covered the issue of showing proper respect for Southern California. He even called on history, telling them the story of the "Trojan Horse," where a confident Troy was caught unawares and was defeated. And he used the old Teddy Roosevelt saying, "Speak softly and carry a big stick."

When he gathered with his team in California, as he stood in the ballroom of the Hyatt Regency Century Plaza, he told his team that they should feel good about themselves. He said, "This is just like the Michigan game last year, only the stakes are much higher. We want you to have fun. You have a right to be proud to be here. Your coaches, the staff, and you should understand that. You have earned the right to play for the national championship. This is the most scrutinized game in sports. In no other sport do people have a month to talk about the game. You worked to get here; now think about why you are here."

Then he set out a theme that would run through every practice, all the way through the game. "Picture that moment in your mind where you can do something to help us win this football game. What we are asking every one of you to do is to be accountable. For the next eight days, be unselfish, and do whatever it takes to help us win. Figure out what your part is, and think about winning all week."

The events of the next days seemed a blur, moving faster than they ever did through a similar schedule the year before. There was the trip to Disneyland and the ESPN Zone; dinner at Lawry's Beef Bowl; daily practice at the Home Depot Center. And with each day, the lobby of the Century Plaza grew more crowded with Longhorn fans.

On Monday, January 2, it rained. In fact, it poured. The Longhorns spent their last official day of practice working out on the concrete floor of the velodrome at the Home Depot Olympic Center. For the first time in fifty years, it rained on the world-famous Rose Parade.

That night, as the Longhorns made their way through the crowded hotel corridors to their meeting room, they learned who was on the seventy-player travel squad. They were surprised to learn something else.

"Tomorrow, before we go to the Rose Bowl for the walk-through and photo session, pack an overnight bag," the members of the travel squad were told. "Spend time with your friends and family tonight, because you won't have a chance to visit with them tomorrow night."

The next day was like those one of those moments in life when you reach that twilight zone between imagination and reality, where you wonder if you will wake from a dream only to find that what you thought was real wasn't real at all. As a kid, you would race to a place, seeking a landmark or some sign of familiarity just so you could be reassured that the constant was indeed the norm.

And as the Gold Coast buses pulled onto the expanse of pavement at the foothills of the San Gabriel mountains, sure enough, there it was: The Rose Bowl.

After a season of speculation and a month of anticipation, the Texas Longhorns returned to the most famous venue in college sports for a brief walk-through visit and photo session prior to the next day's national championship Rose Bowl game against Southern California. This was the final official team activity before the game, and they made the best of it. A church choir or a rap group could not have better acquitted itself. As they stood on the risers in front of the stadium, they rocked, chanted, and generally announced to any and all who were hanging out in the area that they were loose and ready for some football.

The folks from In-N-Out Burgers hauled their eighteen-wheeler down the ramp and turned out the burgers that are unique to, and the pride of, California fast-food cuisine.

As the team suited up for the picture, equipment manager Chip Robertson and his crew re-established game operations in the visiting-team dressing room at the Rose Bowl.

By now, the familiar sight of the Rose Bowl was both a comfort to and a relief for a football team that was ready to play. It had been a month since the two teams had played a game, and neither bunch was interested in one more day or one more minute of practice.

As the buses left the canyon and made their way onto one of the busy freeways, the ones carrying the staff and the non-travel squad headed west toward Century City. But the coaches and the squad that would play in the game turned north, toward Burbank

Only a handful of staff members knew the destination, and that was critical. There was no way to even imagine the crowd at the Century Plaza. Hotel staff had to restrict the dozen elevators of the hotel to residents who presented their room keys for identification. Well-meaning fans, parents, and a legion of other people had packed the lobby so that it was impossible to move from one end to the other. Most people were reduced to going out the south door and back in the north door to get from one end of the lobby to the other. But miles away, only a few guests realized that they were sharing space with one of the two principals in the biggest college football game of its time.

The next day, the staff buses headed from the Century Plaza to the stadium, and the rest of the Longhorn squad rejoined their teammates in Burbank for the trip to Pasadena.

At 3:21 P.M. Pacific standard time, two hours before the scheduled 5:21 kickoff, the number two-ranked Texas Longhorns arrived at the plaza in the valley of the Arroyo Seco, got off their buses, and walked through a sea of burnt orange into the Rose Bowl, en route to their date with destiny.

MB

We had actually started preparing for Southern Cal, along with Oklahoma, last year after they played their bowl game. In the spring, we worked on both of them, along with Ohio State.

I regretted being in New York and missing the team meeting after the announcement. Some of our kids felt like they had to be bold in their statements to the media, and I didn't like that. So when I got back at the end of that week and we got ready to start bowl practice, the first thing we said was, "This is going to be a game of respect. You always

217

respect your opponent, regardless of who they are, but this team has won thirty-four straight games. If you can't say something positive about a team that's won thirty-four straight games, then don't speak. And be sure you don't present yourself as representing this team, because your coach is very respectful of what they've accomplished. We've only won nineteen, so let's not go there."

We started to build a place for them where we didn't yell at them or say "you're wrong" or "show respect because you should," but where we'd use an example of someone in history who kept his mouth shut, worked, and was able to be successful. And the entire bowl week, we got a lot of motivational help from all the media, which kept talking about how good Southern Cal was.

We had an incredible feeling when we left the Michigan Rose Bowl last year because our fans had responded so well. The whole thing was so special. Texas had never been there. It was Michigan, Coach Royal, and Bo Schembechler. It was a place where a small-town boy from Tennessee never thought he'd be able to go as a player or as a coach. Then we won in a national setting and ended up in the top five. I walked out of the Rose Bowl and told myself that I didn't know if it would ever be better than that.

In some ways, the selection day this year probably wasn't as exciting because we knew where we were going, and we had known for a while we would probably be playing SC. Last year, we didn't know where we were going until we stepped off the plane in New York. That had been so dramatic. This was more of a business trip, with the stakes much higher.

It was exciting to be going to the championship game, but it was also exciting to be going back to the Rose Bowl. The year before, we could not have been treated better than we were by the Rose Bowl people, and we have great friends out there now. And I'm so proud of our fans. They got more tickets to both games than anybody could have imagined. There was a time when Texas fans had a reputation of not traveling to bowl games and of sitting on their hands. But there were more of them, and they were louder than both Michigan and Southern Cal. We were behind and in trouble in both games, and we didn't play great at times in both games, and our fans never got discouraged. That's a major change from eight years ago.

It's a dream for a guy raised in a high school coaching family to coach against a Michigan, an Ohio State and a Southern Cal and win all three. Playing or coaching at the University of Texas is big. People listen to what's said here. You have to take very seriously what you say, so it was important that our players and coaches reflected class, and there were several things that helped us to be prepared for this particular game.

First, we have played before huge crowds, home and away, so we knew what to expect on game day. As for the trip itself, the fact that we had flown the same flights to L.A. made it easy. Our kids knew how to get out there easily, and even though the Century Plaza had changed from the Westin group to the Hyatt after the Michigan trip, the hotel was still the same and many of the same personnel were still there. The year before I'd told the team, "Get used to this hotel; this is only practice for next year and the national championship game."

As a staff, we always go over the notes I keep from year to year, and even though we were successful against Michigan, there were some things I thought we needed to change. I thought we had done too much hitting in practice once we got to the bowl site last year, and I thought we had made that mistake against Washington State in 2003. We did a lot of research with coaches who had just won their bowl games to see what they were doing differently.

We found that they had what amounted to two-a-day practices or a spring practice at home. Then, when they got to the bowl, they took the pads off and tuned things up. You are on your feet so much with all of the organized bowl activities. You have the intense media pressure that's bigger than you had at home. If you are not careful, your team can get tired by game time because it's so different from the normal game week. We still coached hard out there, but we didn't run sprints, which we have always done. We didn't hit nearly as much out there as we did at home. We were really physical at home, and out there we were physical, but we only practiced in full pads one time and were in shoulder pads and shorts the rest of the time. I thought that was one of the reasons that we were able to maintain our energy and our speed at the end of the game.

We made a great decision in moving the travel squad to a different hotel. Not only did our players need to be away from all the fans and the media to focus, but our coaches needed to be away from their families. If you are not careful, when you get close to game time, you'll be short with your wife because you're tired. There's a tremendous amount of pressure. You'll be short with your kids and other family members because they're having fun and it's been a wonderful week for them, but it's still work for you. The bowl week's a long week and everybody gets on edge a little bit at the end. We felt like it would be better for the families, the players, and for the coaches themselves to move.

It is important for a coach to understand that this is an important week in his life, but it also is important for his family. I tried to spend some time each day with my family. I would eat lunch with them, or if I had a chance, they would come by the room, but they all understood that I needed to watch film and have my time to think. I didn't want to go everywhere they wanted to go, and they all embraced that.

I told the players to have fun, and I thought it was important for all of us to enjoy the moment. When we went to a dinner with the Southern Cal coaches, I made sure that Pete Carroll and Coach Royal sat beside each other. It's not often that coaches who have won back-to-back national championships and have had winning streaks of more than thirty games are sitting at the same table. I wanted Coach Royal to be included in that moment. I think Pete appreciated that, too.

We had planned the move to another hotel after studying what some other teams had done, and it worked perfectly. I didn't know where we were going, and the players didn't know where they were going. We told them that would make it a lot easier on them, because if anybody knew, they'd want to follow us. We told them to spend time with their families that night, and tomorrow, pack two bags and keep their mouths shut. As soon as we left the Rose Bowl picture day, we were heading to get ready for this game.

We never told them where we were staying. In fact, I can't tell you what hotel it was today. We just got dropped off and didn't know where we were, but it was wonderful because there were no distractions. The other kids who didn't dress and weren't on the seventy-man travel squad were wonderful, too, because they stayed at the Century Plaza, had the same routine exactly, and they pulled their bus up and met us and we all went to the stadium together. Those kids understood it wasn't about any individual; it was about winning.

One of the most meaningful moments of my life came when we were pulling into the stadium again, just like we had before the Michigan game, and we saw all those excited Texas fans. That makes a coach feel great, because whether he'll admit it or not, every coach in the world, no matter how gruff or tough he is, wants to see happy people. At that moment, looking at all the burnt orange everywhere, I don't think I've ever seen that many happy Texas fans at one time.

The game turned out to be everything everybody thought it would be. It was like a heavyweight fight. Sometimes when there is so much hype, the game doesn't live up to it. This one did.

The tone of the game got set early, and we didn't panic. I could tell the defense worked hard to have a three-and-out on their first series. Then Aaron Ross, who is one of our great players, was trying to fight for extra yards on the punt return. He had the ball protected, but the defender hit his helmet right on the ball. So we patted Aaron on the back and told our team, "It's an away game for us, and those guys on the other side will have a lot of emotion early. They're bringing thirty-four straight wins into this game, so expect them to jump on you."

When it was 16-10 at halftime, we told the players it was "an illusion." We said, "They've been behind before, we've been behind before; this thing's gonna go back and forth. Neither team's gonna quit, because this is too important. These teams are too good, so don't get panicked, because they are gonna come back and get after your tail now. They are gonna get right back on you."

We had the three-and-out to start the second half, and Southern Cal scored immediately. I felt as if our team was prepared for the volleyball match with the momentum changing back and forth because it was so much like our OU game—the stadium was half UT fans and half SC fans. I thought we played really well after the interception by Michael Griffin, which stopped an SC drive. That play, by the way, was also great for instant replay, because it was a pivotal play in the game, and the on-the-field call was overruled. After that play, it was just a back-and-forth match with some incredibly talented athletes on both sides who were confident and determined to win.

I have never been prouder of a team than I was of our guys after USC scored and we were down by twelve with 6:42 left. We drove immediately back down the field and scored. There was no bad body language; no one had his head down. It was like going back to work, and the guys understood that.

Starting that drive, the defensive coaches and I sat with the kids and said, "We just need one more stop." We had our timeouts. Our coaches had prepared well for the end of the game. We knew we could move the ball. Southern Cal was really good on offense and they were moving the ball down the field. So we knew it wouldn't be easy. At the same time, we felt if we could make that one stop, we would go on to win the game, and I thought the whole bench knew that.

The fourth-and-two play where we held them will go down in UT history. Our guys decided at that moment that they were going to win the national championship. The offense knew it was over, and we just had to do our business. I've never seen a happier bunch with a game still on the line. It was as if they said, "Men, this thing's over. Let's go finish it." And they did.

People have asked me if I had any doubts on the fourth-and-five play from their eight when Vince scored, and the short answer is "no." We had done it too many times. With Vince's ability to run and his feel of the game—he had hit thirty of forty passes—we had so many options on that play, it was going to be hard to stop. He had four guys in the end zone who could catch the ball, a great protection package, and the ability to run five yards if the pass wasn't there.

Vince got all the credit, but Justin Blaylock might have been the star of that play. He made a great block on their nickel blitz. They had a zone blitz that dropped off with Selvin on the other side, and it turned into an easy play for us. But I didn't have any question when the play was called that we would make it.

The other thing that I was very proud of was that after Vince scored, our coaches were so organized that they already had us going for two and knew the play that we would call. It had to be a unique play because you couldn't fumble; if they picked it up and ran it back, they'd get two points. You couldn't throw an interception because if they ran it back, you'd get beat instead of having some security by going up by three. Not only did our team score and prepare for the two, there was no celebrating. The bench did, but not the guys on the field. There was no one running out on the field to kick the extra point or get us a penalty, which would have taken us out of range to run the two-point play.

The play we called might not have been the best call, because they were loaded for it, but our guys were not going to be denied. The offensive line, Selvin Young, and Vince just took it upon themselves to get in the end zone.

Both offenses got so much credit in the game, but both defenses were really good. I actually thought the first half was dictated by defense because the defenses came into the game hearing how strong the two offenses were. But in the second half, the offenses were able to overcome the great defenses and score points. After it was over, Coach Royal described it best. "Time ran out," he said. "Whoever had enough time was gonna score."

When the game was over, I caught up with Pete, who told me that they had had a great run, but if it had to end, they wanted it to be to someone deserving. Then he told me he thought we'd be great champions. I thought his comments represented the respect that each team had for the other.

After our team and fans sang "The Eyes of Texas," I was rushed to the awards presentation.

When you're in that position, and you've wanted to be in that position for thirty-three years of your life, you don't have time to think. I know last year when they handed us the Rose Bowl Trophy, I thought that was the coolest thing in the world. But this year I was hoping the trophy presentation would go fast so I could get that crystal ball, because it overshadows the bowl trophy.

I thought at that moment, "I don't remember John Saunders's question," because I had some things I wanted to say. The first would be what we believe in, and that was respect for the other team. Those guys had won a lot of games in a row, and had they won a third straight AP national championship, they would have done something that had never been done. I thought we would be classless not to say congratulations to Southern Cal for all that they had accomplished.

Second, I thought that my dad and granddad were watching from above, and they were very proud. My heritage is being reared in a family that revolved around high school football. We would not be where we were without high school football, and I thought of all the help and support we had received from the high school coaches. They had called and sent us notes and letters, and they had shown us hospitality when our staff came to their schools. They encouraged kids to come here to represent their state on the national scene. It was a great moment for them, and I did not want it to go without notice. So my "thank you" wasn't about recruiting at that moment. Some of it was about respect for Dad and Granddad and gratitude for the life they gave me, but it was more about, "Thank you to the high school coaches...you're underpaid, you're under-appreciated, you've done a great job. And I want to take this one moment on the national scene for all college coaches to say thank you to the high school coaches."

When we finally got to the locker room after the game, I wanted to tell the team first of all that we loved them. What you want for your children, and what you want for your players, is happiness. So many times guys have something great happen early in their lives, and it stops there. If they are not careful, at sixty they are still talking about that moment that happened at twenty-one.

That's why I told the players, "Don't let this be the greatest moment in your lives. Let that be for your wife, your children, the things you've given back to other people. The things you've done in a community... helping a child...helping the elderly...all of those things are so important in making your life happy. Winning a national championship and making a lot of money doesn't make you happy. I think it is all of the other things that you do."

At that moment, I knew they would listen to me. The message was, this is really cool, and it is a great moment, and one in sports that we'll remember for the rest of our lives. I want this to be something that helps give you confidence and resources and contacts to make sure it can help you help your children, help your wife, so you can be happy outside of football. But I don't want you, at fifty-four years old, to be talking about this game as the greatest thing that ever happened in your life.

Celebrating the Dream

"FINALLY, THIS IS THE MOST IMPORTANT THING
I WANT YOU TO HEAR TONIGHT. REMEMBER THAT
WE LOVE YOU. BE PROUD OF WHAT YOU
HAVE ACCOMPLISHED AND ENJOY THIS MOMENT.
LET THIS BE A GREAT THING IN LIFE, BUT DON'T LET IT BE
THE BEST THING THAT EVER HAPPENS IN YOUR LIFE.
GO ON FROM HERE, BE GREAT HUSBANDS AND
GREAT DADS AND MAKE A DIFFERENCE.**"**

—Mack Brown

"The single rose is, in essence, a symbol of completion,
of consummate achievement and perfection."
                                    —*J. E. Cirlot, A Dictionary of Symbols*

For a month, the irony had been delicious. The year before, the Rose
Bowl theme had been "Celebrate Family," and it seemed to fit Texas
perfectly. The president of the Rose Parade gets to select the grand
marshal of the famous parade, as well as the theme for the parade and
the game.

Libby Evans Wright, the first woman president of the Rose Parade,
took her duties seriously. She chose as the grand marshal retiring U. S.
Supreme Court Justice Sandra Day O'Connor. For the theme, she
thought of the annual trip the teams take to Disneyland, which is known
as "the Magic Kingdom."

So she determined that the theme for the 2006 Rose Bowl, and therefore the 2005 national championship game, should be "It's Magical."

The year before, Texas had talked of miracles in a season of come-
backs, including winning the Rose Bowl on the final play. But the 2005
season had been a workman-type season, where the Longhorns hadn't
needed miracles or magic. They had dominated almost every opponent,
averaging more than fifty points per game and rarely being challenged.
They had whisked away Oklahoma State and Texas A&M, two teams that
had held early leads, and had out-dueled a fine Ohio State team.

But now, there they were, trailing Southern California by twelve
points with 6:42 remaining in the game. As the Longhorns drove quickly
for a touchdown to cut the lead to 38-33, only four minutes and three
seconds remained.

In the press box of the venerable stadium, a contingent of writers
and school media personnel waited for the elevators. Among them was
Shannon McLaughlin, a UT student who had worked tirelessly in the
Texas Media Relations office and had been part of the Texas Angels

225

football support group.

Despite battling bronchitis, she had dutifully helped file feature stories on the UT website. She was as pretty on the inside as she was on the outside, but now, as she stood waiting for the elevator, she was pale, prompting an old friend to ask, "Shannon, are you okay?"

"I'm just scared, I'm so nervous," she said, obviously reflecting the state of every Longhorn loyalist on the planet.

Her friend put his hand on her shoulder and looked straight into her questioning blue eyes.

"Shannon," he said calmly. "It's magical."

On Wednesday, the morning clouds had given way to bright sunshine, and as the Longhorn staff buses maneuvered toward the Rose Bowl, downtown Los Angeles was a picture-perfect foreground that included a rare sighting of the snow-capped mountains beyond.

It is unusual, the natives say, to see the mountains, which are usually shrouded in clouds, fog, or smog—or any combination thereof. But on this special day, you could see the top of the snow-capped San Bernardino Mountains in the Sierra Nevada range just east of the City of Angels and its accompanying sister cities, including Pasadena.

It was prophetic that you could see the peak, because the top was exactly where Texas was headed before the day would end.

The college football world had talked about this game all season. At a dinner in Dallas two nights before Texas beat Oklahoma in October, the veteran announcer Keith Jackson had talked about the dream match-up.

"If we get Texas and Southern Cal unbeaten," he said, "I may just start the telecast by saying, 'God, are you awake? This is the one we've been waiting for.'"

It was obvious, judging by the splendor of the day, that Somebody really cool had created it. Folks had said it would be "A Game for the Ages." They would not be wrong.

The venue itself, the Rose Bowl, spoke to the purity of college football. While other bowls have forged partnerships with title sponsors, the Rose Bowl has reserved the game for the schools. There was a spiced-up pregame to placate the BCS, but at halftime, the bands marched in the tradition of the college game.

And in that place, in that space, the college game wedged itself right into the heart of Americana.

Southern Cal's reign over college football had lasted for thirty-four straight victories. Networks and news media were poised to anoint the Trojans of 2005 as the greatest team in the history of the college game.

And so it was that Texas came to Los Angeles on December 28, and now the Longhorns were aboard buses riding right into the gates of the city.

The pregame was tastefully spectacular, capped by an appearance by a B-1 bomber, which had come out of Dyess Air Force Base in Abilene—

just one more airplane headed from Texas to California. The big jet flew over the Rose Bowl Stadium and then blasted straight up, freezing the crowd of almost ninety-five thousand (more than half of them in burnt orange) with a deafening roar.

In fact, after country-music star LeAnn Rimes sang the National Anthem, she told Brown, "Hook 'em, Coach. I'm on my way to change into my burnt orange."

In his pregame speech, Mack Brown told his team that he had worked thirty-three years in coaching to finally get to make that talk, and now he didn't know what to say. "So just go out and have fun," was all that he said.

The teams were everything number one and number two should have been. The offenses were relentless, the defenses stubborn. The two most powerful offenses in the country fought for yards and the defenses grudgingly surrendered them. Each team punted only twice in the entire game.

A good tennis match didn't have as many serve-and-return moments. But when the Trojans answered a Texas field goal with a touchdown midway through the fourth quarter, Southern Cal had a twelve-point lead at 38-26.

Only six minutes and forty-two seconds remained in the Rose Bowl Game for the 2005 national championship. As Shannon and her friends gathered their things and began to head to the field for the postgame duties, Vince Young trotted onto the field to take the ball at his own 31-yard line. Gene Chizik talked from the press box to his fellow co-defensive coordinator Duane Akina on the Texas sideline, and then got middle linebacker Aaron Harris on the headset.

"Here is what we are going to do," said the ever-positive Chizik, who was in the process of extending his personal streak—including Auburn—of unbeaten seasons to two in a row. "We're going to go score, and then we've got to have a stop. And it may have to come on fourth down."

Young carried or passed on every play, running the final seventeen yards for the touchdown, which cut the score to 38-33.

The clock showed four minutes and three seconds remaining, and Shannon and the impatient media were waiting for what seemed an extremely slow elevator.

With all of the praise that the extremely talented Reggie Bush had received, this game had validated the one thing about the USC offense which many seasoned observers already knew: the secret to their success was the equally talented Matt Leinart. Now it was Leinart's moment to seize. The Trojans had scored each of the four times that they had the ball in the second half.

Leinart's team was at its own thirty-four. Mack Brown had three time-outs left. On the first play, LenDale White gained four yards. Leinart completed a pass for nine yards. USC had a first down at its own forty-seven. On first down, White gained three yards to midfield.

Brown told an official that he would spend his first time out immediately after the Trojans ran their second down play, fully anticipating that the Trojans would keep the ball on the ground. Leinart, however, threw a flat pass that fell incomplete, stopping the clock. The official glanced at Brown.

"I guess you don't want that time out now, do you?"

It was third down, and White powered over right tackle to the Texas forty-five. With two minutes and thirteen seconds left, Texas called time out.

Now, the fourth-down play Chizik had talked about had come.

On the USC sideline, Pete Carroll knew that a first down would allow USC to basically run out the clock. If he punted, he reasoned, he put the ball in Vince Young's hands. From anywhere on the field, that had proved lethal in that stadium for two years against both Michigan and USC.

The Texas coaches gathered the defense around them. They determined that White, who had been the workhorse for USC, would get the ball.

"We're going to get LenDale White on this play," they said. "So let's bring everybody."

When the ball was snapped, it was the ultimate power battle in the line. Southern Cal had loaded the left side of their line, and Texas was in a power blitz. It was a jumbo package for the Trojans, with two tackles on the same side. Two linemen double-teamed Rod Wright, who still got good penetration. One tackle took on Brian Robison, who grabbed the 295-pounder by the shoulders and threw him to the side like a rag doll. Robison penetrated two yards in the backfield and knocked down the fullback, who was to have been the lead blocker. White tripped over his own man as he tried to adjust, and Michael Huff and Drew Kelson came crashing through the gap. As White tried to push forward, Aaron Harris came over the top of Wright and delivered the final blow.

Texas had won the chess game. They had completely vacated the secondary. If Leinart had faked the run and passed, it would have been a walk-in for a touchdown. But if he had gotten the first down, the game would have been over either way. White got a great spot, but when the chain stretched, he was still one yard shy. It had been, as Chizik had warned it might be, fourth down. Two minutes and nine seconds were all that remained.

A screen pass and an incompletion brought up third and twelve. Quan Cosby caught Young's pass for seven yards, and a five-yard face mask penalty moved the ball to a first down at the forty-six. Brian Carter had two critical catches on the drive, including one that took the ball to the thirteen-yard line.

Young threw incomplete for Sweed, then ran for five. On third down, he found Sweed open in the end zone, but the ball slipped from his grasp. The play was known as Menu Two, and Sweed was one of four options for Young.

Just under thirty seconds remained. It was fourth and five at the USC eight. Texas called its second time out.

Receivers coach Bobby Kennedy was on the field, and he and Young talked with Greg Davis in the press box. When Young and Davis discussed choosing plays during a game, it was more than the normal sideline conversations between a coach and his quarterback. The two had become close, talking together and watching films, studying football and learning about life, all at the same time.

Menu Four, another option play, was discussed. Davis gave Young the choice. "I like all of the Menu plays," he said, "but I like Menu Two the best."

In the huddle, the team awaited the decision.

History will wonder what was said in that huddle, when a band of brothers who had spent a hot summer and a full season preparing for that moment faced what could be the last play of a dream.

In the press box, Keith Jackson told America, "Fourth and five at the Trojan eight. This is for the national championship."

David Thomas says the team said, "This is it. This is for all of it." Seconds later, Lyle Sendlein snapped the ball to Vince Young.

He looked quickly at his pass options, which were covered. Then, the man who had passed or run the ball for the Longhorns on all but two plays in the second half tucked the ball and started to run.

The receivers knew to be ready, and immediately went into blocking mode. USC had come with a complete blitz. The charging cornerback on the left side had a chance to turn Young inside, where all of the traffic was. Texas right tackle Justin Blalock hit the cornerback in the chest, knocking him completely off his feet.

Young ran for the corner, and walked into history.

It was 39-38.

Southern Cal, caught off guard when the Longhorns decided to go for two, spent their final time out. When Young followed his offensive line right up the middle for the two-point conversion, it was 41-38. Nineteen seconds were all that remained in the reign of USC.

On the Texas sideline, Shannon McLaughlin, the UT media assistant, knelt, covering her eyes. A kickoff and two plays later, USC's final pass sailed out of bounds. Her co-worker, Jeremy Sharpe, tapped her on the shoulder. "Shannon, it's over. Now, go have some fun."

Glittering confetti rained on the field. "The Eyes of Texas" had never been sung louder or more passionately.

In the locker room, after all of the trophy presentations and the hugs and general mayhem, Mack Brown talked to his team for the final time in a locker room as part of the 2005 Championship season.

He did all of the usual things, congratulating them and again complimenting USC for its long accomplishment.

And then he said this: "Finally, this is the most important thing I want you to hear tonight. Remember that we love you. Be proud of what you have accomplished, and enjoy this moment. Let this be a great thing in life, but don't let it be the best thing that ever happens in your life. Go on from here, be great husbands and great dads, and make a difference."

The message was clear. The young men who had ascended to the pinnacle of college football can say forever that in the year 2005, they were the best in America at what they did. But the beauty of mountain peaks is that when you have scaled one, there is another higher one just ahead.

Mack Brown began checking his cell phone messages as he rode the bus back to the hotel, hours after the game. There was a call from his friend Roy Williams, an excellent coach who had won a national championship at North Carolina in basketball after years of being "in the neighborhood."

"When you win tonight," Williams said in a long voice message, "your life's gonna change, and you won't feel it. Your friends will be proud of you, you'll be proud of the team and the players, your family will be really proud of you, but they've watched you for years. But others' perception of you—because you've won the championship—will change, and it will confuse you some. And you'll have to go right back to work while they still are wanting to talk about the championship."

Austin, the hometown of the Longhorns, erupted in celebration. As fans jumped in their cars and headed toward the UT campus to witness the Tower bathed in orange and lit with the number "1," neighborhoods surrounding the university experienced traffic jams at 1:00 A.M. Jubilant fans in Escalades and pickups were high-fiving out their windows with folks in vintage used cars.

Before the game ended, one fan had hurried to Longhorns, Ltd., the UT Athletics Department's stadium store. He had heard that national-championship memorabilia would go on sale at 12:30 A.M. if the Longhorns won. He was the only person standing outside the store as the Longhorns fell behind by twelve. As the comeback came, store workers saw him outside the window and invited him in. He had his pick of the prizes when Young scored the final touchdown, and the workers cracked open the boxes and began stocking the shelves.

The lobby of the Century Plaza remained people-packed; when the Longhorns got back from the game, they unloaded the buses at a loading dock, allowing the players to access the elevators from the ground floor and avoid the main floor. The hotel was a total mess, as folks who had guaranteed reservations had to be turned away because guests refused to leave their rooms after the victory.

Brown's phone would ring at 6 A.M. in California, signaling a call from the president of the United States. Coaches throughout the country would call Brown the next day, proud for their colleague who had won it all, and had done it the right way. Media members, some of whom had questioned his ability but always genuinely liked the man, offered sincere congratulations. It was nice to see that the old baseball saying, "Nice guys don't win pennants," was wrong. A truly nice guy, and a very good football coach, had won it all, and they were happy for him.

It was almost eleven o'clock at night when Brown finished his final interviews at the Rose Bowl and headed back to his hotel. Vince Young would hug the women in his life, and finally, when he had quiet time in his hotel room, the tears would come.

They were a mixed bag, these tears. Some were of grateful happiness; others were for those he grew up with who, for whatever reason, didn't find the same path he had found. In life, and in football, the essence of Vince Young is in trying to help people. He makes you better than you thought you could be. And with all of his talent, that is his greatest gift.

Within a week, Young had declared himself eligible for the NFL draft, ending a Longhorn career that saw him lead the team to twenty straight wins and a 30-2 record as a starter.

Ten days later, a celebration recognizing the team drew fifty-thousand fans to Darrell K Royal-Texas Memorial Stadium. A month after the championship game, Austin stores had netted over $10 million in sales of national-championship memorabilia.

On Valentine's Day the Longhorns made their last official trip together. This one was to Washington, D. C., where the team was warmly welcomed by President Bush on the lawn of the White House.

As the Longhorn buses had pulled away for the final time from the Hyatt Regency Century Plaza, there was one last reminder of the theme that President Libby Evans Wright had chosen.

Part of the sign was missing, but there was just enough of it left to see the word that told the story of the evening, and—as this game goes down as perhaps the greatest college football game in history—the word that will always best describe it.

You could say "Amazing," as some did.

You could say "Unbelievable."

You could say, for the first time in thirty-five years, "The Texas Longhorns are the National Champions of College Football."

But Rose Bowl President Libby Evans Wright, Shannon McLaughlin, and a legion of Longhorn fans had the answer.

It was, they would say, simply "Magical."

▶ 1. National Champions – Darrell Royal and Mack Brown. 2. Defensive stop – Michael Griffin (27) and Michael Huff (7) converge. 3. It's good – David Pino hits a field goal as Jonathan Scott (73) blocks. 4. Touchdown – Billy Pittman (5) outruns a defender.

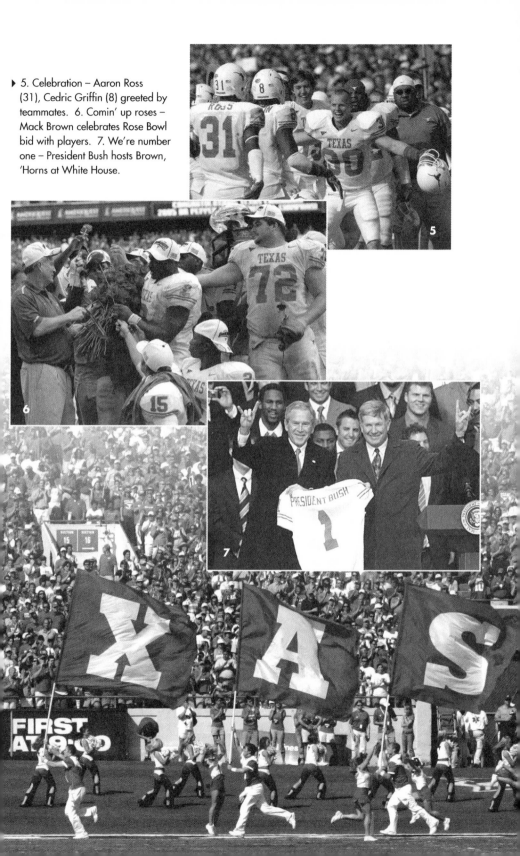

▶ 5. Celebration – Aaron Ross (31), Cedric Griffin (8) greeted by teammates. 6. Comin' up roses – Mack Brown celebrates Rose Bowl bid with players. 7. We're number one – President Bush hosts Brown, 'Horns at White House.

" WHEN I LOOK BACK OVER THIRTY YEARS OF COACHING,
IT ISN'T ONLY THE GAMES THAT I REMEMBER.
CERTAINLY I RECALL THOSE, BUT MORE IMPORTANT,
I REMEMBER THE PEOPLE WHO WERE A PART
OF IT ALL. AND THOSE MEMORIES
LAST LONG AFTER THE GAME IS OVER. **"**

—Mack Brown

EPILOGUE

One Heartbeat Revisited

BL

When Coach Royal talked about *one heartbeat*, no one understood better than Tom Kirksey how it worked. An avid sports fan, a serious golfer, and a mustachioed, distinguished member of the human race, he knew all about the heart.

Over 5,000 times, he had held it, stopped it, started it, repaired it, replumbed it. As Chief of Cardiovascular Surgery at Seton Medical Center in Austin, he, of all people, understood. And every time he touched a heart, he rediscovered the miracle.

In our enlightened society, we are taught that it is the brain that runs the body. We hear of electrical impulses and brain waves. We understand that cherished memories hang like photographs in the hallways of the mind. Ideas, solutions, even our plans are all part of the brain, in one lobe or another. We are even told that the heart is simply a muscle driven by the brain.

All of that we know in logic, but it is in emotion where the heart lives.

Men like Dr. Tom Kirksey can understand why. Long before science defined the responsibilities of parts of the body, mankind spoke of matters of the heart.

And that is what we have tried to do here in this book.

For it is in matters of the heart where courage and will, love and compassion—all of the attributes of caring and determination—reside. It is there where dreams take hold. It is there where brotherhood and sisterhood and the magic of teamwork germinate.

These things are why we coach and why we play the game. The reasons are all there, in the heart.

Dr. Kirksey says the heart is an amazing thing. "It just keeps working," he says. "It is the strongest of the muscles. It goes continuously."

Even, says Kirksey, if the four chambers are not working together, it still works.

"It isn't as efficient, but it will go on," he says. "That's where Coach Royal's concept of *one heartbeat* is correct. When the electrical impulses are out of line, and one of the chambers is doing something different from the others, it still functions, but not nearly as well."

We value the heart because it pumps life, because with one common thrust of uncommon power it sends new blood through thousands of tiny vessels that, if laid end to end, would cover 60,000 miles—almost three times around the world, or a little over one million football fields. Then it turns around and does it all over again less than a second later.

But Dr. Kirksey tells us something else about the heart, and it is here where science and spirituality merge.

"Even after the rest of the body has shut down," says Dr. Kirksey, "The heart keeps on beating. When it is the only thing remaining, it still is trying to keep on going."

And in that space, it is no longer the heart, but the soul.

From a very young age, all I ever wanted to be was a coach.

After an injury shortened my career as a college player, I spent three years at Florida State as a graduate assistant making $1,500 a year. I worked on my master's degree so I could keep coaching. I wrote 106 Division I head coaches to see if I could be a full time coach for them. Out of the 106 letters I wrote, I got four responses. I was proud of that because they, at least, answered.

One day I was in a staff meeting at Florida State, and I got a phone call from Bobby Collins. He offered me the receivers job at University of Southern Mississippi in Hattiesburg. He wanted to know when I could start. I asked him how far it was from Tallahassee. He asked me if I wanted to see Hattiesburg before I made my decision. I said I didn't need to. I packed my stuff, got a map, and drove to Hattiesburg, Mississippi, that night and started the job the next day.

It has been a long ride since that trip, but I can honestly say I wouldn't trade a single mile. There is something to being happy and feeling good about yourself. There is something about the coaching life that says if you lose, you can't wait to go back and get started again. If you win, you'd better get back to work sooner than if you'd lost. Because when you win, everyone is after you, and you have to be careful not to lie down and get lazy.

These are the things that I live by.

Be positive in everything you do. Don't talk about the negatives. You can eat your life up being negative. The old statement about the glass being half-full or half-empty has merit, as far as I am concerned. If you want to sit around and be miserable in your job, you can. Most folks don't get paid what they are worth, and they are never going to get what they deserve. If you're in your job only for the money, you won't be happy.

When you look at your goals, you have to understand what you are really looking for. If you don't enjoy coaching, quit and do something else. Coaching is hard. You have to have a passion for the game. You have to love those kids. You have to get excited watching them play. It has to mean something to you.

Work hard, but don't take that to mean you have to work long. Get your work done and get out of the office. At Texas, we go to work at 7:00 in the morning and go home right after practice. We go home and eat dinner with our families. We don't spend all night at the office. There has never been a good decision made after ten o'clock at night.

Live right. It doesn't help to talk to your team about not drinking if you go out and get drunk that night. It is hard to be a role model for kids all of a sudden—you have to live it all the time.

Above all, live your dream. We gave each player on our 2001 football team a "dream catcher," a web made of netting and feathers that's hung in a window or over a bed. The legend says it will catch the bad dreams, and leave only the good. And, as important as it is to dream, you can only reach that dream one step at a time. It's good to have your eyes on the mountaintop, but as you're going up that mountain, watch where you're walking.

When I look back over thirty years of coaching, it isn't only the games that I remember. Certainly I recall those, but more important, I remember the people who were a part of it all. And those memories last long after the game is over.

Coaching is about watching players grow from boys to men…following their careers and families after they finish playing for you. It is about the pride you feel in seeing doctors, lawyers, NFL players, weddings, and babies…getting Christmas cards, calls for advice, and visits from those who have gone through the program.

It is also about moms and dads. Our senior tackle, Mike Williams, will be a great NFL player. Before the 2001 season started, his mother called to say that no matter what the win-loss record was, she wanted us to know how much she appreciates what her son has gotten from being at Texas.

It is about moments and miracles.

We dedicated the North Carolina game to the memory of Cole Pittman, and the emotion before the game was tremendous. But what happened late in the game was even more amazing.

Chance Mock, our third quarterback, was Cole's best friend. When we had gotten to thirty-one points, he figured out that two touchdowns and an extra point would make it forty-four points. Cole's number was 44, and the whole day had been about him.

Later, when we were leading, 38-14, with a little over a minute left, we recovered a fumble. Chance asked to go into the game as a tribute to Cole, but I know he intended to score when he got the ball. Unfortunately, he slipped down. But he learned something about teamwork. He didn't have to score by himself. Chance inspired the rest of the team to get that touchdown, and when they did we decided not to kick the extra point. We took a knee on the conversion attempt to leave the score at 44.

When you have a safety and a missed two-point conversion, and touchdowns and field goals, it is hard to land on forty-four points, but we did. Cole's Dad, Marc, and most of us in the stadium, figured there was a

Higher Power involved in that. It was also significant that we had a forty-four-yard punt return for a touchdown that helped add up the scoring.

Your challenge as a coach is to make a difference for people, and everybody who was in that stadium that day left with a little different feeling about life. It wasn't because of me; it was because of the kids and the fans who wanted so much to be a part of it.

That's part of the joy of coaching, but the hard times teach lessons. There are times when your faith in yourself will be tested. That's when you need to remember to take pride in what you do and have the courage not to give up. Will Rogers once said, "Never let yesterday take up too much of today."

When it's all over, your career will not be judged by the money you made or the championships you won. It will be measured by the lives you touched.

And that is why we coach.

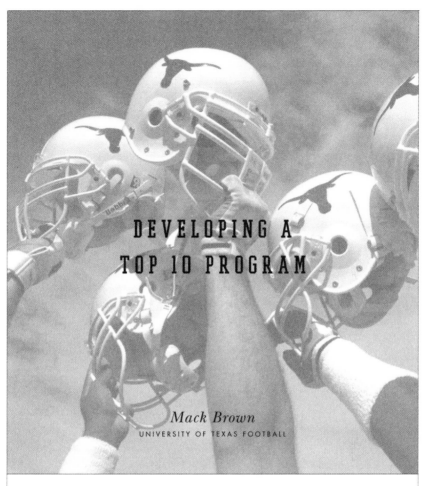

DEVELOPING A TOP 10 PROGRAM

Mack Brown
UNIVERSITY OF TEXAS FOOTBALL

OUR COACHING PHILOSOPHY

Be passionate about coaching and about winning.

Believe in yourself.

Be a positive role model at all times.

Develop a plan and stick with it. Have flexibility within
your system, but stick with what you believe.

Discipline, pride, and unselfishness contribute to
good team and staff morale.

WHAT CONSTITUTES A GOOD COACH

He possesses thorough knowledge of fundamental techniques.

He is a teacher. The most important characteristic of a successful coach is his ability to teach. Games are not won by what a coach thinks he knows; they are won by what his players have learned.

He is prepared—at meetings, practices, games.

He is inquisitive, constantly improving his knowledge and teaching methods.

He has a positive attitude.

He is a tireless worker willing to devote time to all phases of the program.

He has a winning attitude and knows what it takes to win. He recognizes a winner by judging a player's performance.

He pays attention to details. Persistence and perseverance regarding the details makes for a winning program.

He is willing to assume responsibility for thinking out an assignment and for creatively solving problems.

He is loyal, honest, and dedicated to the head coach, his fellow coaches and the staff, the school, and the players.

He does not over-coach. This can take the initiative and instinct out of a player, causing him to be overly cautious.

He is enthusiastic.

He is demanding. A good football team is built on good habits and discipline.

He is self-disciplined. The following will not be tolerated:
- Drinking during work
- Drinking with players or in the same establishment as players
- Use of drugs
- Receiving a ticket for Driving Under the Influence of alcohol or drugs
- Dating a member of the athletic department staff or a student
- Cheating or breaking any NCAA rules
- Cursing
- Abusive behavior toward any player
- Gambling
- Dealing with player agents
- Abuse of expense accounts, telephones, internet accounts
- Sexual harassment

HIRING AND DEVELOPING A TOP-NOTCH STAFF

Building a successful program starts with hiring a great staff. Hire guys who love to coach.

Develop great communication among staff members.

Develop unity as a staff. Team unity will follow.

Develop well-defined job descriptions for each staff member.

Assign each coach tasks taking into consideration his areas of strengths and areas of concern.

Earn the complete trust of your team, staff, and their wives.

Get everyone—coaches, their families, staff, administration, players—to buy into the program and be positive.

BUILDING A UNIFIED STAFF

Get to know coaches and their families away from football.

Involve the wives with the games and with the team and staff.

Reward coaches' accomplishments.

Give coaches enough time to be with their families: be organized.

Offer financial seminars for coaches.

Be loyal to your coaches.

Plan a preseason staff trip.

Evaluate coaches semi-annually or annually.

Praise coaches publicly, criticize them privately.

Always be honest.

Set short- and long-term goals–professional and personal.

Be aware of public relations:
- Staff should attend booster clubs.
- Staff should be visible in the community and at faculty meetings and school functions.
- Coaches must have positive attitudes. Anticipate problems and head them off.

Demonstrate strong character, act with integrity at all times, and always be a role model for your players.

Emphasize the team, not individuals; use "we" instead of "I."

Promote unity among offensive, defensive, and special teams coaches.

STAFF MEETINGS

Be on time. Don't waste other people's time.

Always bring a calendar, paper, and pencil to meetings.

Keep meetings as short and simple as possible.

Don't discuss things that don't affect the entire staff. Save one-to-one conversations for later.

Keep a daily, weekly, yearly schedule in front of your staff. This helps them schedule work and family time.

Encourage coaches to look ahead. Complete all assignments before the due date.

Be a good listener, but encourage coaches to answer only if they've researched the question.

HOW WE COACH

Practice winning every day; demand the best from each player on and off the field.

Keep your poise on and off the field. Don't argue with coaches or players on the field.

Be responsible for your player's progress. If one player is performing poorly, re-evaluate him. If your players are playing poorly, re-evaluate yourself.

Be clear on what is important to winning. Not everything can carry the same weight.

Always treat your players as you would treat your sons.

Practice simplicity regarding the technical aspects of the game.

Encourage them to be self-confident; walk with a swagger.

Never grab your player or his facemask. Never kick him or curse him.

Never verbally attack your players. Encourage them to do their best.

Never encourage a hurt player to practice; defer to the team doctor and the trainer.

Minimize distractions.

Play as many players as possible without jeopardizing team's success.

Have players learn assignments early in the week; too much coaching the day of the game shows a lack of confidence in yourself and in the players.

We control our own destiny. We must build better men and be better coaches than our opponents.

FIRST PLAYERS' MEETING

Emphasize trust: of themselves, their teammates, and coaches.

Demand clear and honest communication with teammates and coaches.

Show them how winning will benefit them.

Let them know you want them to have fun.

Show them how they can be part of something special.

GRADING PLAYERS

Be consistent, thorough, and fair.

Grade technique, effort, and production separately; give priority to production.

Allow adequate time for grading; make sure you're alert when grading.

Share evaluation and comments with players before watching film. Don't share actual grade with player.

Move players up and down depth chart based on daily performance.

Play the guys who love to play and who take great pride in their performance.

EARNING PLAYERS TRUST

Be trustworthy.

Respect must be reciprocal between coach and player.

Be committed to excellence.

Be a good listener. Talk to them about things other than football.

Make being a member of the team special:
- Do community service as a team.
- Attend to details: give them travel shirts, pocket itineraries.
- Take the team to a movie the night before a game.
- Give jackets, t-shirts, hats, rings, or highlight films.
- Have pregame and victory meals.
- Make all players learn the words to the fight song.

Give them educational advantages:
- Offer study hall, tutors, and rewards for honor roll.
- Check their class attendance, know their schedules and course loads.
- Communicate with their professors (*through the academic counselor only*).
- Offer seminars:
    Major Exploration Night, Career Night
    Faculty Guest Coach Program
    Agent Seminar
    Drug and Alcohol Awareness
    Sexual Health Seminar

Emphasize fair discipline.
- Discipline breeds success; harassment breeds contempt.
- Establish leadership committee: the team controls the team, the coaches run the program.
- Have clear team rules:
    Represent their team with honor at all times.
    Establish hair and dress code.
    Be on time.
    Use proper language.
    Attend class and keep up grades.
- Together, coach and player call parent if he breaks a rule. Coach determines punishment in cooperation with parents.
- Treat every case individually; keep these matters private.
- Don't punish team for individual discipline problems.

Treat each player as you would want your son to be treated.

Have players repeat conversations back to you; make sure he understands what you've told him.

PLAYER MEETINGS AND PRE-PRACTICE

Be on time for all meetings, stretching, and practice.

Meetings will never last more than forty-five minutes.

Demand that players sit up and pay attention. Coaches should pay attention to lighting, room temperature, angle to the board.

Ask players questions to see how much they're understanding and retaining.

Use pre-practice to emphasize different parts of kicking game daily.

Use ninja team as the kicking opponents.

PRACTICE PREPARATION

Mottos: "Practice Winning Every Day." "Do Whatever It Takes."

Post daily practice schedule. We practice either 24, 21, or 18 periods of four or five minutes.

Be consistent. If you schedule 2½ hours for practice, stay on the field for 2½ hours. This is part of building trust.

Don't waste time and energy. Do drills that are safe and will help you win. Chart injuries.

Keep a good practice tempo. Keep all players involved and working as much as possible.

Teach in meetings, pre-practice, and individual periods, not at practice. Each player should know his assignments so he can have quality repetitions during practice.

Always practice at full speed, but have a "fit, wrap, and strip" mentality. Only take people to the ground on 24 goal line plays. Injuries are more likely with pile-ups.

Use a lot of fundamental drills.

WEEKLY PRACTICE SCHEDULE

SUNDAY:
- Watch game film
- No individual awards, only team goals
- Show highlight film of plays that made a difference
- Trainers Check
- Coaches go home on Sunday nights

MONDAY:
- Players are off
- Coaches work from 7:00 A.M.–5:30 P.M.
- Offensive coaches might stay until 9:30 P.M.
- Defensive coaches go home
- *(Offense takes more preparation time than defense.)*

TUESDAY:
- Staff schedule same as Monday
- 2½ hour practice - full pads
- 45 minute meeting

WEDNESDAY:
- Staff schedule same as Tuesday
- 2 hour practice - shells
- 45 minute meeting

THURSDAY:
- Staff arrives at 7:00 A.M.
- 2 hour practice - shorts
- 45 minute meeting
- Staff goes home after practice

FRIDAY:
- 30 minute practice is optional. Be brief but organized. We want fresh players and coaches for the game.

HOW TO PREPARE TEAM FOR A GAME OR A SEASON

Be honest about season or upcoming game.

Have a theme for the season and for each week.

Set and break down the season's/game's goals.

Do little things to help motivate team: t-shirts, dedicate games to someone they love, invite former players to talk, rely on tradition.

Emphasize that they must be good every day in order to become great.

Have players visualize themselves winning the game. They should actually see the celebration and press conferences.

Handling Big Wins: Act as if you expected to win. Let the team enjoy the victory. We have a victory meal after all wins. Have three distinct things to say to the media. Be prepared; don't ramble. On Sunday review the game, then drop it and move forward. Don't mention it again.

Handling Tough Losses: Be brief after the game, but be honest. Study film as a team, review checklist of objectives. Discover why we lost and how we can improve. Then, drop that game and move forward. Teach players how to turn negatives into positives.

Plan to win and expect to win. Keep it simple. Don't coach in pregame. Be confident and positive. Make all decisions possible during the week e.g. what play to run on 3rd and 4, etc.

Make all players and coaches feel important. Let them know exactly what you expect of them.

HOW WE WIN

Have a burning desire to win.

Each practice should be intense. Get better every day.

Play with confidence. Field a team that expects to win every game.

Keep your poise after a bad break. Be strong enough to change momentum.

On offense, score every time we're inside the 20. Get points on every drive.

On defense, lead the nation in scoring defense. Don't allow long passes or runs for touchdowns.

Kicking game must be organized and fundamentally sound. Allow no more than 20 yards per kickoff return. Allow no more than 2.5 yards on punt returns.

Kicks, punts, and snaps must be consistently good.

Don't quick kick or punt if snap is juggled on 1st, 2nd, or 3rd down.

Be excellent fundamentally: blocking, tackling, kicking, punting, catching, throwing.

Don't beat ourselves. Force turnovers, don't commit them. Make the big play, don't give it up. Play great field position football and great goal line football. Have a great kicking game.

Know our assignments. Make no mental mistakes.

Eliminate penalties.

Be in top-notch physical condition.

Physically dominate your opponent.

Pursue your opponent relentlessly and gang tackle aggresively.

Play guys who get results. Potential means "ain't done it yet."

Take away your opponent's best plays and players. Take away their strengths.

Summary:
· Eliminate mistakes
· Have superior mental toughness
· Have superior physical preparedness
· Win the explosive plays
· Win on the goal line

Acknowledgments

The authors would like to thank all those friends, staff members, and players who contributed to this book. Special thanks to Rue Judd, Carol Cates, and Haley Savage at Bright Sky Press. Thank you to Tina Taylor for her very creative design work. The book would not have been possible without the help of our editor, Jenna McEachern—the daughter of a high school coach and the wife of a former Longhorn player.

Thanks also to Joe Jamail and David Little, attorneys at law, and to Patricia Ohlendorf, UT vice president for institutional relations and legal affairs, as well as DeLoss Dodds, Chris Plonsky, and Butch Worley of UT Athletics. Thanks to Cleve Bryant and the entire Longhorn football staff, and John Bianco and Rick Brewer and the members of the media relations staffs at Texas and North Carolina, as well as to Jim and Susan Sigmon, the best sports photographers around, and UT publications director Mary Elliott.

Thanks to authors such as Douglas Looney, Dan Jenkins, and Bud Shrake for their wisdom and guidance, and to Eddie Joseph and the staff at the Texas High School Coaches Association, Dr. Richard Coop, Chuck Neinas, Wright Waters, Greg Davis, Kathleen Hessert, Gil Brandt, Paul Deitzel, Barry Switzer, Jim Garner, John Swofford, Jerry Stovall, Kasey Johnson, and Sara Hays.

Finally, our sincere appreciation to Darrell Royal and Red McCombs for their willingness to contribute to the book, and to Sally Brown and Kim Scofield for their help, love, and support.